ISSN 2651-8988 (Print)
Volume 1 Number 1 2020

MW00995070

JOURNAL OF

VAMPIRE

STUDIES

Editor
Anthony Hogg

Assistant Editor
Andrew M. Boylan

VAMPIRE STUDIES ASSOCIATION

in arrangement with **EAGLE HEIGHTS PRESS**

Journal of Vampire Studies

Journal of Vampire Studies (ISSN 2651-8988) is published twice a year on behalf of the Vampire Studies Association, PO Box 3005, Syndal VIC 3149, Australia, in arrangement with Eagle Heights Press, 414 N. Church St., Fayette, MO 65248, USA.

Subscription not currently available, but under consideration for future issues.

All business and editorial correspondence should be addressed to Anthony Hogg by email at thevampirologist@hotmail.com. Include reason for contact in subject line. Physical mail can be sent to the Association's address, but only after prior agreement through email. Do not send unsolicited mail.

Advertising space available for non-fiction vampire books, academic journals, call for papers, lectures, conferences, and courses about vampires. Email Editor for consideration.

CONTENTS

Journal of Vampire Studies

Volume 1 Number 1 2020

THE VAMPIRE, HIS KITH AND KIN

A Critical Edition

By
MONTAGUE SUMMERS

Edited by
JOHN EDGAR BROWNING

In all the dark pages of the supernatural there is no more terrible tradition than that of the Vampire, a pariah even among demons. Foul are his ravages; gruesome and seemingly barbaric are the ancient and approved methods by which folk rid themselves of this hideous pest. The tradition is world-wide and of the greatest antiquity. How did it arise? How did it spread? Does it indeed contain some vestige of truth, some memory of savage practice, some trace of cannibalism or worse? These and similar problems inevitably suggested by a consideration of Vampirism in its various aspects are fully discussed in this work which may not unfairly claim to be the first serious and fully documented study of a subject that in its details is of absorbing interest, although the circumstances are of necessity macabre and ghastly in the highest degree.

Included in this critical edition are the authoritative text, rare contextual and source materials, correspondence, illustrations, as well as Greek and Latin translations. A biographical note and chronology are also included.

"Although published too late to help Professor Van Helsing defeat Dracula, every modern vampire-hunter needs Summers's seminal compendium of folklore and mythology. Browning's critical edition, with commentary by leading vampirologists and rich biographical material, is a treasure-trove for students and scholars alike!" —LESLIE S. KLINGER, editor, *The New Annotated Dracula*

"Summers's extensive albeit curious research on vampires has long been a classic in the field, and it's exciting to see it being rescued from oblivion, as well as framed by such a renowned yet diverse group of scholars." —KATHERINE RAMSLAND, *The Science of Vampires*

"This new edition cannot be recommended too highly to anyone with the faintest interest in Montague Summers or the origin of vampires." —NIGEL SUCKLING, *Book of the Vampire*

Paperback $22.95

APOCRYPHILE PRESS

apocryphilepress.com

Reflections on an Undying Fascination

With the release of the premier issue of this publication, we are about to embark on a new excursion into the dark waters of vampirism. I can certainly relate to all of the challenges involved in putting out a journal of this kind. I was the editor and publisher of the first regular periodical that featured the subject of vampires. First published in 1977, it was called the *Journal of Vampirism*.

That was an opportune time to capitalize on the unearthly subject, for the 1970s provided one of the first major waves of popular interest in these bloodsucking marauders. My friend, Donald F. Glut, came out with the first nonfiction work on the subject in the modern era with his book *True Vampires of History* in 1971.

The American daytime soap opera *Dark Shadows* cultivated a large viewing audience with its vampire character Barnabas Collins. Barnabas evolved into an antihero, revealing elements of both villain and hero in his development.

The blatantly sexy comic book character Vampirella was also very popular in the 1970s. With her bold and unapologetic style, she was, in fact, the first true vampire superhero. For some, she was also an icon of female liberation. Don Glut was also one of the writers for the very first issue of *Vampirella*.

In that same period, vampire films, in particular Hammer films featuring Christopher Lee as Dracula, were popular around the world. At that time, Lee was receiving more fan mail than any other actor in Great Britain. Other Hammer films, such as those of Ingrid Pitt, were suggestive of alternative sexuality under the guise of vampirism.

By the later 1970s, a revival of the play *Dracula* was a huge hit on Broadway, with the seductively handsome actor Frank Langella in the title role. He went on to portray the Count on screen, as did other alluring actors at that time, such as Louis Jourdan and George Hamilton.

Also in the 70s, best-selling vampire novels by authors such as Stephen King and Whitley Strieber were making a big splash. Most notably there was the breakthrough novel by Anne Rice, *Interview with the Vampire*. In her work, the vampire Louis gives his first-hand perspective on what it means to be a vampire. It has been called the first existential vampire novel.

It was in this cultural backdrop that I unleashed the *Journal of Vampirism* onto the world. It explored all aspect of the subject, including folklore, fiction, film, fantasy, and fact. The project was a result of my own fascination with these deathless revenants.

As a child I loved the old Universal monster movies, but among my least favorite were vampires. They often just seemed to be standing and posing in ominous positions, and I found them rather boring.

Much later when I was in college, I saw the film *Dracula Has Risen from the Grave* (1968) on television with Christopher Lee as the Count. I found his portrayal of the vampire to be much more dynamic and frightening than what I was used to.

Around the same time, I attended a lecture by Dracula scholar Leonard Wolf, who was speaking at my university. He discussed the strange mystique and appeal of the vampire and the way it affected people. This sparked my interest. I read Wolf's book *A Dream of Dracula* (1972), and I began collecting more and more books about vampires, including the works of Montague Summers, a writer prominent in the 1920s. He assembled an impressive number of stories and accounts from around the world of what people believed were real unearthly vampires.

In the later 1970s I started writing and lecturing on vampires myself, and it was clear that there was a strong popular interest in all things vampiric. I decided to make a major leap forward and put out a publication that focused primarily on these nocturnal undead. Once I gathered enough material for the first issue, the *Journal of Vampirism* was born. Vampire fans and researchers responded right away, and I was receiving ample contributions to print. I was also developing an extensive correspondence network with those who shared my fascination. It was a great ride, but after a couple years the workload just became too much for me, and my journal bit the dust.

Plenty of other publications about vampires followed my lead, and in later years the internet was awash in vampirology. Under the auspices of Dr. Jeanne Keyes Youngson and her Count Dracula Fan Club (now called Vampire Empire), a collection of my essays was published in 1983 with the title *The Lure of the Vampire*.

J. Gordon Melton was a very early supporter of the *Journal of Vampirism*. With his encouragement and support I was able to compile a comprehensive vampire bibliography and filmography, published as *Vampires Unearthed: The Complete Multi-Media Vampire and Dracula Bibliography* in 1983.

There was a huge proliferation of vampire organizations and publications in the 1990s. I took advantage of this, and asked them to spread the word that I was collecting people's dreams and fantasies about vampires. My purpose was to examine the reasons why so many people were drawn to these otherworldly night-feeders. Once I had assembled a massive collection of dreams and fantasies, it was a relatively simple matter of putting them in various categories. My findings were enumerated in my book *Liquid Dreams of Vampires* (1996).

One basic conclusion of the book was that there are a wide variety of reasons for the attraction that people feel toward vampires. In many ways, these creatures provide an all-purpose fantasy outlet. They are an expression of the dark side of human nature. They represent mystery, fear, danger, darkness and death. They offer an escape into the romance of the night. They provide an outlet for dark desires, forbidden passions and hypnotic surrender. They offer the promise of power and immortality.

Digging even deeper, the vampire gives a sobering perspective on other dark aspects of the human condition such as isolation, alienation and addiction. They can be a symbol for all the evil in the human heart that can be vanquished with a stake into the chest, only to be resurrected when the stake is pulled out. Vampires can be all things to all people. While it is said that vampires cannot see themselves in a mirror, ordinary mortals can see in the vampire a dark reflection of their own souls.

With the publication you are now reading, we are moving on to the next chapter, vampirologically speaking. Great minds continue to dissect the vampire into its component parts. It's time for new blood and fresh outlooks. When it comes to unearthing the secrets of the vampire, we can count on Anthony Hogg to break new ground.

Martin V. Riccardo
Vampire Studies, USA

Introduction to the *Journal of Vampire Studies*

Welcome to the first issue of the *Journal of Vampire Studies* (*JVS*). This is the official journal of the Vampire Studies Association, a not-for-profit organisation I founded on October 31, 2018 at City Library, Melbourne, "to establish vampire studies as a multidisciplinary field by promoting, disseminating and publishing contributions to vampire scholarship."[1] The association's multidisciplinary focus was inspired by the epistemological work of David Lavery (1949–2016) for the adjacent field of Buffy Studies, which unravelled the diversity of disciplines, methods and approaches taken to the subject.[2] It occurred to me that vampire scholarship could be consolidated in a similar way.[3]

Although this is not the first vampire studies journal,[4] *JVS* aims to be the field's flagship periodical by providing a central platform for exclusive research findings, critical analysis, discussion and debate, covering all areas of vampire studies. In this context, *JVS* has more in common with standard academic journals than the pioneering fanzine-style publications that preceded it. It is hoped that the journal will cultivate a network of correspondents who will refine and consolidate the nascent field of vampire studies. *JVS* will eventually have the functionality of a trade journal, especially beneficial to undergraduates, postgraduates, lecturers, scholars, researchers, publishers and conference organisers.

Excepting this issue's foreword kindly provided by Vampire Studies (formerly

---

[1] Vampire Studies Association, "Association Rules" (Unpublished manuscript, October 31, 2018), rule 4.1(i).

[2] [Lavery], "*Buffy* Studies by Discipline/Method/Approach," in *The Encyclopedia of "Buffy" Studies*, ed. David Lavery and Rhonda V. Wilcox (*Slayage: The Online International Journal of Buffy Studies*, [2003]), http://www.slayage.tv/EBS/buffy_studies/buffy_studies_by_discipline .htm (site discontinued) (accessible via the Internet Archive's Wayback Machine); and Lavery, "'I Wrote My Thesis on You!': *Buffy* Studies as an Academic Cult," *Slayage* 4, nos. 1–2 [13–14] (October 2004), https://www.whedonstudies.tv/uploads/2/6/2/8/26288593/lavery_slay age_4.1-2.pdf. Lavery, in turn, built his classification schema on the back of Derik A. Badman's bibliographic contributions the field, partly seen in Badman, "Academic *Buffy* Bibliography," *Slayage* 2, no. 3 [7] (December 2002), https://www.whedonstudies.tv/uploads /2/6/2/8/26288593/badman_slayage_2.3.pdf.

[3] The overlap between vampire studies and Buffy studies is evident in Lavery's encyclopedia entry; one of the subdivisions is "Vampirology."

[4] Precursors include *Journal of Vampirism* (1977–1979), quarterly newsletter of the Vampire Studies Society; *Journal of Vampirology* (1984–1990), independently published by John L. Vellutini; *Transylvanian Journal: Dracula and Vampire Studies* (1995–1998), a joint publication of the American and Canadian chapters of the Transylvanian Society of Dracula; and *Internet Vampire Tribune Quarterly: De Natura Hæretica's Electronic Journal of Vampire Studies* (1996–1997?) (http://www.generation.net/~valmont/ivtq) (site discontinued), an electronic journal published by Benjamin Hugo Leblanc. I aim to discuss these publications in a future issue of this journal.

Vampire Studies Society) founder, Martin V. Riccardo, there are several journal sections operating as signposts for the type of content expected of the journal:

- Editorials (500–1,500 words) are written by members of the Editorial Board or a Guest Editor when appropriate. They typically address a specific topic or provide updates on the journal's staff and formatting.

- Peer-Reviewed Articles (3,000–6,000 words) require specialist input from field experts. The Editorial Board selects two peer reviewers; both reviewers must approve a submission for publication. The peer review model used is open review, where the names of all participants in the review process are known to each other. I have chosen this model for the sake of transparency.

- Articles (3,000–6,000 words) are only subject to review by the Editorial Board.

- Review Essays (2,500–5,000 words) focus on vampire scholarship encapsulated in a single book or a scholar's vampire oeuvre.

- Book Reviews (1,000–2,000 words) for non-fiction vampire books still in print, written by reviewers with an expertise on the specific topics covered, or relevance to the topic, chosen by the Editor. Supplemented by Books Received, which document books received by the Editorial Board for review, or books sent to selected reviewers via the publisher, Editor or original author.

- Conference Reports (1,000–2,000 words) provide an overview of academic vampire conferences either through critical analysis or objective reporting on line-up and respective talks.

- Rejoinders (500–3,000 words), written by authors whose contributions to *JVS* have been criticised by another contributor. They are responses, or countercriticism, and the primary forum for debate in the journal.

- Notes (500–2,000 words) are short form articles dedicated to sharing findings or elaborating on existing work, without need for extensive analysis or elaboration.

- Obituaries (1,000–2,000 words) are dedicated to scholars who have had considerable impact on the field and passed away within three years of journal issue publication.

- Appendices (various) are supplementary material to articles that may otherwise be inaccessible to readers.

I hope to include other sections in future issues, including Bibliographies, Correspondence and Interviews.

The journal also fills a void. Although academic journals have a demonstrable impact on the development of academic disciplines,[5] only two other current journals, to my knowledge, approximate our aims and scope—and those cater to specific niches in the field. *Journal of Dracula Studies* (1999–), annually distributed to members of the Transylvanian Society of Dracula, solicits articles on "Bram Stoker, the novel Dracula, the historical Dracula, the vampire in folklore, fiction, film, popular culture, and related topics."[6] Cercle V's electronic journal, *L'Upir* (2004–2017?) (http://www.cercle-v.org/upir.htm), seeks "originals relacionades amb els vampirs i el folklore sobrenatural des de qualsevol vessant històric, antropològic, biològic, mèdic, forense o mitològic"[7] (original articles related to vampires and supernatural folklore from any historical, anthropological, biological, medical, forensic or mythological point of view).

The dearth of vampire-specific outlets means vampire scholarship is often diversified through countless other journals on various topics, many hidden behind paywalls. This not only frustrates readers who cannot access this content without paying significant sums, but greatly inhibits the free exchange of information for scholars. That is why I am committed to providing affordable access to *JVS* content. I used a print on demand service to reduce overheads; the cover price is set at almost the lowest option available; and all content is published through a Creative Commons Attribution-NonCommercial-NoDerivatives 4.0 International license agreement (CC BY-NC-ND 4.0) (https://creativecommons.org/licenses/by-nc-nd/4.0), allowing readers free copying and distribution rights—provided due credit is given and the work is used non-commercially. Copyright is owned by respective contributors.

I am also committed to establishing an open access version of *JVS*, using membership requirements of the Directory of Open Access Journals (https://doaj.org) and Open Access Scholarly Publishing Association (https://oaspa.org) as guidelines.[8] But this process will be a significant undertaking, so I ask for patience in advance. In the meantime, contributors may opt to upload their submissions to free hosting platforms, like Academia.edu, after the print edition is published. I should also note that the open access version will not supersede the print version. The transient nature of online material highlights the necessity of print media.

---

[5] Hye-Young Lee, "Contribution of Journals to Academic Disciplines," *Journal of Information Science Theory and Practice* 3, no. 1 (2015): 66–76, https://doi.org/10.1633/JISTaP.2015.3.1.5.

[6] "[UPDATE] Journal of Dracula Studies," Department of English, University of Pennsylvania, Call for Papers (website), January 27, 2020, https://call-for-papers.sas.upenn.edu/cfp/2020/01/27/update-journal-of-dracula-studies.

[7] "Instruccions per a publicar," *L'Upir*, Cercle V, accessed May 19, 2019, http://www.cercle-v.org/instruccions.htm. I have been unable to confirm whether *L'Upir* is still being published; the journal's latest issue is the September 2017 edition, but there is no notice on the website of the journal folding.

[8] I am also considering moving onto a rolling publication model to ensure a greater coverage of content. Although the current publication format and editorial process enforces greater quality control, it is also very restrictive on output.

Lastly, I would like to take this opportunity to acknowledge those who have made *JVS* possible. Thank you to Andrew M. Boylan, the journal's Assistant Editor, for screening submissions and providing thoughtful notes and discussions on content; Delia Remington (Eagle Heights Press) for formatting and publication assistance; Erin Chapman for moral support and proof-reading; Sharon Garewal (Taxonomy Manager, ITHAKA/JSTOR) for article keyword assistance; the Advisory Board for lending their credibility to the journal; and all contributors—including those whose work did not make the final cut—for their submissions, patience and co-operation with the editorial process.

The success of this journal will be ultimately measured by the quality of its content. In that spirit, we welcome your corrections, feedback and suggestions. If you would like to contact us, send an email to thevampirologist@hotmail.com. We look forward to hearing from you.

Anthony Hogg
Editor

BIBLIOGRAPHY

Derik A. Badman, "Academic *Buffy* Bibliography," *Slayage* 2, no. 3 [7] (December 2002). https://www.whedonstudies.tv/uploads/2/6/2/8/26288593/badman_slayage_2.3.pdf.

Cercle V. "Instruccions per a publicar." *L'Upir*. Accessed May 19, 2019. http://www.cercle-v.org/instruccions.htm.

[Lavery, David]. "*Buffy* Studies by Discipline/Method/Approach." In *The Encyclopedia of "Buffy" Studies*, edited by David Lavery and Rhonda V. Wilcox. *Slayage: The Online International Journal of Buffy Studies*, [2003]. http://www.slayage.tv/EBS/buffy_studies/buffy_studies_by_discipline.htm (site discontinued).

———. "'I Wrote My Thesis on You!': *Buffy* Studies as an Academic Cult." *Slayage* 4, nos. 1–2 [13–14] (October 2004). https://www.whedonstudies.tv/uploads/2/6/2/8/26288593/lavery_slayage_4.1-2.pdf.

Lee, Hye-Young. "Contribution of Journals to Academic Disciplines." *Journal of Information Science Theory and Practice* 3, no. 1 (2015): 66–76. https://doi.org/10.1633/JISTaP.2015.3.1.5.

University of Pennsylvania. "[UPDATE] Journal of Dracula Studies." Department of English, Call for Papers (website), January 27, 2020. https://call-for-papers.sas.upenn.edu/cfp/2020/01/27/update-journal-of-dracula-studies.

Vampire Studies Association. "Association Rules." Unpublished manuscript, October 31, 2018.

Etymologies of *vampire* with *pirъ* "a feast"

Kamil Stachowski

Jagiellonian University, Poland

ABSTRACT *An addendum to Kamil Stachowski and Olaf Stachowski's "Possibly Oriental Elements in Slavonic Folklore.* Upiór ~ wampir"(2017). *Etymological propositions involving Old Slavonic* pirъ *"a feast" are discussed: one by Jan L. Perkowski from* The Darkling: A Treatise on Slavic Vampirism *(1989); three by Bruce A. McClelland from* Slayers and Their Vampires: A Cultural History of Killing the Dead *(2006); and one by Michael Dilts, from the remarks in his peer review of this paper.*

KEYWORDS *etymology; libations; naming conventions; phonetics; historical linguistics*

ABBREVIATIONS

Blrs.	Belarusian	Gr.	Greek	Slav.	Slavonic
Bosn.	Bosnian	O-	Old	Slvk.	Slovak
Bulg.	Bulgarian	P-	Proto	Sw.	Swedish
Croat.	Croatian	Pol.	Polish	Syr.	Syriac
Cz.	Czech	Russ.	Russian	Ukr.	Ukrainian
E	east	Serb.	Serbian	W	west

INTRODUCTION

Many etymologies have been put forward to explain Slav. *upiór ~ wampir* "vampire." I discussed twenty-three of them in a paper co-written with Olaf Stachowski,[1] but did not include in it a distinct group of propositions which were unknown to us at the time of writing. Unlike the other etymologies examined, these interpret our word as a composition of two elements, the second of which is OSlav. *pirъ* "a feast"; the compound would be coined in the Balkans, around the tenth century ad. Therefore, this paper serves as an addendum to *"Upiór ~ wampir,"* and fits into it as follows: subsection "Jan L. Perkowski" would be subsection number 2.1.12, "Bruce A. McClelland" subsection 2.1.18 (after current 2.1.16), and "Michael Dilts" subsection 2.1.20 (after 2.1.17).

I would also like to use this opportunity to cite two cases, previously unknown to me, when our word was used as a given name.[2] N. M. Tupikov lists three such

---

[1] Kamil Stachowski and Olaf Stachowski, "Possibly Oriental Elements in Slavonic Folklore. *Upiór ~ wampir,"* in *Essays in the History of Languages and Linguistics: Dedicated to Marek Stachowski on the Occasion of His 60th Birthday,* ed. Michał Németh, Barbara Podolak, and Mateusz Urban (Kraków: Księgarnia Akademicka, 2017), 643–93.

[2] Stachowski and Stachowski, *"Upiór ~ wampir,"* subsection 2.42.

examples:[3] the well-known priest Упирь Лихый (Upir' Lihyj), a 1495 source mentioning a peasant by the name of Макарнкъ Упирь (Makarnk" Upir'),[4] and a 1600 source mentioning an Ovruch peasant Климъ Упиръ (Klim" Upir'). Since it is unlikely that *upirь ~ upirъ* was intended to mean "vampire" in the well-known sense in either of those cases, they can probably be viewed as additional arguments to support Anders Sjöberg's explanation of the name of Упиръ Лихый (*see* "Bruce A. McClelland" below).[5]

ETYMOLOGIES

Jan L. Perkowski

The gist of Jan L. Perkowski's idea is that our word is a composition of *Ban*, the borrowed name of a Manichaean god + OSlav. [?] *pirъ* "a feast," which would then become through an unspecified semantic shift the name of an undead monster.[6] The entire development would take place in the Balkans starting in the ninth century[7] or in the fourteenth–fifteenth century.[8]

   Perkowski prefaces his etymology with a lengthy exploration of the religious history of the Balkans in search of dualistic motifs on the one hand, and echoes of Bogomilism in the region's vampire lore on the other.[9] I understand that this is to justify the borrowing by Slavs of a Manichaean character and its name. I find the argumentation less than convincing but will not summarize it here because in my eyes this is in fact the least controversial aspect of his proposition, and likely beside the point anyway. Let it just be noted that the assumption that our word came into being in the Balkans in the early High Middle Ages, or all the more in Late Middle Ages, and then spread throughout the Slavonic world, raises at least two problems. They are presented in subsection "Bruce A. McClelland", together with the rest of the discussion of the historical aspect.

   Here, let us first discuss the foreign element, *Ban*. According to the Manichaean tradition, the world was constructed in the Second Creation, through the mediation of "the Great Builder," Syr. *bān rabbā*.[10] I am not sure why Perkowski introduces

---

[3] N. M. Tupikov, Словарь древнерусских личных собственных имен (St. Petersburg: Tip. I.N. Skorokhodova, 1903; Moscow: Directmedia, 2013), s.v. упирь, https://books.google .pl/books?id=MIjsBQAAQBAJ.

[4] "Makarenko" in Felix J. Oinas, "Heretics as Vampires and Demons in Russia," *Slavic and East European Journal* 22, no. 4 (Winter 1978): 436, https://www.jstor.org/stable/307666, where he is additionally described as residing in Novgorod.

[5] Sjöberg, "Pop Upir' Lichoj and the Swedish Rune-Carver Ofeigr Upir," *Scando-Slavica* 28, no. 1 (1982): 109–24.

[6] Jan L. Perkowski, *The Darkling: A Treatise of Slavic Vampirism* (Columbus: Slavica Publishers, 1989), 33–34.

[7] Perkowski, *Darkling*, 32.

[8] Perkowski, *Darkling*, 24.

[9] Perkowski, *Darkling*, 24–34.

[10] Michel Tardieu, *Manichaeism*, trans. M. B. DeBevoise (Urbana: University of Illinois

this character only through his other function which is to prepare a tomb for Darkness to be imprisoned in at the end of the world.[11] As a possible link between the Middle East and the Balkans, Perkowski adduces a tenth century Greek record of a certain heretic by the name of βααυης. He mentions that "The Armenian form of this name is *Vahan*, which means 'shield' in modern Armenian,"[12] but does not explore the possibility that βααυης might be nothing more than a Greek rendering of an Armenian given name. He even references Nina G. Garsoïan,[13] who does in fact state very clearly that this is exactly what βααυης is.[14]

Perkowski derives Slav. **van-* in *wampir* &c. from Gr. βααυης,[15] so at this point we must either put aside the connection to Ban, or βααυης as the intermediary between Syriac and Slavonic. In the former case, it is entirely unclear to me why the word would have been borrowed or in what meaning, so let us pursue the other possibility. I must, however, begin by noting that it is not at all likely. Ban is a fairly peripheral character in Manichaeism itself; for knowledge about him to penetrate outside of the relatively narrow community of Bogomils, and for his name to be apparently only preserved in just a single word, and one that is not in any way related to religion but is the name of a widely-known monster, would be an exceptional coincidence. Notwithstanding, according to Perkowski, **vanъpirъ* meant "Van's festival."[16] He does not precise the actual language but judging by *pirъ*, I assume he has Old Slavonic in mind. In this case, I am guessing that **vanъ* – or, in fact, **vańъ* – would be the adjective from **vanъ*, similar to *konstantińъ* < **konstantin-jь* < *konstantinъ* < Gr. Κωνσταντίνος.[17]

Press, 2008), 77–79, https://books.google.pl/books?id=e9wk7DQRoPoC; see also Paul Van Lindt, *The Names of Manichaean Mythological Figures: A Comparative Study on Terminology in the Coptic Sources* (Wiesbaden: Otto Harrassowitz, 1992), 78–80, https://books.google.pl/books?id =CHL4ih89v_QC; and Werner Sundermann, "Cosmogony and Cosmology III. In Manicheism," in *Encyclopædia Iranica*, vol. 6, fasc. 3 (Columbia University, 1993), article published December 15, 1993; last updated October 31, 2011, http://www.iranicaonline.org/a rticles/cosmogony-iii.

[11] Perkowski, *Darkling*, 33. Regarding this, see also Byard Bennett, "*Globus horribilis*: The Role of the Bolos in Manichaean Eschatology and Its Polemical Transformation in Augustine's Anti-Manichaean Writings," in *'In Search of Truth': Augustine, Manichaeism and Other Gnosticism; Studies for Johannes van Oort at Sixty*, eds. Jacob Albert van den Berg, Annemaré Kotzé, Tobias Nicklas, and Madeleine Scopello (Leiden: Brill, 2011), 429, https://books.google.com.pl/books?id=qeYE234vlgwC&dq.

[12] Perkowski, *Darkling*, 33.

[13] Specifically, Garsoïan, *The Paulician Heresy: A Study of the Origin and Development of Paulicianism in Armenia and the Eastern Provinces of the Byzantine Empire* (The Hague: De Gruyter, 1967), 119–21, https://books.google.pl/books?id=sk9Q-A0zwq0C.

[14] Garsoïan, *Paulician Heresy*, 145, 183.

[15] Perkowski, *Darkling*, 33.

[16] Perkowski, *Darkling*, 33.

[17] Jussi Halla-aho, *Problems of Proto-Slavic Historical Nominal Morphology: On the Basis of Old Church Slavic* (Helsinki: Helsinki University Press, 2006), 275, but see also pp. 97, 273, regarding the palatalization.

The phonetics Perkowski explains by "the expected phonological development *vam → ǫ → u" on the way from South through East to West Slavonic.[18] He does not reference any other source that would also expect such a development. Among Slavicists, the consensus is that PSlav. *ǫ > ESlav. *u-*, SSlav. *a, ə, o, u*, and WSlav. *ǫ, u*; in some languages this coincided with a not entirely regular prothesis of *v-*. In particular, in Bulgarian, PSlav. *ǫ-* generally > *vǎ-*, while in the east > *vu-* in Belarusian and Ukrainian, and > *u-* in Russian.[19] This is why the great majority of etymologists favour an original *ǫ-* in our word,[20] and also why OSlav. *vaňvpirъ* has effectively no way of accounting for northern Slavonic data.

The semantic side raises at least three questions. It is wholly unclear to me how the Manichaean "Great Builder" relates to the "revenant" from Slavonic folklore, and how "revelry" or "drinking bout" fit into this scheme. In fact, it is even unclear to me why Perkowski translates *pirъ* in this way[21] when the word appears to have had an overall more moderate meaning of "hostina; Gastmahl, Gelage; δοχή, ἄριστον, πότος, συμπόσιον; convivium."[22] I am likewise at a loss to imagine a realistic series of semantic changes that would lead from "Van's festival" to the name of a creature, dead, alive, or in between.

In conclusion, Perkowski's proposition must be rejected for morphological, phonetic, semantic, and probably also historical/cultural reasons.

Bruce A. McClelland

Bruce A. McClelland offers as many as three etymologies, all similar to each other, and also to Perkowski's idea.[23] But to understand them, the reader requires some background which is scattered throughout the book,[24] so let us begin by briefly summarizing it here.

The overall impression from McClelland's book is that the supposed first attestation of our word, in a signature in a 1047 Glagolitic manuscript of the *Book of*

---

[18] Perkowski, *Darkling*, 33–34.

[19] For example, Ronald Sussex and Paul Cubberley, *The Slavic Languages* (Cambridge: Cambridge University Press, 2006), 115, 125. Strictly speaking, Perkowski does not specify which language had which sound so, giving him the benefit of doubt, one could complete his formula in the most favourable way as "PBaltoSlav. *vam > PSlav. *ǫ > Bosn., Croat., Serb. u" (cf. e.g. Matej Šekli, *Od praindoevropščine do praslovanščine*, vol. 1 of *Primerjalno glasoslovje slovanskih jezikov* [Ljubljana: Znanstvena založba Filozofske fakultete, 2014], 250, 329; and Sussex and Cubberley, *Slavic Languages*, 116). But even this interpretation cannot account for the loss of *v- and, in addition, requires that Ban be borrowed at the Proto-Balto-Slavic stage which very significantly weakens the hypothesis.

[20] Stachowski and Stachowski, "*Upiór ~ wampir*," 666–7.

[21] Perkowski, *Darkling*, 33.

[22] Josef Kurz, ed., *Slovník jazyka staroslověnského: Lexicon linguae palaeoslovenicae*, vol. 3 (Prague: Nakladatelství Československé Akademie Věd, 1982), s.v. *пиръ*.

[23] Bruce A. McClelland, *Slayers and Their Vampires: A Cultural History of Killing the Dead* (Ann Arbor: University of Michigan Press, 2006), 187–91.

[24] McClelland, *Slayers and Their Vampires*, "etymology," listed in the index, 259.

the Prophets, was seminal for him.[25] The inscription reads *попъ оупирь лихый* (pop" oupir' lihyj), and it is indeed not immediately clear why a priest should refer to himself as "evil vampire", as the traditional translation suggests. McClelland's explanation is that originally the word had no connection with the supernatural at all; it denoted a group of people, impossible now to precisely identify, who had nothing unusual about them other than their non-Christian beliefs and/or ritual practices.

The argument for this claim is based on two premises: 1) In mediaeval Europe, Christianity had to fight for its position and unity. At first, it would rebrand and incorporate the local pagan beliefs and rituals, but as its strength grew, its attitude quickly turned into condemnation and open hostility; when pagans disappeared, heretics took their place and were persecuted by the Church with equal vigour; 2) McClelland's view of the vampire in a mediaeval society is purely functional: "The vampire serves as etiological factor behind visible events requiring an explanation, and ritualized group aggression against the vampire serves to alleviate collective anxiety by making of the vampirized corpse a scapegoat."[26]

Now, "taking a cue from the evident relationship between vampires and such persecuted groups as witches and magicians,"[27] McClelland asserts that "early in the history of the word *vampir*, its meaning was tied closely to heresy,"[28] "the scapegoat function of the vampire is traceable to Christian hostility toward pagans before heretics"[29] and that the "link between the vampire and heresy is a later phenomenon, resulting from an extension of the semantic range of the word *vampir*, provoked by the displacement of pagans by heretics as targets of Christian polemic."[30] McClelland stresses one particular reason for this opposition from the Church[31]: ritual sacrifices, or at least a specific kind of sacrifices, followed by feasts during which "polluted pagans" were accused of "foul services," debauchery, music and dancing.[32]

In short, McClelland's argument, as I understand it, is this: 1) the Church persecuted pagans and heretics for, among other things, sacrifices and feasts; 2) vampires [men or monsters?] were associated with paganism/heresy; 3) vampires [monsters] served as scapegoats, a link that is "traceable to Christian hostility toward pagans before heretics"[33]—therefore, *vampir* was originally [before point 2?] a term for (a particular group of) pagans or heretics, and its supernatural meaning only evolved later. "Later" must mean here after the tenth or eleventh century,[34]

---

[25] See especially McClelland, *Slayers and Their Vampires*, 187–91.
[26] McClelland, *Slayers and Their Vampires*, 75.
[27] McClelland, *Slayers and Their Vampires*, 75.
[28] McClelland, *Slayers and Their Vampires*, 76.
[29] McClelland, *Slayers and Their Vampires*, 77.
[30] McClelland, *Slayers and Their Vampires*, 77.
[31] McClelland, *Slayers and Their Vampires*, 36–41.
[32] McClelland, *Slayers and Their Vampires*, 41.
[33] McClelland, *Slayers and Their Vampires*, 77.
[34] McClelland, *Slayers and Their Vampires*, 35–37.

and before the fifteenth century when vampires were listed together with bereginas, vilas, Mokoš, Perun and other pagan characters in a manuscript of the *Oration of Saint Gregory*.[35] I appreciate that McClelland's reasoning might have actually been different because the one outlined above shows evident rifts in the logical continuity. It is unfortunate that I failed to extract a more coherent understanding from *Slayers and Their Vampires*, but luckily not critical for the remarks presented below.

Let us now look into McClelland's propositions.

It is impossible to disagree with the claim that the Church was hostile toward any idea and any people who threatened its position or unity. It is also beyond doubt that pagans and heretics were not only rhetorically condemned and accused of wickedness, but also physically persecuted and, surely, sometimes blamed for various calamities, too. Likewise, I cannot debate the assertion that, especially among the less theologically inclined populace, the various heretic groups could easily be conflated with pagans and other people to just "foreigners."

Next, the very functional, pragmatic view of the vampire's place in the belief system of a mediaeval society is no doubt true: in the sense that the creature was blamed for certain specific tragedies.[36] There is, however, no evidence to suggest that is was viewed as a vehicle for the sins of the local folk, as the usual anthropological understanding of the term *scapegoat* would suggest—or at least as an individual who can be conveniently blamed for somebody else's wrongdoing, as the more colloquial interpretation of the term would have it. McClelland's is a modern, detached, analytical insight, but also one that is very unlikely to have been widespread among mediaeval peasants—not least because it does seem that, had they shared his perspective, it would have rather drained the sense of purpose from any aggression they might have wanted to exercise against what they would have seen as nothing more than a corpse. No, they must have honestly believed in the reality of vampires and thought it reasonable to blame them for the deaths of members of their community.[37] As, indeed, they would treat any other of the many

---

[35] Michael Dilts points out in his peer review of this paper that the dating of *Oration* to the fifteenth century is in fact debatable: "the date of this item is disputed, with some scholars (e.g. Boris Rybakov) dating it to the beginning of the 12th [c]entury" (Michael Dilts, email message to Anthony Hogg, July 30, 2018; repr. "Re: Vampire Etymology Article," *Journal of Vampire Studies* 1, no. 1 [2020]: 130. Subsequent citations refer to *JVS* version), a fact which McClelland is not unaware of (*Slayers and Their Vampires*, 39, 202) but does not pursue in great depth. It may be that the time frame should be specified as tenth–twelfth rather than tenth–fifteenth century, but it is not entirely clear to me how this uncertainty impacts McClelland's proposition as a whole.

[36] Jerzy Strzelczyk, *Mity, podania i wierzenia dawnych Słowian* (Poznań: Rebis, 1998), s.v. *upiór*.

[37] Such beliefs have in fact persisted well into modernity. For example, in nineteenth century New England, it was not unusual to blame victims of tuberculosis for spreading the illness after death. Michael E. Bell, "Vampires and Death in New England, 1784 to 1892," *Anthropology and Humanism* 31, no. 2 (December 2006: 124–40, https://doi.org/10.1525/ahu.200 6.31.2.124; see especially pp. 124–8. At the fringes of Western rationalism, one can witness

supernatural creatures that populated the Slavonic folklore—a circumstance which McClelland appears to entirely overlook in his focus on vampires alone.

The early mediaeval association between vampires and paganism or heresy is less evident to me than it is to McClelland. Vampires were part of a worldview similar, in many ways, to what ghosts are to many people today. The belief is not a religious one, it is cultural. The clergy may have associated them with the pre-Christian culture and, by induction, with paganism, but I am only aware of this happening at a later date. McClelland himself only cites a fifteenth century source to this effect.[38] To posit that this change of attitude occurred (considerably) earlier would require much stronger evidence than I was able to find in McClelland's book, and the same reservation applies to his claim that the function of the vampire as a scapegoat is "traceable to Christian hostility toward pagans before heretics."[39]

But even if we suspend doubt and accept these premises, the conclusion which McClelland draws from them is going to be difficult to defend. Effectively, he is asking the reader to believe that, because a group of people was persecuted, their name took on the meaning of "an undead monster"—because both could be blamed for various calamities that befell the local community. McClelland does not explore in detail exactly what calamities heretics were blamed for, and whether the list included deaths of the kin of a recently deceased person, as this appears to have been the primary field of interest of vampires. Similarly, he does not dwell on any of the multitude of mythical creatures of the Slavonic folklore which were likewise regularly blamed for one tragedy or another, and reasons as if vampires were the only potential scapegoats on offer. I can only guess that the semantic evolution he had in mind is this: *"(a particular group of) pagans" > *"people blamed for various things" > *"a scapegoat" > "vampire (functioning as a scapegoat)."

If my guess is correct, then we must also assume that the belief in a corpse rising from the grave actually predated the last one in this chain of semantic changes. The opposite would be only possible if whoever initiated this change had the same analytical insight and utilitarian view of the vampire as McClelland does several hundred years later. If that is the case, then two further reservations need to be voiced.

Firstly, McClelland seems to imply, though he does not say so directly, that our series of semantic changes took place in Bulgaria. The country was baptized in 864, and we must allow some time for the new religion to actually take root among the populace before such semantic shifts can occur. McClelland estimates that could have happened in the tenth or eleventh century.[40] We must also allow some time for the new name to spread from Bulgaria across the Slavonic world, which could not have been a rapid process in early High Middle Ages. It is quite surprising

---

them even today in the form of Koryak "vampires." Alexander D. King, "Soul Suckers: Vampiric Shamans in Northern Kamchatka, Russia," *Anthropology of Consciousness* 10, no. 4 (December 1999): 57–68.

[38] But see note 35 above.

[39] McClelland, *Slayers and Their Vampires*, 77.

[40] McClelland, *Slayers and Their Vampires*, 42.

then, that supposed anti-vampiric burials appear in Poland as early as the tenth century. It is, in fact, possible that the existing archaeological interpretation of those burials is inaccurate,[41] but it is not extremely likely. Secondly, one may find it difficult to believe that a new name for an already existing creature should spread not only so rapidly and so far, throughout the entire Slavonic world, but also so deeply as to seemingly erase completely any trace of whatever name vampires bore previously. Especially if the epicentre of this change was Bulgaria, an Orthodox country, and Western Slavonic states followed the Roman rite and therefore were not so much under its influence at all.

As far as semantics is concerned, however, there may be another possibility. McClelland mentions Felix Oinas' 1978 article, "Heretics as Vampires and Demons in Russia,"[42] which discusses the use of the word *еретик* in Russia's Siberia effectively in the meaning of "vampire." Oinas suggests the change took place in the sixteenth–seventeenth century[43] but does not thoroughly discuss semantics. I imagine the following sequence: "heretic" > *"heretic, pagan, any non-Orthodox Christian" > *"+ witch, sorcerer, &c." > "[a sorcerer who became a] vampire," where the last link was informed by the folklore of Tatars and other neighbouring Turkic peoples.[44] However, for such an explanation to be acceptable, it requires the presence of a strong and early association between sorcerers and vampires which, to the best of my knowledge, is lacking from Bulgarian folklore. It is present in Chuvash[45] but I do not know if it is original there, and therefore had had an opportunity to penetrate to Bulgarian mythology, or a later innovation or a borrowing from Tatar, and therefore did not.[46]

Lastly, regarding the 1047 attestation as *попъ оупирь лихый*. I certainly agree with McClelland that it would be strange if a priest, or anyone for that matter, referred to themselves as "evil vampire." But unlike McClelland,[47] I fail to see how it would be less strange if a priest signed himself—be it in a humble, self-deprecating way, as McClelland suggests—as "weak heretic" (*weak* as in "susceptible to evil"). I believe that a far more plausible explanation is the one

---

[41] Leszek Gardeła and Paweł Duma, "Untimely Death: Atypical Burials of Children in Early and Late Medieval Poland," *World Archaeology* 45, no. 2 (2013): 314–32, http://dx.doi.org /10.1080/00438243.2013.799040; Leszek Gardeła and Kamil Kajkowski, "Vampires, Criminals or Slaves? Reinterpreting 'Deviant Burials' in Early Medieval Poland," *World Archaeology* 45, no. 5 (2013): 780–96, http://dx.doi.org/10.1080/00438243.2013.849853; Stachowski and Stachowski, "*Upiór ~ wampir*," 677.

[42] McClelland, *Slayers and Their Vampires*, 187, 230n3.

[43] Oinas, "Heretics as Vampires," 437.

[44] Stachowski and Stachowski, "*Upiór ~ wampir*," 653, 668–9.

[45] Stachowski and Stachowski, "*Upiór ~ wampir*," 669–70.

[46] Incidentally, a form of such an association is also present in the entirely contemporary, "transhuman" vampire (see Wojciech Kosior, "Kompleks upiora-wampira i jego realizacja we współczesności. Duchowość wampiryczna," *Ex Nihilo: Periodyk Młodych Religioznawców* 1 [2009]: 64–81) but I doubt that the two are linked by anything more specific than the general human fascination with the extraordinary.

[47] McClelland. *Slayers and Their Vampires*, 187–91.

proposed by Sjöberg where our priest is identified with the Upplandic rune-carver Upir Ofeigr, and his name interpreted as a combination of a Slavonic rendering of OSw. *upir* ~ … "screamer, shouter," with a translation of *ofeigr* "bold, daring."[48] In fact, it is not even necessary that the priest and the rune-carver be the same person; the priest might have simply been the first recorded Slav to bear this particular borrowed Scandinavian name. This idea is additionally strengthened by fifteenth and seventeenth century attestations of eastern Slavonic peasants *Макарнкъ Упиь* and *Климъ Упиръ*.[49]

To sum up, the entire premise of McClelland's proposition is at best debatable. The etymologies are not.

McClelland offers three propositions, without specifying the language, the time, or the geography.[50] He states that the morphemes in his reconstructions "correspond to O[ld] C[hurch] S[lavonic]" words, and refers to Old Slavonic word-formative patterns;[51] based on previous mentions in the book,[52] I am guessing they should be dated to around tenth–eleventh century; and the overall impression from the book is that he sees our word as originating from Bulgaria.[53]

1. *vamъ* "you dat.pl" + *pirъ* "a feast, libation" > *vampirъ* "a feast (or libation" for/to you [pl.]." The word would designate a group "known to offer libations to multiple deities (since the Orthodox Christian God was always addressed, in prayers, by the singular, ты)."[54] McClelland himself voices doubts about this etymology, in particular whether "such an ethnonymic construction follows a productive pattern in Old Slavic,"[55] whether ethnonyms could contain personal pronouns in them and, touchingly, whether the word order is natural. I could not agree more with McClelland's reservations.

2. *vъ* "into" + *pirъ* "a feast, libation" > *vъpirъ*, *vъmpirъ* "into the feast." In fact, McClelland translates *vъ* as "in, into" and the entire compound as "in (or into) the feast,"[56] but since he consistently proposes *pirъ*, i.e. nom. or acc., the meaning could not have been static because that would have required the loc. form *pirě* or *piru*.[57] The word would designate "someone who participated in feasting."[58] McClelland admits that this idea necessitates the

---

[48] See Stachowski and Stachowski, "*Upiór* ~ *wampir*," 675–6.

[49] See introduction.

[50] McClelland, *Slayers and Their Vampires*, 187–91.

[51] McClelland, *Slayers and Their Vampires*, 189.

[52] McClelland, *Slayers and Their Vampires*, 42.

[53] See in particular McClelland, *Slayers and Their Vampires*, 190.

[54] McClelland, *Slayers and Their Vampires*, 189.

[55] McClelland, *Slayers and Their Vampires*, 189.

[56] McClelland, *Slayers and Their Vampires*, 190.

[57] Kurz, *Slovník jazyka staroslověnského*, s.v. *pirъ*.

[58] McClelland, *Slayers and Their Vampires*, 190.

assumption of a later insertion of *m* between the two words, but this aspect is actually not impossible.[59] The weak side is the change from "into the feast" > "someone who participated in feasting," a rather unusual development which McClelland sadly does not support with any parallel examples, and for which I too am unable to adduce or indeed conceive of any. In this context, I find it ironic that McClelland ends the paragraph with a criticism of J. B. Rudnyćkyj's etymology, saying that "It is harder to justify the notion that **пиръ** was ever some sort of *nomen agentis*, such that *vъ pir* [sic, no -ъ] would mean 'he who drinks in.'"[60] Lastly, I am not certain about the use of *vъ* with *pirъ* in general because the only relevant attestation I could find actually employs *kъ*: *инъ къ богатого пирови пришьлъ бы* "ad … convivium."[61]

3. *vъnъ* "outside" + *pirъ* "a feast, libation [offered at an initiation]" > *vъmpirъ* "outside the feast." The word would designate someone who did not participate in the libation offered at an initiation, hence "uninitiated," "outside the circle of initiates."[62] According to McClelland, this idea is especially attractive as it would allow us to translate the confusing 1047 attestation of *оупирь лихый* as "an estranged uninitiate," a humble, self-deprecating signature of someone who "had lapsed from Christianity by participating in pagan Slavic feasting."[63] But it would not. If he had participated in such feasting, he would no longer have been an uninitiate—unless the meaning of our word would have already shifted to "pagan" or "heretic" by 1047, but this is unlikely for reasons mentioned above, and anyway even in such case he could only be "an estranged pagan or heretic," not "an uninitiate." Also, we must not forget that the author was in fact a priest, a circumstance which does not quite fit into McClelland's explanation at all. The 1982 proposition by Sjöberg mentioned above is considerably more plausible. Be that as it may, the main difficulty with this idea is the shift from "outside the libation" to "someone outside the libation." McClelland does not explain how such a change could have occurred and does not offer any parallel examples, and neither can I. Lastly, OSlav. *vъnъ* stands with loc. so the expected, and indeed attested, form is in fact *pirě* or *piru* rather than *pirъ*.[64]

In addition to the reservations listed above, it needs to be noted that none of the forms proposed by McClelland can be directly connected to northern Slavonic

---

[59] Stachowski and Stachowski, "Upiór ~ wampir," 680–82.

[60] McClelland, *Slayers and Their Vampires*, 190.

[61] Kurz, *Slovník jazyka staroslověnského*, s.v. пиръ.

[62] McClelland, *Slayers and Their Vampires*, 190.

[63] McClelland, *Slayers and Their Vampires*, 191.

[64] Kurz, *Slovník jazyka staroslověnského*, s.v. пиръ.

shapes with *u-*: Blrs. *úpir, úpiŕ*, Cz. and Slvk. *upír*, Pol. *upiór*, Russ. and Ukr. *upýŕ*, etc. All three scenarios entail either some rather unusual phonetic adaptations during the word's journey north from Bulgaria, or that the two groups of words (southern *vam-* and northern *u-*) are not related which is quite unlikely in light of their close semantic and phonetic similarity.

To sum up, McClelland assumes that the word *vampir* originally referred to people—pagans or heretics but perfectly human—and only later, sometime between the tenth and fifteenth centuries, its meaning shifted towards the supernatural. This assumption is maybe not entirely impossible to defend, if considerably stronger arguments can be found. He proposes three etymologies within this scheme. Those, however, must be rejected for morphological, phonetic, semantic, and probably also historical/cultural reasons.

Michael Dilts

In his review of this paper, Michael Dilts suggested another way in which *upiór ~ wampir* could be linked with *pirъ*. At this stage, it is more a bundle of facts than a fully formed proposition. In short, he speculates that originally "the *upiri* [. . .] were spirits of the ancestors who frequented the gravesites where their remains were laid to rest, and libations kept them satisfied so that they did not harass the living."[65] The word for "libation," *pirъ*, would be thus connected with the creatures themselves in a similar way as has happened in Christianity "in which Christ is the sacrificed 'lamb of god' who identifies his body with the offered bread and his blood with the wine drunk by the celebrant,"[66] or in Germanic languages where "a convincing etymology of the word for 'god' [...] derives it from the Proto-Indo-European root **gheu-* 'to pour, to libate'."[67] In the initial *u-*, Dilts sees the same verbal prefix as is attested in ORuss. *оупити са* "to become inebriated, to get drunk." He offers several more parallels for the ethnographic side of his idea which I will omit here for brevity, and because it is primarily the linguistic side that raises my reservations.

It is easy to see why Dilts made a connection between the facts he adduces, for they do appear to outline a reasonable narrative. The details, however, do not all fall into place. I understand he would propose OSlav. *upiti sę* "to become inebriated" → **upirъ* "libation" (similarly to **obĕsti* > **obĕdъ*) which would then transform into "one who 'gets drunk' from the libation" or "one [. . .] offered libations by the living," which in fact may be the same meaning. But such a shift is problematic. As was mentioned in subsection "Bruce A. McClelland," I am not aware of an Old Slavonic mechanism that would allow a deverbal noun of this kind to take on the meaning of a person. The Germanic parallel in *god* is only typological, and thus unlikely to convince etymologists on its own.

Dilts does not specify the time or place, but if the tradition from which he

---

[65] Dilts, "Re: Vampire Etymology Article," 131.
[66] Dilts, "Re: Vampire Etymology Article," 130.
[67] Dilts, "Re: Vampire Etymology Article," 130–1.

would derive the vampire is Indo-European then I imagine it would be sensible to assume a Proto Slavonic provenance for our word. This raises phonetic problems. *u- can of course explain modern u- in upiór etc. but it cannot account for vam- in wampir-like forms. As discussed previously in my paper, -m- may be a later addition,[68] but v- cannot be ascribed to prothesis mentioned in subsection "Jan L. Perkowski" above or any other process that I am aware of, and neither can the quality of the vowel. To explain all three simultaneously would require a very strong set of arguments. In this situation, it would be perhaps easier to posit that upiór and wampir are not related after all, but such a claim would also demand a rather compelling counterproposition.

While the ethnographic and historical/cultural side of Dilts' idea is not without appeal, morphology and phonetics appear to me to be the main weak points which must be addressed before a fully formed etymological proposition can be put forward.

CONCLUSION

The paper examines a group of etymologies of Slav. upiór ~ wampir "vampire" which deconstruct the word into a composition with OSlav. (?) pirъ "a feast."

One was proposed by Jan L. Perkowski. In it, the initial element is *vanъ "Ban," i.e. an entity borrowed from the Manichaean tradition where it is known as "the Great Builder," responsible for the creation of the world and the construction of the tomb in which to imprison Darkness. The following three etymologies were put forward by Bruce A. McClelland. These assume that the first element was either vamъ "to you" which would result in a compound meaning "a feast for you," or vъ "into" yielding "into the feast," or alternately vъnъ "outside" which would produce "outside the feast." All four postulate that the compound was created in the Balkans around the tenth century (Perkowski also mentions fourteenth–fifteenth century at one point) and spread from there throughout the Slavonic world. The last proposition was suggested by Michael Dilts. It deconstructs our word into the verbal prefix u-, as in оупити са "to become inebriated", + pirъ "libation."

The historical and cultural side of Perkowski and McClelland's ideas raises some reservations. Morphology is problematic in all the etymologies discussed here, primarily because it is not clear how pirъ "feast" could turn into the name of a person or monster without the help of any suffix at all. The postulated phonetic shapes will be also quite difficult to defend as they have no way of accounting for northern forms with u- or, conversely, for southern shapes with vam-. Lastly, the proposed semantic development must be considered rather exceptional and as such it will require far stronger argumentation than has been so far presented.

The idea of employing pirъ in our etymology is certainly unconventional and thus interesting. It is therefore with regret that I must judge it highly improbable for reasons outlined above—and then several more, as discussed in the respective

---

[68] Stachowski and Stachowski, "Upiór ~ wampir," 680–82.

subsections—and uphold my support either for the Turkic provenance or maybe for native *ǫpirъ* "unrotten."[69]

ACKNOWLEDGEMENTS

I would like to thank Anthony Hogg for providing me with copies of Perkowski's *The Darkling*, McClelland's *Slayers and Their Vampires* and Oinas' "Heretics as Vampires and Demons in Russia" for this paper. Any remaining inaccuracies and errors are mine alone.

BIBLIOGRAPHY

Bell, Michael E. "Vampires and Death in New England, 1784 to 1892." *Anthropology and Humanism* 31, no. 2 (December 2006): 124–40. https://doi.org/10.1525/ahu.2006.31.2.124.

Bennett, Byard. "*Globus horribilis*: The Role of the *Bolos* in Manichaean Eschatology and Its Polemical Transformation in Augustine's Anti-Manichaean Writings." In *'In Search of Truth': Augustine, Manichaeism and Other Gnosticism; Studies for Johannes van Oort at Sixty*, edited by Jacob Albert van den Berg, Annemaré Kotzé, Tobias Nicklas, and Madeleine Scopello, 427–40. Leiden: Brill, 2011. https://books.google.com.pl/books?id=qeYE234vlgwC&dq.

Gardeła, Leszek, and Paweł Duma. "Untimely Death: Atypical Burials of Children in Early and Late Medieval Poland." *World Archaeology* 45, no. 2 (2013): 314–32. http://dx.doi.org/10.1080/00438243.2013.799040.

Gardeła, Leszek, and Kamil Kajkowski. "Vampires, Criminals or Slaves? Reinterpreting 'Deviant Burials' in Early Medieval Poland." *World Archaeology* 45, no. 5 (2013): 780–96. http://dx.doi.org/10.1080/00438243.2013.849853.

Garsoïan, Nina G. *The Paulician Heresy: A Study of the Origin and Development of Paulicianism in Armenia and the Eastern Provinces of the Byzantine Empire*. The Hague: De Gruyter, 1967. https://books.google.pl/books?id=sk9Q-A0zwq0C.

Halla-aho, Jussi. *Problems of Proto-Slavic Historical Nominal Morphology: On the Basis of Old Church Slavic*. Helsinki: Helsinki University Press, 2006.

King, Alexander D. "Soul Suckers: Vampiric Shamans in Northern Kamchatka, Russia." *Anthropology of Consciousness* 10, no. 4 (December 1999): 57–68.

Kosior, Wojciech. "Kompleks upiora-wampira i jego realizacja we współczesności. Duchowość wampiryczna." *Ex Nihilo: Periodyk Młodych Religioznawców* 1 (2009): 64–81.

Kurz, Josef, ed. *Slovník jazyka staroslověnského: Lexicon linguae palaeoslovenicae*. Vol. 3. Prague: Nakladatelství Československé Akademie Věd, 1982.

McClelland, Bruce A. *Slayers and their Vampires: A Cultural History of Killing the Dead*. Ann Arbor: University of Michigan Press, 2006.

Oinas, Felix J. "Heretics as Vampires and Demons in Russia." *Slavic and East European Journal* 22, no. 4 (Winter 1978): 433–41. https://www.jstor.org/stable/307666.

Perkowski, Jan L. *The Darkling. A Treatise on Slavic Vampirism*. Columbus: Slavica Publishers, 1989.

Šekli, Matej. *Od praindoevropščine do praslovanščine*. Vol. 1 of *Primerjalno glasoslovje slovanskih jezikov*. Ljubljana: Znanstvena založba Filozofske fakultete, 2014.

Sjöberg, Anders. "Pop Upir' Lichoj and the Swedish Rune-Carver Ofeigr Upir." *Scando-*

---

[69] Stachowski and Stachowski, "*Upiór ~ wampir*," 670–2, 664.

Slavica 28, no. 1 (1982): 109–124.

Stachowski, Kamil, and Olaf Stachowski. "Possibly Oriental Elements in Slavonic Folklore. *Upiór ~ wampir.*" In *Essays in the History of Languages and Linguistics: Dedicated to Marek Stachowski on the Occasion of His 60ᵗʰ Birthday*, edited by Michał Németh, Barbara Podolak, and Mateusz Urban, 643–93. Kraków: Księgarnia Akademicka, 2017.

Strzelczyk, Jerzy. *Mity, podania i wierzenia dawnych Słowian.* Poznań: Rebis, 1998.

Sunderman, Werner. "Cosmogony and Cosmology III. In Manicheism." In *Encyclopædia Iranica.* Vol. 6, fasc. 3. Columbia University, 1993. Article published December 15, 1993; last updated October 31, 2011. http://www.iranicaonline.org/articles/cosmogony-iii.

Sussex, Roland, and Paul Cubberley. *The Slavic Languages.* Cambridge: Cambridge University Press, 2006.

Tardieu, Michel. *Manichaeism.* Translated by M. B. DeBevoise. Urbana: University of Illinois Press, 2008. https://books.google.pl/books?id=e9wk7DQRoPoC. Originally published as *Le manichéisme*, 2nd rev. ed. (Paris: Presses Universitaires de France, 1997).

Tupikov, N. M. Словарь древнерусских личных собственных имен. Moscow: Directmedia, 2013. First published in 1903 by Tip. I.N. Skorokhodova (St. Petersburg). https://books.google.pl/books?id=MIjsBQAAQBAJ.

Van Lindt, Paul. *The Names of Manichaean Mythological Figures: A Comparative Study on Terminology in the Coptic Sources.* Wiesbaden: Otto Harrassowitz, 1992. https://books.google.pl/books?id=CHL4ih89v_QC.

Plot Variations in the Nineteenth-Century Story of Lord Ruthven, Pt. 1

Kevin Dodd

Vanderbilt University, USA

ABSTRACT *The first installment of a two-part comparative study of the Lord Ruthven character in the nineteenth century. Twenty permutations are examined; comedies excluded. Ten examples are discussed in this installment. Works by Lord Byron; John William Polidori; Uriah Derick D'Arcy; Cyprien Bérard; Charles Nodier, Pierre-Frédéric-Adolphe Carmouche, and Achille de Jouffroy; J. R. Planché; the anonymous author of* The Bride of the Isles; *W. T. Moncrieff; Heinrich Ludwig Ritter; and Heinrich Marschner and Wilhelm August Wohlbrück.*

KEYWORDS *adaptations; narratives; nineteenth-century literature; theatre; opera*

INTRODUCTION

> Oh, Geoffrey, the wretch is odious. I never look at his black piercing eyes and white glistening teeth without thinking of Ruthven the Vampire.
> *Birmingham (UK) Daily Post,* "The Banker's Secret"[1]

Lord Ruthven (pronounced *Riven*) was the most famous vampire during the nineteenth century. But it is questionable how much people during that time were aware of the extent to which their vampire entertainment was dependent on him. We look back at the period and consider it obvious, but these tales were spread out in German, French, and English literature, playhouses, and concert halls. One might come into contact with one or two instances, but more was unlikely. In 1871, an anonymous individual, possibly Charles Dickens, Jr.,[2] observed that "Fifty years ago, vampyre literature had a temporary run of public favour. The Vampyre, or the Bride of the Isles, a drama [1820], and The Vampyre, a melodrama in two acts [the same play, 1820], were presented at the theatres: the hero being enacted by some performer who had the art of making himself gaunt and ghastly on occasions. There was also a story under the same title, purporting to be by the Right Honourable Lord Byron, which attracted notice [1819]."[3] In other words, to him, Ruthven, and the vampire generally, was someone or something long in the past and was popular for a very short time. And this is with over a half century littered

---

[1] "The Banker's Secret," codicil to "Larkin's Legacy," *Birmingham (UK) Daily Post,* December 27, 1870, 6, Newspapers.com.

[2] Robert Eighteen-Bisang and Richard Dalby, eds., *Vintage Vampire Stories* (New York: Skyhorse Publishing, 2011), 313.

[3] [Charles Dickens, Jr.?], "Vampyres and Ghouls," *All the Year Round,* May 20, 1871, 600, https://archive.org/details/allyearround05dickrich.

by Lord Ruthven stories behind him.

LITERATURE REVIEW

The importance of this character in the nineteenth century, as we noted, has been well understood and investigated by current scholarship. There have been several lengthy studies on the subject by, for instance, Stefan Hock, Montague Summers, Roxana Stuart, Nina Auerbach, and Noel Montague-Etienne Rarignac.[4]

Hock looks at Byron, Polidori, Nodier, Bérard, Ritter, Marschner, and Lindpaintner.[5] He is less interested in comparing the pieces than in passing judgment on them. He is quite severe with Polidori, Nodier, Bérard, and Ritter. Of Polidori he says he is unable to arouse any interest, much less sympathy, for his characters.[6] He writes of Nodier that his melodrama lacks any artistic merit and is not even good entertainment.[7] Bérard's novel is "ganz elenden"[8] (very miserable). Ritter's translation is extremely clumsy and sometimes downright mistaken.[9] He is fairly positive of Byron,[10] but is truly favorable only of the two operas: Marschner's music and text[11] and Lindpaintner's libretto.[12]

Summers seems not to have a unified perspective. There is no uniformity of vision and little attention to plot divergences except indirectly in the ones he outlines. He gives a long rehearsal of Polidori,[13] followed by passing references to translations and Bérard[14] then gives another lengthy summary of Nodier with some critics' reviews[15] and Dumas' notes on his viewing of a revival in 1823.[16] Thereafter he turns to Dumas's own 1851 play.[17] He follows this up with a return to 1820 and Planché's adaptation of Nodier which consists of Planché's own comments on it,

---

[4] Hock, *Die Vampyrsagen und ihre Verwertung in der deutschen Litteratur* (Berlin: Alexander Duncker, 1900), 89–108; Summers, *The Vampire, His Kith and Kin* (London: Kegan Paul, Trench, Trubner, 1928), 280–303; 306–8; 311–18; Stuart, *Stage Blood: Vampires of the 19th-Century Stage* (Bowling Green, OH: Bowling Green State University Popular Press, 1994), 26–103, 110–120, 136–39, 145—55, 268–301; Auerbach, *Our Vampires, Ourselves* (Chicago: University of Chicago Press, 1995), 13–25; and Rarignac, *The Theology of Dracula: Reading the Book of Stoker as Sacred Text* (Jefferson, NC: McFarland, 2012), 21–90.

[5] Hock, *Vampyrsagen*, 72–79, 89–108.

[6] Hock, *Vampyrsagen*, 78.

[7] Hock, *Vampyrsagen*, 94.

[8] Hock, *Vampyrsagen*, 90. Unless otherwise noted, all translations in this article are my own.

[9] Hock, *Vampyrsagen*, 96–97. Hock calls it a translation, but it is better to refer to it as an adaptation because Ritter took substantial liberties with the text.

[10] Hock, *Vampyrsagen*, 74–76.

[11] Hock, *Vampyrsagen*, 97–102.

[12] Hock, *Vampyrsagen*, 102–108.

[13] Summers, *Vampire*, 282–90.

[14] Summers, *Vampire*, 290.

[15] Summers, *Vampire*, 290–94.

[16] Summers, *Vampire*, 294–97.

[17] Summers, *Vampire*, 297–303.

the cast, and their attire.[18] He notes Marschner, examining mainly background issues,[19] covers Boucicault's 1852 drama by quoting a single review,[20] then proceeds to deliver a long synopsis of Boucicault's 1856 update.[21]

Stuart dedicates a significant portion of her book to Ruthven,[22] but she is looking specifically at Ruthven as a character in drama. Although much of her work has to do with social and political context, the actors, the theaters, costumes, reviews, etc., some forty pages are still dedicated solely to sketches of the major plays.[23] But these are summaries, not comparisons. Also because of the limits of the study to the stage some stories are minimized—Bérard,[24] Lindpaintner,[25] and Harris[26] receive just a paragraph apiece—and others are missing altogether. Still, this is the most complete list of which I am aware; her book covers Polidori, Bérard, Nodier, Planché (1820), Moncrieff, Marschner, Lindpaintner, Planché (1829), Dumas, Boucicault (1852; 1856), and Harris.

Auerbach draws comparisons, but the sources are limited to English language ones, which do not even represent half of the variations: Byron, Polidori, Planché, and Boucicault's 1856 text.[27] She makes references to oaths, patriarchal friendship between males and the exploitation of women, changes in relationships from friendship to paternal devotion, the role of the moon, and embodied and disembodied states.

Rarignac is also selective and focuses only on the most famous tales: Byron, Polidori, Nodier, Planché, and Dumas.[28] A lot of space is taken up with summaries—in fact, almost Dumas' entire play is retold in third-person prose[29]—and analysis favors the interpretation of symbols, often using classical Greek references; Celtic and Christian allusions are utilized far less. Thus, however many comparisons there are between the stories it is not the intention of the book to draw them and anyway the selection is too restrictive for meaningful examination of similarities and contrasts.

Many important vampire scholars do not show much interest in the subject at all. To name three, Christopher Frayling devotes himself to Polidori;[30] Carol A. Senf

---

[18] Summers, *Vampire*, 306–308.

[19] Summers, *Vampire*, 311–12.

[20] Summers, *Vampire*, 312–14.

[21] Summers, *Vampire*, 314–18.

[22] Stuart, *Stage Blood*, 35–178, 268–306.

[23] Stuart, *Stage Blood*, 268–301.

[24] Stuart, *Stage Blood*, 47.

[25] Stuart, *Stage Blood*, 118–19.

[26] Stuart, *Stage Blood*, 151. In all fairness, I also give it a short overview.

[27] Auerbach, *Our Vampires, Ourselves*, 13–27.

[28] Rarignac, *Theology of Dracula*, 21–90.

[29] Rarignac, *Theology of Dracula*, 56–79.

[30] Frayling, *Vampyres: Lord Byron to Count Dracula* (London: Faber & Faber, 1991), 6–18. However, he does not deal with the text, but with its background. He mentions Nodier and Planché, but no more.

examines only Polidori and Planché;[31] and James Twitchell merely investigates Byron and Polidori,[32] which is the most common choice.

So, there has yet to be an exhaustive, comparative study. Even this article cannot ultimately claim this distinction, for there is one source I have been unable to obtain: Cäsar Max Heigel's adaptation of Ritter's play, retitled *Ein Uhr! Romantisches Schauspiel mit Musik in 3 Akten* (1822).[33] I have limited myself mostly to serious works, so that comedies play little part here. Nor do pieces that have Lord Ruthven as one of several sources for the development of another character. I want an actor, if not Ruthven himself, who is almost totally modeled on him.

PLOT VARIATIONS

[O]ften, as she told him the tale of the living vampyre, who had passed years amidst his friends, and dearest ties, forced every year, by feeding upon the life of a lovely female to prolong his existence for the ensuing months, his blood would run cold, whilst he attempted to laugh her out of such idle and horrible fantasies; but Ianthe cited to him the names of old men, who had at last detected one living among themselves, after several of their near relatives and children had been found marked with the stamp of the fiend's appetite; and when she found him so incredulous, she begged of him to believe her, for it had been remarked, that those who had dared to question their existence, always had some proof given, which obliged them, with grief and heartbreaking, to confess it was true.

   John William Polidori, "The Vampyre"[34]

Ruthven's origin poses no difficulty to an investigator; it lies squarely with Lord Byron. It is a well-rehearsed story, so we can be brief. In 1816, Byron and his personal physician, John William Polidori, were joined in Switzerland by Percy Shelley, Mary Godwin (soon to be Mary Shelley), and Mary's stepsister Clare Clairmont. It was, as fate would have it, "The Year Without a Summer"[35] so it was

---

[31] Senf, *The Vampire in Nineteenth Century Literature* (Madison: University of Wisconsin Press, 1988), 33–42.

[32] Twitchell, *The Living Dead: A Study of the Vampire in Romantic Literature* (Durham: Duke University Press, 1981), 101–15.

[33] As far as I can tell, Hock, *Vampyrsagen*, 103n1, is the first comment on it. He does not include an author, however, Heigel's authorship and further details on the play can be found in Karl Goedeke, *Vom Weltfrieden bis zur französischen Revolution 1830*, bd. 11, bk. 8, 4. Abt. (Drama und Theater), Halbbd. 1, of *Grundrisz zur Geschichte der deutschen Dichtung aus den Quellen*, ed. Carl Diesch, 2 Aufl. (Düsseldorf: L. Ehlermann, 1951), 173, 225, 608, https://archive.org/details/GoedekeGrundrissZurGeschichteDerDeutschenDichtung-2-111.

[34] [Polidori], "The Vampyre; A Tale," *New Monthly Magazine*, April 1, 1819, 199, https://hdl.handle.net/2027/hvd.32044025671017.

[35] For further information on this event, see William K. Klingaman and Nicholas P. Klingaman, *The Year Without a Summer: 1816 and the Volcano That Darkened the World and Changed History* (New York: St. Martin's Press, 2013); and Gillen D'Arcy Wood, *Tambora: The Eruption That Changed the World* (Princeton, NJ: Princeton University Press, 2014).

cold and rainy outside the villa where they were staying. To occupy themselves Byron suggested they each compose a ghost story. Byron began to compose one but quickly lost interest; Polidori, however, was quite attentive to it.[36]

"A Fragment" ([1816]; 1819), by Lord Byron

In Byron's fragment,[37] the unnamed narrator has finished his studies at university and is ready to begin his travels. He wishes to have the companionship of an older peer, Augustus Darvell, who is fascinating but distant, passionate yet cool. He gains his consent to join him. The first part of their journey goes very well, except that Darvell begins to grow more and more enfeebled as their attention turns to the East. As they are on their way to the ruins of Ephesus and passing through a desolate region, they enter an abandoned Turkish cemetery. This obscure place is strangely well-known to Darvell. Darvell is now so weak that he is talking of his immanent death and he extracts an oath from the narrator that he tell no one of his demise. The vow also includes throwing his ring, at a specific day and time, into a designated salt spring, and visiting a ruined temple, both of which are associated with the Eleusinian mysteries, and hence with resurrection. A stork with a snake in its beak lands on a nearby tombstone which Darvell takes as a sign. When it finally flies away, he dies and almost immediately turns nearly black. He is buried in the grave marked by that stone, as he wished.

There are several observations we can make with reference to what follows. Darvell is not a total stranger, but attended all the same schools as the narrator, although, of course, earlier. He has no obvious vices but is mysterious. There is nothing that smacks of revenge against the narrator. It is peculiar that Darvell would be familiar with a Turkish wasteland, that he spoke Turkish, and that he had a ring with Arabic characters on it. Those, no doubt, add to his enigmatic quality and could play to an Islamophobia,[38] or serve as an illustration of a penchant for the exotic. There appears to be something supernatural to Darvell by his corpse discoloring so quickly. If he does revive, the moon will play no part in it. The narrator is telling this tale much later in life, so he survives the episode. Polidori would later use this as the template for his much-celebrated novella.

"The Vampyre" (1819), by John William Polidori

Polidori's novella, "The Vampyre; A Tale" (1819),[39] starts off roughly the same as

---

[36] Frayling, *Vampyres*, 10–17, gives further background to this ghost story session.

[37] First published as "A Fragment" in Byron, *Mazeppa, a Poem* (London: John Murray, 1819), 59–69, the story is dated "*June 17, 1816*" (59).

[38] Byron was an ardent supporter of Greek independence from the Ottoman Turks. See Roderick Beaton, *Byron's War: Romantic Rebellion, Greek Revolution* (Cambridge: Cambridge University Press, 2013).

[39] Famously misattributed to Lord Byron, the story was first published as "The Vampyre; a Tale" in *New Monthly Magazine*, April 1, 1819, 195–206, prefaced by "Extract of a Letter from Geneva, with Anecdotes of Lord Byron, &c.," 193–5. The story was later published in

Byron's fragment, except it is in the third person and with a stranger; Byron's narrator is now named Aubrey and his companion, Lord Ruthven. The beginning of their trip is a revelation to Aubrey because he learns that Ruthven is sadistic and cruel. He withholds charity from the deserving and gives more than needed to the degenerate which results in them getting in trouble with the law, sometimes being caught committing capital crimes. Of his own class, he preys on older, desperate men and on naïve young men and women, shaming them and their families. Aubrey decides to alert the parents of a girl Ruthven is planning to ruin and parts company with him. This fuels Ruthven's vengeful behavior in what follows.

Aubrey goes to Athens and begins translating obscure inscriptions on the ruins, but the family with whom he stays has a free-spirited and lithe daughter, Ianthe, who is devoid of all the artificiality of London social circles. He is constantly distracted from his studies by her and finds himself falling in love. He is also charmed by her beliefs in superstitions like vampires. One day, he needs to travel some distance through woods to work on some artifacts, but Ianthe is disturbed by this for he shall pass through the haunts of vampires. She wants him back before dark. He is not and is caught in a storm as he is crossing the woods. Aubrey's horse bolts, then stops at a hovel from which a woman's screams and a man's laughter are heard. Aubrey goes inside and is attacked by someone with superhuman strength who declares "again baffled."[40] He begins to strangle him, but Aubrey is saved by an approaching search party which finds Ianthe dead and her killer gone.

Aubrey becomes violently ill and, in his condition, associates Ruthven with the assailant. But when he is recovering, he finds that he has been cared for by none other than Ruthven. Their friendship restored, they begin traveling across the area when they are waylaid by robbers and Ruthven is mortally wounded. He extracts an oath from Aubrey that he will not reveal his death for a year and a day to keep Ruthven's honor intact. Aubrey leaves and Ruthven then arranges with the thieves to have his body placed in the open where it can receive the first rays of the moon. When Aubrey finds out, he goes there to bury the corpse but finds nothing.

He spends some further time abroad, where he finds out Ruthven was indeed Ianthe's murderer, before returning home to his loving, younger sister, referred to only as Miss Aubrey. Now taciturn and withdrawn, he still joins her for her formal debut when his arm is seized and he hears someone say, "Remember your oath."[41] Naturally, it is Ruthven. Aubrey becomes very protective of his sister, for no stated reason, but he begins also to lose his reason. His actions become bizarre and soon he is confined to his room.

As the promised year of silence comes to an end, he learns his sister is marrying. But when he discovers it is to Ruthven, he enters a paroxysm of impotent rage, which is interpreted as insanity. He finds out from Ruthven that she will lose her

---

book form as *The Vampyre; a Tale* (London: Sherwood, Neely, and Jones, 1819) along with "Extract."

[40] Polidori, "Vampyre," 200.

[41] Polidori, "Vampyre," 203.

virginity to him, for "[w]omen are frail,"[42] if there be no wedding; so it is either marriage or disgrace. Overcome by the dilemma, a blood vessel in his head ruptures and he is confined to bed. In a weakening state, he dictates his story now that the time limit is passed and then dies. His sister, married and departed, is sought following Aubrey's revelations and she is found dead or, put another way, she has "glutted the thirst of a VAMPYRE!"[43]

Polidori's narrative is the first and the last of the variations discussed here that ends with the triumph of the vampire and where religion plays no part. Many things we currently associate with the vampire monster are here. For example, Ruthven is fully human-like with a distinct personality; aristocratic, a member of elite society; attractive and seductive. More unfamiliar is that he can travel long distances needing only the moon wherever he is in case he is killed. The lunar preoccupation has been replaced by a solar one for us, even though Dracula was able to walk in the daylight. There is no sense that he depends on hypnosis or mesmerism; rather he has his own fascinating charm: "Who could resist his power? His tongue had dangers and toils to recount—could speak of himself as of an individual having no sympathy with any being on the crowded earth, save with her to whom he addressed himself;—could tell how, since he knew her, his existence had begun to seem worthy of preservation, if it were merely that he might listen to her soothing accents;—in fine, he knew so well how to use the serpent's art, or such was the will of fate, that he gained her affections."[44]

The story was published without Polidori's knowledge.[45] Shortly after it appeared, he prepared an authorized version which was not printed until 1994.[46] Apart from variations in word or phrasing,[47] it is the same, with one exception: the villain's name is no longer Lord Ruthven, but Lord Strongmore.

The next two variants deviate substantially from Polidori but are nonetheless dependent on him.

"The Black Vampyre" (1819), by Uriah Derick D'Arcy

The first variant is probably pseudonymous—a parody called *The Black Vampyre; A Legend of St. Domingo* (1819),[48] by Uriah Derick D'Arcy.[49] It is, as the title indicates,

---

[42] Polidori, "Vampyre," 206.

[43] Polidori, "Vampyre," 206.

[44] Polidori, "Vampyre," 205.

[45] *The Diary of Dr. John William Polidori, 1816: Relating to Byron, Shelley, etc.*, ed. William Michael Rossetti (London: Elkin Matthews, 1911), 17–18, https://hdl.handle.net/2027/uc2.ark :/13960/t0gt5jq1t.

[46] Polidori, "The Vampyre: A Tale," in *"The Vampyre" and "Ernestus Berchtold; or, The Modern Oedipus": Collected Fiction of John William Polidori*, ed. D. L. Macdonald and Kathleen Scherf (Toronto: University of Toronto Press, 1994), 33–49.

[47] Variation between the texts are listed in Polidori, *"The Vampyre" and "Ernestus Berchtold"*, 145–52.

[48] First published as *The Black Vampyre; A Legend of St. Domingo* (New York: printed for the author, 1819), an abridged version of the story was anonymously published in the

about a Black Vampyre to be contrasted with the White Vampyre of Polidori and may deal with Ruthven's ancestry. The author describes his purpose being to show how much nonsense an individual might deliver "without any excuse but idleness, or any object but amusement."[50] But as he also states in the introduction, "The prominent descriptions, which it is here attempted to ridicule, are fresh in the memory of all who have read the 'White Vampyre;' and to those who have not, the Superstition must be so familiar, that it is unnecessary to make useless extracts."[51] So, ridicule is also an object.

Mr. Personne repeatedly tries to drown "a little negro"[52] in the moonlight to no avail. He finally kindles a fire to burn him, but the child bounces him into the flames instead. Before he dies from the burns sustained, he learns his own child has had his insides sucked out like juice from an orange and all that is left is his skin, nails, and hair. Years later his widow, Euphemia, is mourning her third husband's death; she is approached by a regal-looking black man with a young, white servant, Zembo. The Prince is charming and handsome, so within a short amount of time when he proposes to her, she accepts. They get married that night, but not without the priest warning them against miscegenation.

Late that night, the Prince leads his wife and servant out to the graves of her three husbands and several children. Her third child, to whom she showed the most affection, was named Spooner, and when he is dug up, he is uncorrupted and therefore a vampire. In a footnote we read, "This Spooner Dubois having never been heard of since, it is probable that he has been roaming about the world; and it is possible, that he may be the same Lord Ruthven, whose adventures have recently been related."[53] The Prince scoops out his heart, mixes the blood with water and dirt, and unsuccessfully tries to force the child's mother to drink the concoction. She faints and revives as a vampire. As she readies herself to devour a corpse, her

---

Knickerbocker and attributed to Robert C. Sands ("More of Sands' Literary Remains: 'The Black Vampyre,'" January 1845, 73–77; and "Sands' 'Black Vampyre,'" February 1845, 171–3). The original story lay dormant until reprinted under Sands' by-line as "The Black Vampyre: A Legend of Saint Domingo," in *The Best Vampire Stories, 1800–1849: A Classic Vampire Anthology*, ed. Andrew Barger (N.p.: Bottletree, 2011), 139–61. There are a number of variations from the original in Barger's reprinting in spelling, italics, capitalization, breaking of paragraphs, and typographical errors, but none of these affect the story itself. The only problem is he cut the story's introduction, which is essential to understanding the author's intention.

[49] The author's identity has been disputed. Barger, *Best Vampire Stories*, 133–7, proposes "Uriah Derick D'Arcy" was an anagram Sands derived from Richard Varick Dey, a valedictorian of Columbia College, which Sands also attended. However, Katie Bray, "'A Climate . . . More Prolific . . . in Sorcery': *The Black Vampyre* and the Hemispheric Gothic," *American Literature* 87, no. 1 (March 2015): 19–20n4, https://doi.org/10.1215/00029831-2865163, argues in favour of Dey's authorship.

[50] D'Arcy, *Black Vampyre*, v.

[51] D'Arcy, *Black Vampyre*, v.

[52] D'Arcy, *Black Vampyre*, 9.

[53] D'Arcy, *Black Vampyre*, 19n.

first husband, Mr. Personne, gets up from his coffin and they spend a pleasant time catching up. They are interrupted by the resurrection of her other two husbands, but "the African" intervenes and stakes them.[54] He then hands his wife over to Mr. Personne, whom he has forgiven all his abuse, giving up his claim to her and revealing Zembo to be their son.

The African Prince gives them money and points them to a ship sailing to Europe, but instead they, with Zembo leading the way, enter a secret cave and listen to the Prince rally vampires and slaves alike to fight for the emancipation of the slaves.[55] But the rally is broken up by soldiers and the slaves sneak out, leaving the vampires to fight alone, initially gaining the upper hand against the troops because they can bounce back up like roly-poly dolls and the Prince can swirl swords like windmills. Zembo counsels the soldiers how to defeat them and they end up victorious. The family has learned inadvertently of an antidote to vampirism to be found in the cave and they all are cured and resettle on the plantation. Euphemia gives birth to "a mulatto [. . .] of Vampyrish propensities,"[56] but they are helpless to cure him since they have no antidote left.

Spooner would be the child of Euphemia and her second or third husband and hail from Santo Domingo. He is one of two surviving children that we know of, the other being Zembo, until the "mulatto" is born.[57] Spooner was a vampire when dug up from the grave and we have no record of him staying with the family, so he probably set out into the world at that time. We know that vampires can age, at least out of childhood and adolescence, because the Prince does so, thus there is no indication of how old Spooner would be when he left. I realize this is taking the narrative more seriously than intended, and turning possibility into probability, but it does have some relevance to the background of Ruthven in the literature concerning him, other than simply depicting him as the spirit of a criminal incarnate, as he soon shall be.

"Lord Ruthwen" (1820), by Cyprien Bérard

The second variant is a sequel, as *The Black Vampyre* is a prequel, attributed to Cyprien Bérard: *Lord Ruthwen, ou Les vampires*, 2 vols. (1820).[58] As Brian Stableford notes in his English translation, the novel is "a frail and muddled effort,"[59] but important for helping to create a "pattern of established clichés" for future vampires.[60] The story begins with Ruthwen manipulating a young couple,

---

[54] D'Arcy, *Black Vampyre*, 27.

[55] The Haitian Revolt (1791–1804) may have been in the author's mind.

[56] D'Arcy, *Black Vampyre*, 42.

[57] His scooped-out heart probably means he is literally "heartless."

[58] Some scholars believe Charles Nodier was the true author. See, for instance, A. Richard Oliver, *Charles Nodier: Pilot of Romanticism* (Syracuse: Syracuse University Press, 1964), 125–6.

[59] Stableford, introduction to *The Vampire Lord Ruthwen*, by Cyprien Bérard, trans. Stableford (Encino, CA: Black Coat Press, 2011), 15.

[60] Stableford, introduction, 17.

separating the lady, Bettina, from her man, Léonti, and then attacking and killing her. This leads to two significant results. First, Léonti pursues him and finds himself joined by another, who also lost a loved one to Ruthwen, Aubrey. Second, Bettina, now a virgin vampire raised by God to avenge Ruthwen and to protect the innocent, is encountered by them on their travels. Bettina finally locates Ruthwen as Lord Seymour, prime minister of Modena, who has his eye set on the Duke of Modena's daughter, Éléonore. The two men are now joined by a third, bereft of a woman by Ruthwen in Greece.

The prime minister manufactures a crisis, a fire, from which he saves the duke. Although his daughter has her heart set on another, the man who saved her from the fire, the duke insists that she marry Lord Seymour right away and she dare not disobey, even though Bettina appears to her and warns of the monster she is going to marry and the death he will bring in his wake. Éléonore is murdered by Lord Seymour on their wedding night, but Léonti then stabs him and impales himself to join Bettina. But young ladies in the court are falling deathly ill until Aubrey thinks to open Ruthwen's grave and sear his heart and eyes: "Après cette exécution la mort cessa ses ravages"[61] ("After this execution, death ceases its ravages"[62]).

Although this is ultimately a happy ending, the death of Éléonore keeps the final tragedy of Polidori still in view. This will be followed in several of the retellings. Several other tropes begin here, too. A daughter/sister coerced to marry a vampire becomes a feature in many future stories, and a warning from spirits to the intended victim recurs in other early tales. The novel bears the mark of Roman Catholicism. This can be seen in the choice to make Bettina act as a kind of supernatural surrogate for the Virgin Mary as Ruthwen stands in for the Devil. This is the only rendition of the Ruthwen narrative that has an unquestionably good vampire countering Ruthven. She feeds on no one and is genuinely altruistic.

Now we move back to versions of Lord Ruthven that bear some semblance to Polidori's tale.

"Le Vampire" (1820), by Charles Nodier, Pierre-Frédéric-Adolphe Carmouche, and Achille De Jouffroy

They start with the wildly popular adaptation for the stage by Charles Nodier, Pierre-Frédéric-Adolphe Carmouche, and Achille de Jouffroy,[63] *Le Vampire,*

---

[61] Bérard [C. B., pseud.], *Lord Ruthwen, ou Les vampires* (Paris: Ladvocat, 1820), 2:175–6, Gallica.

[62] Bérard, *The Vampire Lord Ruthwen*, trans. Brian Stableford (Encino, CA: Black Coat Press, 2011), 195.

[63] The book version of the play, *Le Vampire, mélodrame en trois actes, avec un prologue* (Paris: J.-N. Barba, 1820), https://archive.org/details/bub_gb_Cda5kpWKRHgC, credits "M.M. ***" as the author. However, "Notice bibliographique: Des ouvrages publiés par Charles Nodier" in Charles Nodier, *Description raisonnée d'une jolie collection de livres (Nouveaux mélanges tirés d'une petite bibliothèque)* (Paris: J. Techener, 1844), 7, https://books.google.com.au/books?id=s_tEsoplZegC, discloses the identities of the co-writers: Pierre-Frédéric-Adolphe Carmouche ("MM. Carmouche") and Achille de Jouffroy ("Jouffrey"). Frank J. Morlock, "The Birth of

mélodrame en trois actes, avec un prologue[64] (Théâtre de la Porte-Saint-Martin, Paris, June 13, 1820).[65] The play was in part responsible for the continued success of Polidori's novella. Rarignac notes "Polidori's *Vampyre* . . . was doomed to oblivion until, as Byron phrased it, 'it was put up as a melo-drame at Paris.'"[66]

Ituriel, angel of the moon, catches Oscar, protector of marriage, watching over Malvina as she lay asleep in a graveyard, led astray from a hunt by a storm, to make sure she is not assaulted by a vampire. Tomorrow, Malvina will have to marry the famous Count de Marsden, a vampire. His vampire spirit arises from its grave and charges at her, but Oscar stops him. The vampire says she is his, but Oscar replies that his destiny is not her but nothingness, meted out by The Great Spirit. Malvina sees this in her dream.

The following morning, she talks to Aubray, her brother, about her intended who is soon to arrive, the brother of Aubray's dearest friend, Lord Rutwen. Rutwen sacrificed his life to save Aubray from brigands abroad and asked only to be placed in moonlight in return. Aubray is overjoyed to discover that the Count de Marsden turns out to be Rutwen himself, who had "[u]n secors puissant"[67] ("powerful help"[68]) to preserve his existence after apparently dying. Malvina agrees to be wed that very night because of her brother's love for the man and because a "charme inconcevable agit sur moi"[69] ("inconceivable charm acts on me"[70]), although she recognizes him as the man she saw in the cemetery.

That day, Rutwen travels with Aubray to Castle Marsden to arrange some things with his estate and to attend a servant's wedding. He believes that he can feed on the servant's bride before Malvina to take the pressure off the 1 a.m. deadline, so he tries to seduce her. She runs, screaming with him in pursuit. The

---

Modern Vampirism," introduction to *Lord Ruthven the Vampire*, by John William Polidori, Charlies Nodier, and Eugène Scribe, adapt. Morlock (Encino: Black Coat Press, 2004), 16; and Stableford, introduction to *Vampire Lord Ruthwen*, 14, 15, credit Jean Toussaint Merle, director of Théâtre de la Porte-Saint-Martin, as a co-author.

[64] Unless otherwise noted, titles and dates for plays and operas have been taken from playbills for first performances wherever possible because titles could vary between performance and publication in book form. This title has been taken from the J.-N. Barba version. Subsequent citations refer to this edition.

[65] The dates of the first performance by Nodier, and the following two by Moncrieff and Planché, are from Frederick Burwick, *Playing to the Crowd: London Popular Theatre, 1780–1830* (New York: Palgrave Macmillan, 2011), 76.

[66] Rarignac, *Theology of Dracula*, 55. Byron rather attributed it to his name being affixed to the tale. Thomas Medwin, *Journal of the Conversations of Lord Byron: Noted during a Residence with His Lordship at Pisa, in the Years 1821 and 1822* (London: Henry Colburn, 1824), 101, https://books.google.com.au/books?id=n7oVAQAAMAAJ.

[67] Nodier, Carmouche, and Jouffroy, *Vampire*, 21.

[68] Charles Nodier [attrib.], "The Vampire," in *Lord Ruthven the Vampire*, by John William Polidori, Charles Nodier, and Eugène Scribe, adapt. Frank J. Morlock (Encino, CA: Black Coat Press, 2004), 105.

[69] Nodier, Carmouche, and Jouffroy, *Vampire*, 25.

[70] Nodier, "Vampire," 109.

groom intervenes, shooting Rutwen. Aubray, unaware of what happened, sees this as a cold-blooded murder and once again follows the dying man's wishes to be placed in the moonlight. He also vows to let no one know what has happened to him for twelve hours. Aubray returns, dreading to break the news to Malvina. When he encounters Rutwen there with her, insisting to go ahead with the wedding and telling him to keep his oath, Aubray strongly reacts and is dragged off as mad, but escapes, returns, and stalls the ceremony long enough for 1 a.m. to strike. Rutwen moans "Le néant! Le néant!"[71] ("Nothingness! Nothingness!"[72]) and is reduced to ashes by a lightning bolt.

Not only does the prologue contain an exchange between Christian angels, who also seem like mild portrayals of the Greek minor deities Hymen and Selene, giving it something of a classical feel as well, but Oscar incarnates himself in the narrative to match the incarnate vampire—at the servants' wedding as a minstrel singing a song of warning to the bride against Rutwen and as a monk counseling Malvina's lady-in-waiting to get Malvina away. This further Christianizes the plot although he is largely impotent both times. Also, with regard to Christianizing the story there is a brief stage direction at the end; while Rutwen is being forced down to annihilation by his victims before he is incinerated, "l'Ange exterminateur"[73] (the avenging angel) crosses the stage in a luminous chariot.[74]

It is puzzling that the same moon who is fraternizing with Oscar in the graveyard and learning about vampires in the prologue has the power to revive the vampire and, in all likelihood, has done so many times before. The whole action shifts to Scotland from part of it being abroad in Polidori. Aubray and Rutwen are peers; Rutwen's vices are reduced to his need to feed on virgin women, Ianthe is eliminated, Rutwen sacrifices his life to save Aubray, and the end is happy with justice prevailing. Lord Rutwen can no longer be a stranger in this scenario; he has to be an acquaintance of someone in the family. From this point on, Polidori's story will be an indirect influence on what follows and this one more direct.

"The Vampire" (1820), by J. R. Planché

The first English adaptation of Nodier, Caramouche and Jouffroy's play was James Robinson Planché's *The Vampire; or, The Bride of the Isles*[75] (English Opera House,

---

[71] Nodier, Carmouche, and Jouffroy, *Vampire*, 56.

[72] Nodier, "Vampire," 161.

[73] Nodier, Carmouche, and Jouffroy, *Vampire*, 56. Frank J. Morlock renders this line "the angel of love" in Nodier, "Vampire," 161.

[74] This Christianization of the story was not enough for some. Colin de Plancy, *Histoire des vampires et des spectres malfaisans: avec un examen du vampirisme* (Paris: Masson, 1820), calls the play "hideuse et imorale" (hideous and immoral) (271), adding "Toute la pièce représente indirectement Dieu comme un être faible ou odieux qui abandonne le monde aux génies de l'enfer" (271) (The entire play indirectly represents God as a weak or odious being who abandons the world to spirits from hell).

[75] Although the title has been taken from the original playbill, citations to follow are from Planché, *The Vampire; or, The Bride of the Isles, a Romantic Drama, in Two Acts*, original and

London, August 9, 1820). The basic plot is the same as Nodier, Caramouche and Jouffroy's. The two angels are now Ariel, a sky spirit, and Unda, a water or flood spirit. They conjure up in the cemetery the vampire ghost, so that the sleeping Lady Margaret, daughter of Baron Ronald,[76] might remember his appearance in her dream and reject him. She is engaged to Lord Ruthven, who is possessed by the vampire spirit. Neither angel incarnates in the story.

Ianthe makes a small cameo in the play. Her story is told by M'Swill, the comic character:

> Once on a time, there lived a lady named Blanche, in this very castle, and she was betrothed to a rich Scotch nobleman. All the preparations for the wedding were finished, when, on the evening before it was to take place, the lovers strolled into the forest— [. . .] They never came out again. [. . .] The next morning the body of the lady was found covered with blood, and the marks of human teeth on her throat, but no trace of the nobleman could be discovered, and from that time to this he has never been heard of; and they do say—I hope nobody hears us—they do say that the nobleman was a vampire [. . .].[77]

The vampire has stronger mesmerizing effects here, his victims said to be "Like birds when gaz'd on by the basilisk."[78] It operates both through vision and by touch (he takes her hand and "a thrill runs through [her] frame"[79]), and so it explains better the ease with which Margaret casts aside the warning from the spirits.[80] Nonetheless it takes time fully to work. Her suitor is not really Lord Ruthven, but Cromal the Bloody inhabiting his body. The narrative insinuates a pact with the Devil to explain Ruthven's need to marry young virgins and kill them at regular intervals, instead of just leaving it to God's permissive providence.

Ronald's relationship with Ruthven begins with his unnamed son being deathly ill in Athens and under Ruthven's care. After his son's death, Ruthven fills the void for his paternal affection. This is the first narrative that relates them as father and future son-in-law. Ruthven finds out one of Ronald's servants, Robert, is going to

---

complete ed. ([London: J. Dicks, 1874?]), https://hdl.handle.net/2027/uc1.31175035148637. This is not the earliest printed version of the play, but the earliest version that could be accessed at the time of writing.

[76] In Planché, *Vampire*, 3, the character is referred to as Lord Ronald after the dramatis personae on the title page introduces him as "Baron of the Isles." A baron is a title of nobility. *Lord* is used of a baron when referring to him less formally. So, he is a baron even though he is addressed and designated as lord. He will be referred to as baron in this text for consistency.

[77] Planché, *Vampire*, 4–5.

[78] Planché, *Vampire*, 3.

[79] Planché, *Vampire*, 7.

[80] Stuart complains about this: "to attribute Margaret's attraction to him to 'magic' undermines Nodier's insight into human nature—our attraction to the danger of the 'dark stranger' (which Ibsen plumbs so deeply in *The Lady from the Sea*)—and completely misses the power of the central myth of vampires." *Stage Blood*, 80.

marry Effie, the daughter of Ruthven's steward, Andrew. Ruthven attends the wedding to steal Effie from Robert and marry her himself. He will kill her and thus grant a temporary reprieve to Margaret. Effie flees from Ruthven's seductions and he pursues her. Her cries alert Robert, who shoots Ruthven. As Ruthven lies mortally wounded, he stops Ronald from talking about retribution for he does not have much time. Ruthven extracts an oath not to reveal his death until the moon sets that night and to throw his ring into a pool that laps up against some caverns. Meanwhile, Robert seeks refuge in those very caverns to wait until Ronald's wrath subsides, so he can explain everything.

Robert reveals himself to Ronald in the caverns and Ronald fights him and throws him into the waves. Leaving him for dead, Ronald returns home and encounters Ruthven alive and his shock, anger, and the paternal passion to protect his daughter are again mistaken for madness and he is removed to his chamber. Robert, who was rescued from the water by Effie and Andrew, learns of Ronald's seclusion and of the wedding and, as a loyal servant, despite his treatment, rescues him. Ronald returns and refuses the marriage. Ruthven passes his time allotment, is struck by lightning, and annihilated. Unda and Ariel reappear; there is no visitation from an avenging angel.

One of the most interesting aspects of this retelling is the development of the sympathetic vampire: "Demon as I am, that walk the earth to slaughter and devour, the little that remains of heart within this wizard frame, sustained alone by human blood, shrinks from the appalling act of planting misery in the bosom of this veteran chieftain. Still must the fearful sacrifice be made, and suddenly, for the approaching night will find my wretched frame exhausted, and darkness, worse than death, annihilation is my lot! Margaret, unhappy maid, thou art my destined prey! Thy blood must feed a vampire's life, and prove the food of his disgusting banquet."[81] He actually decides to spare her life for a time and take that of his servant's daughter, Effie, instead, but his plan goes awry. The insinuation is that he will inhabit another body and become engaged again to her.

"The Vampire" (1820), by W. T. Moncrieff

The second English adaptation of Nodier, Caramouche and Jouffroy's play was W. T. Moncrieff's *The Vampire: A Drama in Three Acts*[82] (Royal Coburg Theatre, London, August 22, 1820).[83] The opening sequence is now between Terra, spirit of the earth, and Lunaria, spirit of the moon. Terra is calling upon Lunaria, whose planet has a strange effect on vampires,[84] restoring them to life, to help him warn Malvina of the

[81] Planché, *Vampire*, 7.

[82] The play's title is taken from Moncrieff, *The Vampire: A Drama, in Three Acts* (London: Thomas Richardson, 1829?).

[83] Burwick misprints the date as "June 22, 1820" in *Playing to the Crowd*, 206; and Burwick, *Romanticism: Keywords* (Malden, MA: Wiley Blackwell, 2015), 177, using the correct date in *Playing to the Crowd*, 76, 221n37, 275, but also cites August 21, 1820 (224n27).

[84] The sun and moon were numbered among the planets at this time, for they were also

vampire she is about to marry by making his spirit take shape when he rises from the grave and claims her as his own. This way she will recognize him. He is "the chief of the vampire race,"[85] here named Ruthwold, a shape shifter who has left ruin and destruction in his wake. The vampire is conjured and does lunge at her but is threatened by Terra with being prey to "The Invisible;"[86] not with nothingness but "flames and pangs eternal."[87] In the body of the story, there are several noteworthy differences. One is a conversation among the servants talking of Ruthwold at his return as a terrible and destructive man, who cannot be respected. In Nodier and Planché he is welcomed back with universal joy. Ianthe is back in the form of "Ida," and is used as the pretext for Ruthwold saving the life of Sir Malcolm, who is Malvina's brother, not father, as in Nodier. More on Ida in a moment.

There is the introduction of Edgar, who is in love with Malvina and is not a servant, and who, from the beginning, distrusts Ruthwold. When Ruthwold finds out that there is a wedding at his estate, he decides on sparing Malvina and taking Jeannie instead: "one victim will suffice,"[88] he declares. Edgar follows him there. Disguised as a minstrel he takes Oscar's place warning the bride and it is he who executes Ruthwold in the chase. Ruthwold, in addition to the vows he exacts from Malcolm, calls for revenge against Edgar, so Malcolm follows him this time, despite Jeannie's protests that he saved her from Ruthwold, to a secluded cavern and believes he has killed him, having pushed him into the water below.

Edgar, a good swimmer, precedes Malcolm home and warns Malvina's maid-of-honor as Oscar did, but is misunderstood. Ruthwold appears shortly thereafter and makes final preparations for the wedding. Malcolm in expressing again his fear and anxiety at finding Ruthwold alive is hauled off as mad. Edgar releases him and then stops the ceremony. Not being bound to a vow he reveals Ruthwold for who he is, thus stalling the ceremony. The clock strikes one and the moon rises. The Invisible exclaims "Ruthwold thou'rt lost forever!—I wait for thee—Come, come!"[89] Ruthwold is dragged down by vampires and Terra and Lunaria descend in the clouds.

The moon is present in this tale, as in Planché, but moves beyond its revivifying rays. It is personified but now has the power, by itself, to make a vampire spirit reveal its physical form. Most vampires are of an inferior status, we are told—they are released from their graves from 1 a.m. until dawn to find and feed on victims. This one, Ruthwold, can work all the time and like in Planché, is able to take different forms to make him hard to detect. The narrative is slightly more Christianized by the introduction of The Invisible. God's providence is still in the

---

πλανῆται (wanderers) in the heavens.

[85] Moncrieff, *Vampire*, 10.

[86] The "Invisible" is not Nodier's "Great Spirit," but Satan. "The Invisible shall have his tribute," Ruthwold remarks as he pressures Malvina to the altar. Moncrieff, *Vampire*, 39.

[87] Moncrieff, *Vampire*, 10.

[88] Moncrieff, *Vampire*, 21.

[89] Moncrieff, *Vampire*, 40.

background. Ruthwold is made sympathetic, but a little less so at the outset than in Planché, in that his intentions are merely in stray comments. He could feel pity for Malvina if he did not need her for his life.[90] Then when Jeannie becomes available, he thinks Malvina can be spared altogether, which is more magnanimous.[91]

There is the reintroduction of Ianthe (Ida). Malcolm relates how he was being strangled in the hut when members of his party entered. Ruthwold then came running thereto followed by "thieves." He threw himself between a robber's bullet and Malcolm, then the thieves were vanquished. The whole situation is clearly a cover-up. Ruthwold had left Malcolm to attend a wedding of peasants he had secretly paid for. He obviously fled with the bride, Ida, took her to the hut, and exsanguinated her. He had to flee when Malcolm's men entered the hut and found the peasant girl dead. Running away he must have run into the wedding search party and had to return to the hut in a hurry, where he acted the hero. This clarifies a point in Polidori's narrative: how Ianthe ended up at the hut. Ruthven must have met her near her home and offered his protection to enter the woods and wait for him there.

It is a significant innovation for Moncrieff to make Edgar a love interest rather than a servant. Instead of service to Malcolm, it is romantic love for Malvina that motivates his intrusion into the narrative. At the heart of the story is a contradiction. In the prologue it states Ruthwold must marry before he can partake of his victim, but he is willing to take Jeannine without marrying her and he still tries to abduct Malvina even though his wedding is suspended.

"The Bride of the Isles" (1820?)

We turn now to an anonymous adaptation of Planché's play, *The Bride of the Isles, a Tale Founded on the Popular Legend of the Vampire* (1820?), misattributed to Lord Byron.[92] The vampire is now explicitly in league with the Christian Devil who has required of him to marry a virgin on Halloween, slay her, and drink her blood before the setting of the moon. That done, he can vacate the body he is in and find another. If he fails, he is annihilated, subject to Nodier's "nothingness." The vampire is the notorious Oscar Montcalm, who inhabits the body of Lord Ruthven when he dies. Oscar had been in love, when alive, with Lady Margaret, Lord Ronald's daughter, but their social stations made a union impossible, so now is his chance for revenge against Ronald. Meanwhile Margaret, twenty with no prospects of marriage, goes to an enchanted cave to see what her future holds. Una, spirit of the storm, in league with Oscar, shows her Lord Ruthven; Ariel, spirit of the air,

---

[90] Moncrieff, *Vampire*, 21.

[91] Moncrieff, *Vampire*, 21.

[92] The title page of *The Bride of the Isles, a Tale Founded on the Popular Legend of the Vampire* (Dublin: J. Charles, 1820?) has "by Lord Byron" as its byline. Reprinted as Anonymous, "The Bride of the Isles: A Tale Founded on the Popular Legend of the Vampyre," in *The Shilling Shockers: Stories of Terror from the Gothic Bluebooks*, ed. Peter Haining (London: Victor Gollancz, 1978), 127–51.

unsolicited, shows her a different young man—as it turns out, her first cousin.

After Margaret's experience in the cave, the real Lord Ruthven joins Lord Ronald home from battle and love blossoms between her and him. The men are called back to war and this time Ruthven is killed. Oscar takes over his body and returns to Margaret. The spirits try to warn her, but she takes no heed. Some months later Ronald and his servant, Robert, return and are shocked to find Margaret hanging on Ruthven's arm. Robert, knowing that Ruthven had died, being versed in vampire lore, thus called the "Vampire hunter,"[93] and suspicious of Ruthven's avoidance of mass and prayer, confides this to Ronald and the latter actually listens and decides he will wait until after moonset on Halloween to let the couple marry.

Shortly thereafter Ruthven makes his move and demands they marry immediately and Ronald refuses; the set date of October 31 is only a month away. Ruthven continues to provoke Ronald and, as his anger flares, he is declared mad and confined. Ruthven initiates the ceremony, but Robert liberates Ronald and together they stop the wedding. Feeling there is nothing left to do, Ruthven seduces Robert's fiancée. He does this so he can take another form with her death and woo Margaret again. As they ride away together, Robert shoots him.

Ruthven, mortally wounded, protests that this proves he is mortal and not a vampire, and extracts an oath not to bury his body until the morrow, to throw his ring into the pool near the cave Margaret had visited, and to give him his ring to wear as an emblem of their reconciliation, in addition to his silence for twelve hours. Robert and Ronald go that night to the pool and throw in the ring and Ariel warns them the marriage is about to start. Ruthven has returned, produced Ronald's ring, said that Ronald was called away, and gave his permission for the marriage. On the way home Ronald and Robert run into Ronald's nephew who is on the road to see him. They join him and together they thwart Ruthven; he is hit by lightning and disappears. Margaret then marries her cousin and they live happily ever after.

Religion plays a smaller part than usual in the narrative. Robert simply accuses Ruthven of not attending church and there are the revelations from the spirits. The coincidence of meeting Ronald's nephew on the road is read as providential and so too the final lightning strike but these are indirect and unstated, with the latter as standard fare. As opposed to Edgar in Moncrieff, Robert has a sound reason to distrust Ruthven beyond Edgar's intuition and undisclosed tales and observations: he is certain Ruthven meets the description of a vampire, which includes really dying. The ring is more integrated into the plot than it was in Planché. It acts pretty much as the moon does, a plot device from Byron, but is now also something to get Ronald and Robert out of the way so the marriage can be rushed and uninterrupted. Ronald and Robert would have been too late without the encounter with Margaret's cousin, for initially they had to go slowly through the woods to avoid getting lost in the storm that had arisen. The vow is minimized, outside

---

[93] *Bride of the Isles*, 21.

throwing the ring in the pool, and has no manipulative value.

Margaret is said to be under Ruthven's "spell" so that she finds the now pallid Ruthven handsome. It is reported that he is in possession of eyes like a basilisk. The relationship between the vampire spirit and Lord Ruthven is clarified considerably: Lord Ruthven and Margaret fall in love; Ruthven dies in battle; the spirit inhabits his body and returns to Margaret to marry and devour her. This is the only variation that has the vampire previously acquainted with the victim in addition to her parent or sibling. The moon gains a role beyond revivification, but it is less than in Moncrieff. The experiment with a sympathetic vampire is over; he is again simply a cruel manipulator. This tale is also unique in that Lord Ronald actually listens to his servant.

"Der Vampyr" (1821), bearb. Heinrich Ludwig Ritter

Heinrich Ludwig Ritter's German adaptation of Nodier's play, entitled *Der Vampyr oder die Todten-Braut, romantisches Schauspiel in drei Acten; in Verbindung eines Vorspiels: Der Traum in der Fingalschöhle; nach einer Erzählung des Lord Byron* (Karlsruhe, March 1, 1821)[94] takes some substantial liberties with the text, but at two points they become significant for us; they both deal with religion. The first is with Oskar watching over Malvina in the graveyard. In the original, the promise made to the vampire spirit is *néant* or nothingness; here it is more Christianized to a theme of "punishment and retribution," as it was in Moncrieff. In addition, after the vampire spirit recedes, Oskar kneels beside the sleeping Malvina and prays.[95]

At the end *néant* is again changed, this time to "der ewigen Rache des Himmels"[96] (the eternal vengeance of heaven). But note the grand Christianization of the text, which ends simply with a lightning bolt and a chariot in Nodier:

> er sucht zu entfliehen, aber krachend stürzen die Säulen des Gerwölbes zusammen. Geister und Furien steigen aus der Erde empor, umschlingen ihn mit Ketten und rietzen ihn mit sich fort. Der Engle des Weltgerichts erscheint mit einem flammenden Schwert in einer Wolke. Auf einen heftigen Donnerschlag öffnet sich der Boden, Flammen schlagen heraus und Rutwen sinkt mit den Schatten hinab [. . .] Während dem [. . .] ein Engel des Friedens mit einer Palme, schützen über Aubray und Malvina. Wenn der Feuerregen sich allmählig verliert, sieht man den Genius der Liebe in Verklärung vor dem hellerleuchteten Kreuze aufschweben, unter solgenden

---

[94] Location and date of first performance taken from Stuart, *Stage Blood*, 112, 265. The first theatre the play was performed in could not be determined by the time this article went to press. The play's title is taken from Ritter, bearb., *Der Vampyr oder die Todten-Braut, romantisches Schauspiel in drei Acten; in Verbindung eines Vorspiels: Der Traum in der Fingalschöhle; nach einer Erzählung des Lord Byron* (Braunschweig: G. C. E. Meyer, 1822), http://resolver.sub.uni-goettingen.de/purl?PPN856879215.

[95] Ritter, *Vampyr*, 12. The text explicitly highlights this theme: "strafende Vergeltung" (punitive retribution) (12).

[96] Ritter, *Vampyr*, 127.

unsichtbaren Chor von Engeln.[97]

he tries to escape but the pillars of the vault break and crash together. Specters and furies rise up from the ground, wrap him in chains and drag him away with them. In a cloud the angel of the final judgment appears with a flaming sword. With a violent clap of thunder, the floor opens; flames leap up and Rutwen sinks down with the shadows [. . .] Meanwhile [. . .] an angel of peace with a palm branch shelters Aubray and Malvina. As the rain of fire gradually lets up, one could see the spirit of love hover in transfiguration, before a bright, shining cross, and behind this there an invisible choir of angels.

The choir sings:

Zur Todtenbraut erlesen
Bist Jungfrau du gewesen.
Doch unsichtbar umschweben
Beschüzend, wir dein Leben;
Vor drohenden Gesahren
Wird Unschuld dich bewahren.
Das Laster unterliegt,
Dem ew'gen Strafsgericht,
Die Tugend aber siegt
Und blendend strahit ihr Licht.[98]

To the chosen dead bride
A virgin you abide.
We invisibly hover
Your life to secure;
Innocence protects
From dangerous threats.
Vice gives way
To the judgment day,
Virtue's victorious
Its light brilliant and luminous.

We now turn to the first of two operas based on Ritter's adaptation, both debuting in 1828.

"Der Vampyr" (1828), comp. Heinrich Marschner; lib. Wilhelm August Wohlbrück

The first is Heinrich Marschner's *Der Vampyr, große romantische Oper in zwei Aufzügen*[99] (Theater der Stadt Leipzig, March 29, 1828). Our interest is in the

---

[97] Ritter, *Vampyr*, 127–8.

[98] Ritter, *Vampyr*, 128.

[99] Although the title has been taken from the original playbill, citations to follow are from Wohlbrück, *Der Vampyr: Romantische Oper in zwei Aufzügen; nach Lord Byron's Erzählung,*

libretto, prepared by Wilhelm August Wohlbrück. We continue with the ruthless, conscienceless male vampire fixated on the blood of innocent maidens. Following Ritter, the plot is deeply Christianized.

The opera commences with a devil substitute—who is also a vampire—named Der Meister[100] (The Master), articulating the conditions for Ruthwen to live another year on earth. By midnight of this day, he must kill three brides. He boasts that he already has two lined up and that a third will be easy to find. But he is caught after killing the first, Janthe, mortally wounded, and unable reach the moonlight. At this juncture Edgar Aubrey, who owes him a favor for saving his life, happens by and, although recognizing that only a vampire would ask to be placed in the lunar light, he does it out of obligation. He also vows to keep everything he knows about him secret for twenty-four hours.

Edgar continues on his journey to his beloved, Malwina, in hopes that her father, on this her eighteenth birthday, will allow them to marry. But in the midst of the couple's reunion, her father, Sir Humpry, bursts in with what he considers to be good news: Malwina can now marry someone of her own station, the Earl of Marsden. Edgar recognizes him as Ruthwen and rages that he must be silent. As the scene ends Sir Humpry, Malwina, and Edgar, from their own perspectives, reiterate their faith in God's help when they act strongly, while Ruthwen exalts his own strength as fortified by the power of hell.

The couple is to be wed that night; during the day he visits his castle where two servants are marrying. Here, Edgar confronts him and explains that he is going to break his vow. This is the moment where Ruthwen outlines the tragedy of the vampire. Edgar would be guilty of perjury and this will require he enter vampiric existence and kill all his loved ones, an act which shall torment him. His family will curse him as they die. There is nothing abstract about this, he says; it happened to him. Thence Ruthwen seduces the servant bride and kills his second victim.

All Edgar can do now is tell Malwina that she is lost, but both then confess their trust in God to reward piety and to overcome the powers of hell. Edgar protests at the wedding against Malwina marrying this monster and is led out in chains as insane. Malwina, despite her father's curses, refuses to marry him; Edgar escapes, re-enters, and breaks his vow. Ruthwen is struck by lightning a moment thereafter; Sir Humpry repents and allows the love of Malwina and Edgar to be consummated. The heavens open and a choir sings:

> Ihm! der der Unschuld Sieg verleiht,
> Dem Laster grause Strafe dräut,
> Dem Ewigen sey Preis und Dank!
> Ihm schalle unser Lobgesang!

---

music by Heinrich Marschener (Leipzig: C. H. F. Hartmann, 1828), https://www.loc.gov/item /2010659686. Citations refer to the Hartmann edition.

[100] "Vampire Master" in Heinrich Marschner [attrib.], "The Vampire," trans. Jutta Romero, Public Domain Opera Libretti and Other Vocal Texts, last updated May 13, 1997, http://opera.stanfo rd.edu/iu/libretti/vampyr.html.

Aus des Verderbens finsterm Schoos
Erschuf er Euch das schönste Loos,
So führet Er aus dunkler Nacht
Den Tag hervor in Strahlen-Pracht;
Dem Ewigen sey Preis und Dank!
Ihm schalle unser Lobgesang.[101]

To him! who brings victory to the innocent,
To the depraved threatens grave punishment,
To the Eternal be acclaim and thanks!
To him we sing our heartfelt praise!
Out of the lap of dark ruination,
He created you the most beautiful fate
So he leads forth from the darkest night
The day of bright luminous light;
To the Eternal be acclaim and thanks!
To him we sing our heartfelt praise![102]

The conditions are the most demanding here, but one aspect is missing: he needs three brides, but they need not be his brides. Janthe (Ianthe) is introduced in a different role, that of a lover to Ruthwen. He is, as usual, equipped with mesmerism. In the case of Janthe, she declares that at first, she was repelled by him:

Aber wie mit Zaubers Banden
Zog es später mich zu Dir.
[. . .]
Ja ich folg' dem innern Drange,
Meinem Herzen folge ich.[103]

But like as with a magical restraint
It delayed my being pulled to you.
[. . .]
Yes, I'm following an urge,
I am following my heart.[104]

---

[101] Wohlbrück, *Vampyr*, 106.

[102] In Marschner, "Vampire," the German text is abbreviated to the following:

Out of ruins lap
Blossomed a beautiful fate;
To the almighty praise and thanks!
To him our song of praise is dedicated!

[103] Wohlbrück, *Vampyr*, 11.

[104] In Marschner, "Vampire," the translation is:

But it never works on Malwina; she never likes him. This is the first that has the oath-taker seriously contemplating breaking his vow. Aubry is again Malwina's lover, not a servant.

The locus of sympathy has changed. With Planché it was remorse that he would have to kill Margaret largely because it will hurt Robert. It is real sympathy, but not for Margaret. Here it is a warning to Aubrey based on his own tragic experience of slaughtering his family. The vampire first kills his wife, sons and daughters. They will recognize him, cursing him and themselves. Then he must take the life of his most precious little girl who hugs her father, prays, and begs for her life. The passage alludes to Lord Byron's *The Giaour* (1813):

> But first, on earth as Vampire sent,
> Thy corse [corpse] shall from its tomb be rent;
> Then ghastly haunt thy native place,
> And suck the blood of all thy race,
> There from thy daughter, sister, wife,
> At midnight drain the stream of life;
> Yet loathe the banquet with perforce
> Must feed thy livid living corse;
> Thy victims ere they yet expire
> Shall know the dæmon for their sire,
> As cursing thee, thou cursing them,
> Thy flowers are wither'd on the stem.
> But one that for thy crime must fall—
> The youngest—most belov'd of all,
> Shall bless thee with a *father's* name—
> That word shall wrap thy heart in flame![105]

This is the only rendition where the servant bride is murdered, and Ruthven gets away. Elsewhere she escapes and he dies. And this is the only one where the bride disobeys her father and refuses to marry the groom. This is important, for it portrays, for the first time in Ruthven narratives, a woman with a degree of independence.

ACKNOWLEDGMENTS

This article could not have been realized without the services of Vanderbilt

---

Like with a magic rope
It pulled me later to you.
[. . .]
Yes, I am following an urge,
I am following my heart.

[105] Byron, *The Giaour, a Fragment of a Turkish Tale* (London: Printed by T. Davison, Whitefriars, for John Murray, Albemarle-street, 1813), 23–24, https://archive.org/details/giao urfragmentof01byro.

University's Interlibrary Loan team, especially James Toplon and Rachel Adams. I wish to express my gratitude to Anthony G. Cirilla and Clemens Ruthner for examining my extended German translations. Any errors remain my own. I wish also to thank Anthony Hogg, whose diligent research has made this a more rigorous study.

BIBLIOGRAPHY

Anonymous. "The Bride of the Isles: A Tale Founded on the Popular Legend of the Vampire." In *The Shilling Shockers: Stories of Terror from the Gothic Bluebooks*, edited by Peter Haining, 127–51. London: Victor Gollancz, 1978. Originally published as Lord Byron [attrib.], *The Bride of the Isles, a Tale Founded on the Popular Legend of the Vampire* (Dublin: J. Charles, ca. 1820).

Auerbach, Nina. *Our Vampires, Ourselves*. Chicago: University of Chicago Press, 1995.

Barger, Andrew, ed. *The Best Vampire Stories, 1800–1849: A Classic Vampire Anthology*. N.p.: Bottletree, 2011.

Beaton, Roderick. *Byron's War: Romantic Rebellion, Greek Revolution*. Cambridge: Cambridge University Press, 2013.

Bérard, Cyprien [C. B., pseud.]. *Lord Ruthwen, ou Les vampires*. 2 vols. Paris: Ladvocat, 1820. Gallica.

———. *The Vampire Lord Ruthwen*. Translated by Brian Stableford. Encino, CA: Black Coat Press, 2011. Originally published as *Lord Ruthwen, ou Les vampires*, 2 vols. (Paris: Ladvocat, 1820).

Birmingham (UK) Daily Post. "The Banker's Secret." Codicil to "Larkin's Legacy." December 27, 1870, 6–7. Newspapers.com.

Bray, Katie. "'A Climate . . . More Prolific . . . in Sorcery': *The Black Vampyre* and the Hemispheric Gothic," *American Literature* 87, no. 1 (March 2015): 1–21. https://doi.org/10.1215/00029831-2865163.

The Bride of the Isles, a Tale Founded on the Popular Legend of the Vampire. Dublin: J. Charles, ca. 1820. Incorrectly attributed to Lord Byron.

Burwick, Frederick. *Playing to the Crowd: London Popular Theatre, 1780–1830*. New York: Palgrave Macmillan, 2011.

———. *Romanticism: Keywords*. Malden, MA: Wiley Blackwell, 2015.

Byron, Lord. "A Fragment." In *Mazeppa, a Poem*, 59–69. London: John Murray, 1819. https://archive.org/details/mazeppaapoem02byrogoog.

———. *The Giaour, a Fragment of a Turkish Tale*. London: printed by T. Davison, Whitefriars, for John Murray, Albemarle-street, 1813. https://archive.org/details/giaourfragmentof01byro.

C. B. *See* Bérard, Cyprien.

D'Arcy, Uriah Derick [Richard Varick Dey? Robert C. Sands?]. *The Black Vampyre; A Legend of St. Domingo*. New York: printed for the author, 1819.

Dey, Richard Varick. *See* D'Arcy, Uriah Derick.

[Dickens, Charles, Jr.?]. "Vampyres and Ghouls." *All the Year Round*, May 20, 1871, 597–600. https://archive.org/details/allyearround05dickrich.

Eighteen-Bisang, Robert, and Richard Dalby, eds. *Vintage Vampire Stories*. New York: Skyhorse Publishing, 2011.

Frayling, Christopher. *Vampyres: Lord Byron to Count Dracula*. London: Faber & Faber, 1991.

Goedeke, Karl. *Vom Weltfrieden bis zur französischen Revolution 1830*. Bd. 11, bk. 8, 4. Abt.

(Drama und Theater), Halbbd. 1, of *Grundrisz zur Geschichte der deutschen Dichtung aus den Quellen*, edited by Carl Diesch. 2. Aufl. Düsseldorf: L. Ehlermann, 1951. https://archiv e.org/details/GoedekeGrundrissZurGeschichteDerDeutschenDichtung-2-111.

Hock, Stefan. *Die Vampyrsagen und ihre Verwertung in der deutschen Litteratur.* Berlin: Alexander Duncker, 1900. Google Play Books.

Klingaman, William K., and Nicholas P. Klingaman. *The Year Without a Summer: 1816 and the Volcano That Darkened the World and Changed History.* New York: St. Martin's Press, 2013.

Knickerbocker. "More of Sands' Literary Remains: 'The Black Vampyre.'" January 1845, 73–77. https://hdl.handle.net/2027/uc1.b5238921.

———. "Sands' 'Black Vampyre.'" February 1845, 171–3. https://hdl.handle.net/2027/uc1.b523 8921.

Marschner, Heinrich. *See* Wohlbrück, Wilh[elm] Aug[ust].

——— [attrib.]. "The Vampire." Translated by Jutta Romero. Public-Domain Opera Libretti and Other Vocal Texts. Last updated May 13, 1997. http://opera.stanford.edu/iu/libretti/v ampyr.html.

Medwin, Thomas. *Journal of the Conversations of Lord Byron: Noted During a Residence with His Lordship at Pisa, in the Years 1821 and 1822.* London: Henry Colburn, 1824. https://books.g oogle.com.au/books?id=n7oVAQAAMAAJ.

M.M. ***. *See* Nodier, Charles, Pierre-Frédéric-Adolphe Carmouche, and Achille de Jouffroy.

Moncrieff, W. T. *The Vampire: A Drama, in Three Acts.* London: Thomas Richardson, 1829?

Morlock, Frank J. "The Birth of Modern Vampirism." Introduction to Polidori, Nodier, and Scribe, *Lord Ruthven the Vampire*, 7–19.

Nodier, Charles [attrib.]. "The Vampire." In Polidori, Nodier, and Scribe, *Lord Ruthven the Vampire*, 77–161.

Nodier, Charles, Pierre-Frédéric-Adolphe Carmouche, and Achille de Jouffroy [M.M. ***, pseud.]. *Le Vampire, mélodrame en trois actes, avec un prologue.* Paris: J.-N. Barba, 1820. https://archive.org/details/bub_gb_Cda5kpWKRHgC.

"Notice bibliographique: Des ouvrages publiés par Charles Nodier." In *Description raisonnée d'une jolie collection de livres (Nouveaux mélanges tirés d'une petite bibliothèque)*, by Charles Nodier. Paris: J. Techener, 1844. https://books.google.com.au/books?id=s_tEsoplZegC.

Oliver, A. Richard. *Charles Nodier: Pilot of Romanticism.* Syracuse: Syracuse University Press, 1964.

Planché, J. R. *The Vampire; or, The Bride of the Isles. A Romantic Drama, in Two Acts.* Original complete ed. [London: John Dicks, 1874?]. https://hdl.handle.net/2027/uc1.3117503514863 7.

[Plancy, Collin de]. *Histoire des vampires et des spectres malfaisans: avec un examen du vampirisme.* Paris: Masson, 1820. Google Play Books.

Polidori, John William. *The Diary of Dr. John William Polidori, 1816: Relating to Byron, Shelley, etc.* Edited and elucidated by William Michael Rossetti. London: Elkin Mathews, 1911. https://hdl.handle.net/2027/uc2.ark:/13960/t0gt5jq1t.

———. *The Vampyre; A Tale.* London: Sherwood, Neely, and Jones, 1819.

———. "The Vampyre; A Tale." *New Monthly Magazine*, April 1, 1819, 195–206. https://hdl.ha ndle.net/2027/hvd.32044025671017. Incorrectly attributed to Lord Byron.

———. "The Vampyre: A Tale." In Polidori, *"The Vampyre" and "Ernestus Berchtold"*, 33–49.

———. *"The Vampyre" and "Ernestus Berchtold; or, The Modern Oedipus": Collected Fiction of John William Polidori.* Edited and introduced by D. L. Macdonald and Kathleen Scherf. Toronto: University of Toronto Press, 1994.

Polidori, John William, Charles Nodier, and Eugène Scribe. *Lord Ruthven the Vampire.* Adapted in English by Frank J. Morlock. Encino, CA: Black Coat Press, 2004.

Rarignac, Noël Montague-Étienne. *The Theology of Dracula: Reading the Book of Stoker as Sacred Text.* Jefferson, NC: McFarland, 2012.

Ritter, [Heinrich] L[udwig], bearb. *Der Vampyr oder die Todten-Braut, romantisches Schauspiel in drei Acten; in Verbindung eines Vorspiels: Der Traum in der Fingalschöhle; nach einer Erzählung des Lord Byron.* Braunschweig: G. C. E. Meyer, 1822. http://resolver.sub.uni-goe ttingen.de/purl?PPN856879215.

Sands, Robert C. [attrib.]. "The Black Vampyre: A Legend of Saint Domingo." In Barger, *Best Vampire Stories*, 139–61.

———. *See also* D'Arcy, Uriah Derick.

Senf, Carol A. *The Vampire in Nineteenth-Century English Literature.* Madison: University of Wisconsin Press, 1988.

Stableford, Brian. Introduction to Bérard, *Vampire Lord Ruthwen*, 9–20.

Stuart, Roxana. *Stage Blood: Vampires of the 19th-Century Stage.* Bowling Green, OH: Bowling Green State University Popular Press, 1994.

Summers, Montague. *The Vampire, His Kith and Kin.* London: Kegan Paul, Trench, Trubner, 1928.

Twitchell, James. *The Living Dead: A Study of the Vampire in Romantic Literature.* Durham: Duke University Press, 1981.

Wohlbrück, Wilh[elm] Aug[ust]. *Der Vampyr: Romantische Oper in zwei Aufzügen; nach Lord Byron's Erzählung.* Music by Heinrich Marschener. Leipzig: C. H. F. Hartmann, 1828. http ://www.loc.gov/item/2010659686.

Wood, Gillen D'Arcy. *Tambora: The Eruption That Changed the World.* Princeton, NJ: Princeton University Press, 2014.

Syncretism and Credulity in Montague Summers' "Philosophy of Vampirism"

Gerard P. O'Sullivan
Independent scholar, USA

ABSTRACT *Montague Summers wrote* The Vampire, His Kith and Kin *(1928) during a time when popular discourse about vampires, after the publication of Stoker's Dracula, was dominated by Theosophical writers. This was a period of regnant "occulture" when American Spiritualism, Theosophy, and various forms of esoteric Masonry shaped British thinking about the supernatural. Summers tried countering the dominant occult discourse with one which was more acceptably Catholic (to him), but which was still tinged with heterodoxy.*

KEYWORDS *supernaturalism; Catholicism; Spiritualist philosophy; Theosophy; Freemasonry*

Montague Summers' *The Vampire, His Kith and Kin* (1928) is a classic work in the canon of revenantology. While Summers characterized his book as the first comprehensive study of the vampire in English,[1] it was not. The book is best regarded as one idiosyncratic Catholic's theological intervention into a popular conversation which was then dominated by Theosophical discourse and works of popular occultism.

For all his Ultramontanist posturing, Montague Summers was anything but an orthodox believer in the doctrines of the Roman Catholic Church. Summers was a syncretist who sought to meld Jacobite political sympathies with Tridentine liturgical practices and occult theories about matter, time and space. These placed him within a camp of upper-echelon, university-based spiritualists like Lord Rayleigh, J. J. Thomson, William Crookes and Oliver Lodge.[2]

It is not unusual to read an essay or book by Summers which flips the reader quickly from discussions on the writings of St. Thomas Aquinas to a consideration of ectoplasm and its role in mediumistic séances. This curious juxtaposition of theological and metaphysical "registers" occurs throughout Summers' posthumously published book, *The Physical Phenomena of Mysticism: With Especial Reference the Stigmata, Divine and Diabolic* (1950):

> One of the most striking instances of divinely supernatural telekenesis is when Pope St. Pius V on -7 October, 1571, was informed of the result of the Battle of Lepanto and

---

[1] Montague Summers, *The Vampire, His Kith and Kin: A Critical Edition*, ed. John Edgar Browning (Berkeley: Apocryphile Press, 2011), xii. All subsequent citations refer to this edition.

[2] Janet Oppenheimer, "Physics and Psychic Research in Victorian and Edwardian England," *Physics Today* 39, no. 5 (May 1986): 62–72, https://doi.org/10.1063/1.881027.

the Victory of Don John. The Holy Father at the very decisive moment was discussing some business of the first importance with a Congregation of Cardinals. Suddenly he rose, left them abruptly, and went to the window which he opened. For a moment his eyes were fixed on the heavens, and then returning to the table he said: "It is not now a time to talk any more about affairs, however pressing; it is the time to give thanks to Almighty God for the signal victory which He has vouchsafed to the Christians." This fact was carefully attested at the very moment and authentically recorded so as to admit of no shadow of doubt. There is (apparently) a natural telekenesis, outside the midnight and murk of the séance-rooms, of which an example was displayed by Mr. Stephan Ossowiecki, a Polish gentleman, whose supra-normal gifts are described in Dr. Gustave Geley's work, Paris, 1924, *L'Ectoplasmie et la Clairvoyance* [46].[3]

For this and other reasons, Summers was often dismissed by more mainstream commentators (like Fr. Herbert Thurston, S.J, cited below) as a costume Catholic. Summers, however, would not be dissuaded: he saw himself as doing battle with diabolical forces which included modernism, Theosophy, surrealism and psychoanalysis. Summers believed that he could carve out a space for himself and his often-reactionary positions by demonstrating an erudite (if misguided) understanding of theology fused with pseudoscience.

OCCULTURE

London in the 1880s and 1890s was rife with popular occultism, or what Christopher Partridge calls "occulture."[4] Summers knew this world well, and he was one of its leading denizens. Over the course of decades Summers built an enviable library of occult titles and rubbed shoulders with some of Great Britain's most notable luminaries in the esoteric world.

By the 1880s, American-style Spiritualism had found a welcoming home in Great Britain. The writings of Andrew Jackson Davis, Paschal Beverly Randolph and others reignited interest in Mesmerism and Swedenborgianism. Likewise, Theosophy—another North American export to Great Britain—was established as the Theosophical Society in New York City in 1875 by Helena Blavatsky, Henry Steel Olcott, and William Quan Judge. Spiritualist and Theosophical speakers toured Europe with some regularity and their teachings found fertile ground among social reformers and urban intellectuals.

As Joy Dixon notes, the links between Theosophy, feminism and women's suffrage were historically as well as statistically significant: her survey of Theosophical Society membership rolls proves that mostly urban leaders of the feminist and suffrage movements were hundreds of times more likely to join the

---

[3] Summers, *The Physical Phenomena of Mysticism: With Especial Reference the Stigmata, Divine and Diabolic* (New York: Barnes & Noble, [1950]), 66, https://archive.org/details/physic alphenomen007373mbp.

[4] Partridge, *Alternative Spiritualities, Sacralization, Popular Culture and Occulture*, vol. 1 of *The Re-Enchantment of the West* (London: T & T Clark Publishers, 2006).

Society than their women counterparts elsewhere in the country.[5] The discourse of "the New Woman" and "New Womanhood" was first introduced into the critical and theoretical vocabulary of suffragism by Theosophists.[6]

Similarly, Spiritualism was strongly linked to radical politics of a socialist nature. Spiritualism's reformist tendencies made it especially appealing to radical Quakers in both New York State and London. The utopian socialist Robert Owen made a late-in-life conversion to Spiritualism and many of spiritualism's earliest leaders were active social reformers. Like Theosophy, Spiritualism advocated for women's rights and women's suffrage among upper middle-class women and proved to be a powerful instance of popular spirituality as well as a cohesive form of resistance to established political, economic and gender norms.[7]

Both Theosophy and spiritualism produced successful and wide-reaching media outlets which included newspapers, magazines, and book publishing houses. Many adherents to both movements were writers, artists and poets who sought to share their philosophical beliefs through short stories and novels. After the wild successes of Bram Stoker's novel *Dracula* (1897), the bulk of popularly available materials on vampires and vampirism were published by Theosophical outlets and bore that movement's philosophical stamp. Indeed, and as Mark Morrison reminds us, British occulture in the 1880s and 1890s was largely a periodical culture aimed at popularizing the underlying messages of a movement which would have been otherwise marginalized.[8]

James Taylor's curious tract, *Occult Novels as Theosophical Propaganda* (1932),[9] makes clear that Theosophical leaders saw gothic and supernatural fiction as means to an end: occult fiction flourished during the heyday of Theosophy and many writers on esoteric matters were also accomplished novelists and short story writers like Mabel Collins, Dion Fortune and Franz Hartmann.[10] Theosophists saw

  [5] Dixon, *Divine Feminine: Theosophy and Feminism in England* (Baltimore: Johns Hopkins University Press, 2001), 6.

  [6] Siv Ellen Kraft, "Theosophy, Gender and 'The New Woman,'" in *Handbook of the Theosophical Current*, ed. Olav Hammer and Mikael Rothstein (Leiden: Brill, 2013), 357–74, https://doi.org/10.1163 /9789004235977.

  [7] Ann Braude, *Radical Spirits: Spiritualism and Women's Rights in Nineteenth-Century America* (Bloomington: Indiana University Press, 2001).

  [8] Mark S. Morrison, "The Periodical Culture of the Occult Revival: Esoteric Wisdom, Modernity and Counter-Public Spheres," *Journal of Modern Literature* 31, no. 2 (Winter 2008): 1–22.

  [9] Taylor, *Occult Novels as Theosophical Propaganda* (Wheaton, IL: Theosophical Publishing House, 1932); *see also* Michael J. Altman, "The Theosophical Quest for Occult Power," chap. 5 in *Heathen, Hindoo, Hindu: American Representations of India, 1721–1893* (New York: Oxford University Press, 2017), https://www.doi.org/10.1093/acprof:oso/9780190654924.003.0005.

  [10] Christine Ferguson, "Conjuring the Market: Literature and Occult Populism at the *fin de siècle*," review of *Popular Literature, Authorship and the Occult in Late Victorian Britain*, by Andrew McCann, *Journal of Victorian Culture* 20, no. 3 (September 2015): 435–8, https://doi.org/10.1080/13555502.2015.1058081; and Christine Ferguson and Andrew Radford, eds., *The Occult Imagination in Britain, 1875–1947* (London, Routledge, 2017).

supernatural literature as one among many ways to proselytize for the gospel of Madame Blavatsky. Montague Summers would have none of this.

"PHILOSOPHY OF VAMPIRISM"

Summers makes clear in *The Vampire, His Kith and Kin* that his goals in writing the book are twofold: 1) To present the "first" comprehensive guide to vampires and vampirism written in English; and 2) To offer to the reading public a compendious "philosophy of vampirism":

> In the present work I have endeavoured to set forth what might be termed "the philosophy of vampirism," and however ghastly and macabre they may appear I have felt that here one must not tamely shrink from a careful and detailed consideration of the many cognate passions and congruous circumstances which—there can be no reasonable doubt—have throughout the ages played no impertinent and no trivial but a very vital and very memorable part in consolidating the vampire legend, and in perpetuating the vampire tradition among the darker and more secret mysteries of belief that prevail in the heart of man.[11]

Summers's book was by no means the first such study written in English. It was the second. But Summers scorned his competitor, Dudley Wright, and his book *Vampires and Vampirism* (1914; 1924), calling it "an insipid olio," chastising both editions as "slovenly" and unscholarly treatises, reliant on second-hand sources.[12]

Despite summers' reproaches, Wright's book was the most comprehensive overview of vampires published in English, to date. Wright was a well-known Freemason and historian of the Lodge whose alternating religious indifferentism and outright hostility to Catholicism made Summers more than a little peevish. Wright, however, was still the first author to write a popular, book-length overview of vampires and vampirism in English.

Why did Summers feel compelled to pen a "philosophy of vampirism?" Most, if not all the materials available for public consumption on vampires, and appearing in print between the late nineteenth century and 1928, when *The Vampire, His Kith and Kin* was first published, were generated by Theosophists and other occultists for reasons discussed earlier. Writers on literature and the arts who did not have access to classical languages were forced to consult contemporary authorities on the vampire that did not accord with Summers's standards of scholarship or, for that matter, his eccentric version of religious orthodoxy. Unlike Wright, Summers did not set out to write a popular compendium of received knowledge about vampires. Instead he wanted to write a scholarly treatise, and this explains why he took no pains to translate lengthy Latin, Greek, French, German and other quotes from their original languages into contemporary English.

Dorothy Scarborough, author of a monumental early study of supernaturalism

---

[11] Summers, *Vampire*, xii–xiii.
[12] Summers, *Vampire*, xi–xii.

in English literature entitled *The Supernatural in Modern English Fiction* (1917), alluded to Theosophical resources on vampirism:

> The idea of occult vampirism used by [Ivan] Turgeniev is also employed by Reginald Hodder in his work, *The Vampire*. Here peculiar power is possessed by a woman leader of an occult band, who vampirizes by means of a talisman. Her ravages are psychic rather than physical. Theosophists, according to the *Occult Magazine*, believe in vampires even in the present. According to their theory, one who has been very wicked in life is in death so inextricably entangled with his evil motives and acts that he is hopelessly lost and knows it, yet seeks to delay for a time his final damnation. He can ward off spiritual death so long as he can keep alive by means of blood his physical corpse. *The Occult Review* believes that probably only those acquainted with black magic in their lifetime can become vampires, — a thought comforting to some of us.[13]

Before the publication of Summers's book, Theosophical and other occult periodicals featured dozens of articles on vampires, written by authors of some repute in the esoteric community (among them Franz Hartmann, Helena Blavatsky, and Henry Steele Olcott). Non-Theosophist writers of fiction, like New Zealand-born journalist Reginald Hodder, author of *The Vampire* (1913), also made contributions to these periodicals.[14] It was not unusual for literary critics like Scarborough, quoted above, to mine occult publications for "facts" about vampires in the absence of less dogmatic studies.

One of Theosophy's most prolific writers, Henry Steel Olcott, had an article on vampires published in an 1891 issue of the *Theosophist*.[15] Olcott, a U. S. Army Colonel and military investigator in the Union Army during the American Civil War, was one of the men credited with making the first arrests after the assassination of Abraham Lincoln. Like Lincoln, Olcott was fascinated by Spiritualism and the occult. An ardent advocate for cremation as a sanitary means of disposing of the dead, he also believed that cremation was the most effective deterrent to vampirism. When Olcott supervised the first public cremation in United States history, at New York's Masonic Hall on May 28, 1876, he almost caused a riot. The papers dismissed the burning of a corpse as a "pagan funeral" and denounced the social reformer for desecrating the dead.[16] Indeed, Olcott took the occasion of writing about vampires to promote cremation: "And it is another argument in favor of cremation — if any were needed by thoughtful persons — that

---

[13] Scarborough, *The Supernatural in Modern English Fiction* (New York: G.P. Putnam's Sons, 1917), 163, https://archive.org/details/supernaturalinm00scargoog.

[14] Hodder, "Vampires," *Occult Review*, April 1914, 225–9, http://www.iapsop.com/archive/materials/occult_review/occult_review_v19_n4_apr_1914.pdf.

[15] Olcott, "The Vampire." *Theosophist* 12, no. 7 (April 1891): 385–93, http://www.iapsop.com/archive/materials/theosophist/theosophist_v12_n07_april_1891.pdf.

[16] Stephen Prothero, *Purified by Fire: A History of Cremation in America* (Berkeley: University of California Press, 2002), 33.

there are no vampires save in countries where the dead are buried."[17] He continues:

> I do not know the derivation of the word vampire. In French it is spelt as in English; in Spanish and Italian *vampiro*; in German and Danish *vampir*; in Serb *wampir*, *wampira*, *wukódlak*; in Wallachian *murony*; in Turkish *massâcet*; in Modern Greek *bronkolakas*, and in several other ways; its Polish name is *upior*, Slavonic *upir*, and Russian *googooka*. The "Am. Cyclopædia" calls it "a fabulous creature", but the pious Benedictine writer, Dom Calmet, describes it as persons "who have been dead a considerable time, sometimes more, sometimes less; who leave their tombs, and come and disturb the living, sucking their blood, appearing to them, making a noise at their doors and in their houses, and often causing their death". They usually, he informs us, visit their relatives and those in the prime of life and full health and vigour. [. . .] In reading upon this gruesome subject, I have been struck with the apparent substantiation of certain facts, viz:
> 1.   The vampire elementary always attacks the robust;
> 2.   The signs of the obsession are invariably nervous prostration and anæmia, and usually a slight puncture over the jugular vein;
> 3.   The corpse of the suspected vampire, when examined, appears well-nourished with healthy blood, and presents the appearance of one in cataleptic sleep, rather than of death.
> 4.   If a pointed stake or weapon be thrust through the heart, the corpse cries out and often writhes in agony;
> 5.   If the corpse be cremated, the vampire ceases to trouble. I have found no exception stated in this respect.[18]

In Theosophical parlance, one type of vampire is an astral revenant which is amorally moved to attack and drain human beings of their energy. Another is the physical vampire, which drains humans of blood. They are not "diabolical" in any recognizably Christian sense of that term, but Olcott's use of the writings of the Benedictine Biblical scholar Dom Augustin Calmet as a legitimizing authority (see below) would have given Summers pause.

DUDLEY WRIGHT AND POPULAR OCCULTISM

In 1910, Dudley Wright wrote an article on vampires for the *Occult Review*,[19] relating a story told to him by an unnamed surgeon of great repute: "The following particulars have been communicated to me by a well-known surgeon, who has held various official appointments in the tropics, and the incidents herein recorded happened exactly as they are described."[20]

The account is the tale of a "living vampire" who feeds upon one British consular officer after another until each one grows so sick and so despondent that

---

[17] Olcott, "Vampire," 385.

[18] Olcott, "Vampire," 385–6.

[19] Wright, "A Living Vampire," *Occult Review*, July 1910, 45–47, http://www.iapsop.com/archive/materials/occult_review/occult_review_v12_n1_jul_1910.pdf.

[20] Wright, "Living Vampire," 45.

they request a transfer to another colonial outpost. All we know of the location is that it is in "the tropics." In the end we learn that the purported vampire is a tall Indian gentleman who is landed and wealthy. His mistake is to feed by night upon the wife of an officer who recalls his face from "a dream" which, as it turns out, was no dream at all. The consul officer approaches the gentleman at their club and the following ensues:

> In the afternoon husband and wife were going together to the Club, when around the corner of the jungle came a tall Indian, the owner of a large number of milch cattle, and reputed to be a wealthy man. The surgeon's wife suddenly stopped, turned pale and said immediately: —
> "That is the man I saw in my dream."
> The husband went directly up to the man and said to him: —
> "Look here, I will give you twelve hours to get out of this place. I know everything that happened last night at midnight, and I will kill you like a dog if I find you here in twelve hours' time."
> The Indian disappeared the same night, taking with him only a few valuables and a little loose money. He left behind him the money that was deposited in the Bank as well as the whole of his property. His forty head of cattle, worth eighty dollars each, were impounded, and no news had been heard of him five years afterwards. Since his departure no one has complained of depression and lassitude in that area.[21]

This bizarre story appears again in chapter ten of *Vampires and Vampirism* (1914) with the following, additional details: "The following account was contributed by me to the *Occult Review* for July 1910. The particulars are given exactly as I wrote them down in shorthand from the narrator's dictation. My informant is a well-known medical practitioner in the West End of London, who has held various official appointments in the tropics, and I received his assurance that the incidents recorded happened exactly as they are described. Whether the Indian referred to is still alive or not is unknown, but certainly the two other principals, at the time of writing, are."[22]

Summers takes a sidelong jab at Wright in *The Vampire, His Kith and Kin*, which appeared in print four years after the second edition of Wright's book was published. In discussing the taxonomy of Indian ghouls and vampires, Summers notes:

> In a private letter to myself Mr. [N. M.] Penzer [author of *The Ocean of Story*] writes: "It is the Rakshasas who are the more prominent among malicious demons. Their name means 'the harmers' or 'destroyers' as their particular delight is to upset sacrifices, worry ascetics, animate dead bodies, etc. They date in India from *Rig-Vedic* days.

---

[21] Wright, "Living Vampire," 47.

[22] Wright, *Vampires and Vampirism* (London: William Rider and Son, 1914), 143, https://archive.org/details/b24876549.

"In the *Atharva Veda* they are described as deformed, of blue, green, or yellow colour, with long slit eyes. Their nails are poisonous and are dangerous to the touch. They eat human and horse flesh, the former of which they procure by prowling round the burning-ghats at night. They possess great wealth, and bestow it on those they favour. Their chief is Ravana, the enemy of Rama. See Crooke, *Folk-Lore of Northern India*, Vol. I, p. 246 *sqq*.

"The Pisachas are very similar to the above, while the Vetalas are perhaps more like Vampires."[23]

Summers seems to suggest that Wright has his vampirological taxonomies confused: the purported vampire described in both the *Occult Review* article and chapter ten of *Vampires and Vampirism* is not a vampire at all, but a *pisacha*, or a flesh-eating ghoul.

While Wright borrows from Theosophical and other occult writers in discussing vampires, he is not unwilling to disagree with them. At one juncture in his book, Wright references Olcott on the question of Indian vampires, but without naming him, to wit: can a religious culture which eschews the consumption of animal blood and that practices cremation rather than burial produce vampires? Here are the words of Olcott taken from the *Theosophist* in which he makes the quite remarkable argument that there can be no Hindu (or for that matter, Buddhist) vampires:

Of all the forms of the real or supposed intercourse between the living and dead, that of the vampire is the most loathsome. The horrid physical effects which follow after the burial of a corpse, have no doubt, had much to do in creating the sentiment of disgust and terror which associates with the thought of this return of the dead to prey upon the living. And it is another argument in favor of cremation—if any were needed by thoughtful persons—that there are no vampires save in countries where the dead are buried. We do not hear of Hindu vampires, but where such cases occur in India, it turns out that the *revenant* is a deceased Mussalman [Muslim], Christian, or Jew, whose body has been interred.[24]

Wright states that while it has been asserted "by some writers" that "vampires are not to be found in Indian lore and legend,"[25] he claims that vampires are just as plentiful on the Indian subcontinent as they are elsewhere in the world. The major difference, claims Wright, is that folktales about them "are more scarce."[26] Summers, as noted, made short work of Wright's misreadings of Indian legends about ghouls and vampires, and is especially uncharitable toward Wright in the opening pages of *The Vampire, His Kith and Kin*:

In English there is a little book entitled *Vampires and Vampirism* by Mr. Dudley Wright, which was first published in 1914; second edition (with additional matter),

---

[23] Summers, *Vampire*, 250.
[24] Olcott, "Vampire," 385.
[25] Wright, *Vampires and Vampirism*, 59.
[26] Wright, *Vampires and Vampirism*, 60.

1924. It may, of course, be said that this is not intended to be more than a popular and trifling collection and that one must not look for accuracy and research from the author of *Roman Catholicism and Freemasonry*. However that may be, it were not an easy task to find a more insipid olio than *Vampires and Vampirism*, of which the ingredients, so far as I am able to judge, are most palpably derived at second, and even at third hand. Dom Calmet, sometimes with and sometimes without acknowledgement, is frequently quoted and continually misunderstood, In what the "additional matter" of the second edition consists I cannot pretend to say but I have noticed that the same anecdotes are repeated, *e.g.* on p. 9 we are told the story of a shepherd of "Blow, near Kadam, in Bohemia," and the relation is said to be taken (*via* Calmet, it is plain,) from "De Schartz [rather Charles Ferdinand de Schertz], in his *Magia Postuma*, published at Olmutz in 1706." On p. 166 this story, as given by "E. P. Evans, in his interesting work on the *Criminal Prosecution and Capital Punishment of Animals*," is told of "a herdsman near the town of Cadan," and dated 1337. Pages 60-62 are occupied with an Oriental legend related by "Fornari, in his *History of Sorcerers*," by which is presumably intended the *Histoire curieuse et pittoresque des sorciers . . . Revue et augmentée par Fornari*, Paris, 1846, and other editions, a book usually catalogued under Giraldo, as by Caillet and Yve-Plessis, although the latter certainly has a cross-reference to Fornari. In greater detail Mr. Dudley Wright narrates this legend which he has already told (pp. 60-62), on pp. 131-137. Such repetition seems superfluous. In the Bibliography we have such entries as "Leo Allatius," "*Encyclopaedia Britannica*"; "Frazer's *Golden Bough*," "Nider's *Formicarius*," "Phlegon's *Fragments*," "William of Newbury," all of which are not merely unscholarly and slovenly, but entirely useless from the point of view of reference. I also remark blunders such as "Philip Rehrius," "Nicolas Ramy's *Demonolatrie*," "Rymer's *Varney the Vampire*." Who Rymer might be I cannot tell. *Varney the Vampire* was written by Thomas Preskett Prest.[27]

Dudley Wright published a book and nine articles which were highly critical of Roman Catholicism.[28] His 1921 series of articles in the *Builder* examining the history of Catholic anti-Masonry were later collected and published as *Roman Catholicism and Freemasonry* (1922). In that book and its precursor essays Wright reviews numerous declarations and actions by Catholic laity and clergy aimed at undermining Freemasonry. In the early thirties, however, Wright left Masonry and became a committed Catholic

As an early proponent of Theosophy, Wright wrote testimonies to the truths contained in Druidism and the Eleusinian mysteries, among other ancient cults. To Wright's way of thinking, the ancient mystery cults and all the historic religions of the world thereafter derived their doctrines, disciplines and liturgical practices from Freemasonry and not the other way around. Writing in his preface to *The*

---

[27] Summers, *Vampire*, xi–xii.

[28] I am deeply indebted to Simon Mayers, who has blogged extensively on Dudley Wright and his spiritually peripatetic ways: Simon Mayers and John Belton, "The Life and Works of Dudley Wright," *Heredom* 23 (2015): 11–54. *See also* Paul Calderwood, *Freemasonry and the Press in the Twentieth Century: A National Newspaper Study of England and Wales* (Farnham, Surrey, Ashgate, 2013), app. 4.

Eleusinian Mysteries & Rites (1919), Wright makes a bold claim: "The Masonic antiquarian maintains that Freemasonry is not a scion snatched with a violent hand from the Mysteries—whether Pythagorean, Hermetic, Samothracian, Eleusinian, Drusian, Druidical, or the like—but is the original institution, from which all the Mysteries were derived."[29]

Through the 1910s Wright combined a fervent philo-Judaism with an ardent belief that Freemasonry preserved the ancient tenets of Merkabah mysticism and the forgotten practices of First Temple Judaism. Wright was also a regular contributor to the *Occult Review*.

Summers was a regular reader of the *Occult Review* and later a contributor, alongside such esoteric notables as Aleister Crowley and Arthur Edward Waite. In all likelihood, Summers was also a reader of Wright's articles as they appeared in the *Occult Review* and the *Theosophist*, among other publications. One cannot imagine Summers finding anything to admire in Wright's heterodox musings on the virgin birth, the prodigal son, immortality of the human soul and other Catholic and Christian themes.

During this phase in his religious thinking, Wright also dabbled in Buddhism. In September 1915, Wright embraced the tenets of Ahmadiyya Islam. Ahmadis, as they are known, are unlike other Muslims in their belief that Mirza Ghulam Ahmad, the founder of the movement, was both the promised Mahdi (Guided One) and the Messiah foretold by Muhammad to appear at the end of time. At heart, Ahmadis are universalists insofar as they believe that all religions are one and spring from the same Divine source which culminates in the teachings of Islam.

Wright's Islamophile period did not last long. In 1933, he converted to Roman Catholicism and became avowedly anti-Semitic in his views. He joined the Catholic Guild of Israel, an ultramontane and extremely conservative organization dedicated to aggressively proselytizing and converting Great Britain's Jews to Catholicism.

In his articles and pamphlets from that time, Wright appears to repeat, almost verbatim, the language used by Fr. Bede Jarrett, O.P., provincial head of the English Dominicans and president of the Guild, and Fr. Arthur Day, S.J., an English Jesuit and the Guild's vice-president. Both Jarrett and Day actively supported the Papacy's position during the so-called Mortara case (Italian: *caso Mortara*), an Italian *cause celebre* in the 1850s and 1860s.

The Papal States seized a six-year-old child from a Jewish family in Bologna, Edgardo Mortara, on the basis of a former housemaid's testimony that she had administered emergency baptism to the boy when he allegedly fell sick as an infant. Mortara grew up as a Catholic under the protection of Pope Pius IX, who steadfastly refused his parents' desperate pleas for the return of their son. Edgardo eventually became a priest.

Both Jarrett and Day used the Mortara case to illustrate the extent of what they

---

[29] Wright, *The Eleusinian Mysteries & Rites* (London: Theosophical Publishing House; Denver: "The Square & Compass," [1919]), 7.

called "Jewish power," inferring that the fall of the Papal States was due to the sinister international reach of world Jewry acting in response to Pius IX's intransigence. Wright himself repeated many of these canards during the time of his Catholicism, and this in spite of his own earlier philo-Judaism. However, by the 1940s the spiritually promiscuous Wright left the Catholic Church, returned to Islam and became—once again—Muhammed Sadiq Dudley Wright. It was under this name that Wright published numerous essays in the *Islamic Review*. By this time, Wright's scurrilous attacks on Judaism ceased.

In his later years, Wright was forthright about his commitment to the *Prisca theologia* or "theology of the ancients"—a belief that underlying all of the world's religions is a core set of truths which should serve to unite rather than divide believers. This belief was in full accord with the implicit universalism of Freemasonry and Wright's avowedly Theosophical leanings. Wright's perennialism, his interreligious profligacy, and his earlier attacks on Catholicism made him a natural foil for Summers.

The 1914 edition of Wright's *Vampires and Vampirism* was published under the long shadow cast by the 1897 appearance of *Dracula*. By 1913 Stoker's novel had already reached its tenth edition. As Montague Summers notes in the opening chapters of *The Vampire, His Kith and Kin*:

> It is hardly an exaggeration to affirm that of recent years there have been few books which have been more popular than Bram Stoker's *Dracula, A tale*, and certainly there is no sensational romance which in modern days has achieved so universal a reputation. Since it was first published in 1897, that is to say one and twenty years ago, it has run into a great number of editions, and the name has veritably become a household word. It will prove interesting to inquire into the immediate causes which have brought this book such wide and enduring fame. It has already been remarked that it is well-nigh impossible for a story which deals with the supernatural or the horrible to be sustained to any great length. Elements which at first are almost unendurable, will lose their effect if they are continued, for the reader's mind insensibly becomes inured to fresh emotions of awe and horror, and *Dracula* is by no means briefly told. In the ordinary reprints (Tenth Edition, 1913) it extends to more than four hundred pages, nor does it escape the penalty of its prolixity.[30]

Summers references Stoker and *Dracula* several times in *The Vampire, His Kith and Kin*. Wright barely mentions the book,[31] and has more to say about Reginald Hodder's then recently published *The Vampire* (1913)[32] than he does about the canonical Stoker novel. It is doubtless that the release of an expanded and edited second edition of Wright's vampire study in 1924 prompted Summers to move forward with his own project.

---

[30] Summers, *Vampire*, 333.
[31] Wright, *Vampires and Vampirism*, 150.
[32] Wright, *Vampires and Vampirism*, 160.

THE USES AND MISUSES OF DOM AUGUSTIN CALMET

Both Wright and Summers rely heavily upon the work of Dom Antoine Augustin Calmet, O.S.B., a famed biblical scholar of the eighteenth-century and a man surprisingly sympathetic to the Philosophes and associated with the Congregation of St. Maur; a community of French Benedictines renowned for their scholarship and often called the Maurist Enlighteners.[33]

Calmet and his close contemporary, Giuseppe Davanzati, drew inspiration from Leo Allatios. The Greek-born Allatios was a convert to Catholicism from Orthodoxy, a Hellenist and the keeper of the Vatican Library. He is oft remembered among historians of science for his bizarre rejoinder to Galileo about the Rings of Saturn. Galileo observed the Rings over time (1610–1616) with his 20x telescope and wondered, in writing, how the immutable and unchangeable planets and stars could seemingly mutate and change over time. Allatios proffered a counter-theory: the Rings were the foreskin (Prepus) of the risen Christ, "caught" on the horns of the planet as Jesus rose through the heavens. Foreskins change with temperature and conditions, reasoned Allatios, ergo the Rings were also (therefore) subject to change.[34]

This "anatomical" argument made a certain amount of sense to the Vatican Librarian because Allatios was trained as a physician as well as a theologian. He was as much concerned with post-mortem life as he was with human (and planetary) anatomy and physiology: Allatios produced the first methodical study of vampires and vampirism written in any language, and within the context of a broader study of Greek beliefs: *De Graecorum hodie quorundam opinationibus* (On certain modern opinions among the Greeks) (1645). Allatios's treatise served as a source for Giuseppe Davanzati's *Dissertazione sopra I vampiri* (completed in 1739; first published in 1774; republished in 1789) and Dom Calmet's three editions.

Summers draws upon Allatios, Davanzati and Calmet in *The Vampire, His Kith and Kin*, citing Allatios three times, Davanzati fourteen times and Calmet twenty-seven times. It was Calmet, after all, who provided the outline for Wright's book as well as the topics for emphasis and amplification. The treatises of Calmet, Wright and Summers focus on Greece (per Allatios, of course) but also dwell on vampirism in the Slavic nations. Indeed, Calmet's treatise provides an enduring topical and geographical outline for numerous vampire studies.

At the height of the Age of Reason, Dom Augustin Calmet published *Dissertations sur les apparitions des anges, des démons et des esprits, et sur les revenants et vampires de Hongrie, de Bohême, de Moravie, et de Silésie*. This extraordinary collection of allegedly true tales of ghosts, ghouls and vampires sold out shortly after its first appearance in 1746. In 1751, a revised and expanded version was published under the title *Traité sur les Apparitions des esprits et sur les vampires ou les revenans de*

---

[33] Christophe Vuillaume, "Dom Augustin Calmet, exegete," *American Benedictine Review* 68, no. 1 (March 2017): 57–72.

[34] Jolene Creighton, "The Mysteries of Saturn," *Futurism*, December 10, 2013, https://futurism.com/the-mysteries-of-saturn-2.

Hongrie, de Moravie etc. Dom Calmet's treatise is the first comprehensive study of the European vampire, and the first work to examine the Slavic vampire in any detail.

Calmet was not interested in vampires, *per se.* Despite its utility for writers like Joseph Sheridan Le Fanu and Bram Stoker, who may have mined the good Father's work for tropes and ideas, Calmet's treatise was sparked by the theologian's campaign to investigate and disprove numerous "outbreak" stories from countries like Silesia, Moravia and Serbia, among others. Through the 1720s and 1730s, priests and physicians reported stories of murderous revenants that allegedly killed so many townsfolk that officials felt obliged to disinter dozens of corpses from cemeteries.[35]

As a cleric, Calmet was horrified by the wanton desecration of sacred ground and the callous disregard shown toward the bodies of the dead by "hunters" searching for evidence of blood-engorged bodies underground. Calmet, heavily influenced by Enlightenment rationalism, could not explain or explain away the numerous case studies about vampirism which appeared in reputable scientific and medical journals across Europe. The vampire epidemics of the 1720s and 1730s led to the publication of seventeen articles in professional journals on vampire outbreaks in 1732 alone. Between 1732 and 1735, twenty-two learned treatises appeared in print on vampires which were published in several European centers of learning, written by highly esteemed medical and scientific scholars.[36] These stories were coherent, consistent in detail across countries and towns, and shared similar characteristics from case to case. The fact that these tales were told by reputable persons also fascinated Calmet.[37]

But why did the Enlightenment writers like Calmet produce such detailed studies of vampires and vampirism? The Annales School historian Philippe Ariès notes that the Enlightenment became increasingly death-haunted over time, and for numerous reasons.[38] Two of the most prominent ones were a growing fear of premature burial and widespread public concern about human dissection. In England, France, Germany and elsewhere fresh corpses were monetized by the traffic among what the English called "resurrectionists" or "resurrection men" — grave robbers who sold their ungodly wares to medical schools, surgical colleges, and independent scientists.[39]

---

[35] Several examples are discussed in Paul Barber, *Vampires, Burial and Death: Folklore and Reality* (1988; repr., New Haven, CT: Yale University Press, 2010).

[36] Nick Groom, "*Dracula's* Pre-History," in *The Cambridge Companion to "Dracula,"* ed. Roger Luckhurst (Cambridge: Cambridge University Press, 2018), 15.

[37] Groom, "*Dracula's* Pre-History," 19.

[38] Ariès, *The Hour of Our Death: The Classic History of Western Attitudes Toward Death over the Last One Hundred Years*, trans. Helen Weaver (New York: Random House, 1982).

[39] Marie-Hélène Huet, "Deadly Fears: Dom Augustin Calmet's Vampires and the Rule Over Death," in "Faces of Monstrosity in Eighteenth-Century Thought," ed. Andrew Curran, Robert P. Maccubbin, and David F. Morrill, special issue, *Eighteenth-Century Life*, n.s., 21, no. 2 (May 1997): 222–32, Project Muse.

As cemeteries became more crowded (and especially in urban areas), clerics and canons also raised probing questions about the proper disposition of the bodies of excommunicants, and notably those of alleged heretics like unrepentant members of the Jansenist movement. Calmet's book is replete with stories of improperly buried excommunicants being unceremoniously if mysteriously disinterred by the hallowed ground itself. Calmet shares one report from the Bishop of Cahors[40] (about an excommunicated knight secretly buried in consecrated ground by his friends) which is especially illustrative:

> The next morning his body was found out of the ground, and thrown naked at some distance from the grave, perfectly entire, and without any token of its having been touched. The soldiers who buried him having opened the grave, found nothing but the linnen [sic] which had been wrapped about his body. They then buried him afresh, and, covered the grave with an enormous quantity of earth and stones. The next day the corpse was found out of the grave again, and no symptom of any one's having been at work. The same thing was repeated five several times, and at last they buried him, as they could, in unconsecrated ground, at a distance from the church -yard. The neighbouring gentlemen were so struck with this remarkable event, that they came to me in a body to make overtures of peace.[41]

Wright cites this story in *Vampires and Vampirism* but without due attribution.[42] He spends fifteen pages discussing the relationship between excommunication and vampirism in the Greek church but says practically nothing about the role of excommunication in the Roman church.[43] Summers, on the other hand, surveys the literature on Orthodoxy, vampirism and excommunication with an eye toward raising empirical questions about the allegedly physical postmortem consequences of excommunication in the Orthodox church.

Both Wright and Summers note that it is a strongly held belief in the Orthodox (and especially the Greek) church that the bodies of excommunicants and the contumaciously wicked do not decompose unless, and until, a bishop lifts the curse of ecclesiastical exile. Summers cites several instances of the bodies of Orthodox excommunicants undergoing corruption without episcopal intervention: however, a considerable difficulty arose. It was discovered that excommunication sometimes failed to produce the expected physical result, and the body crumbled to dust in the ordinary way. Accordingly, this had to be reckoned with and explained and Allatios, in his *De Graecorum hodie quorundam opinationibus*, cites a *nomocanon de excommunicatis* which sets out to explain how it is that sometimes excommunication can fail of its result: "Concerning persons excommunicate the which sadly incur

---

[40] Calmet, *Dissertations upon the Apparition of Angels, Dæmons, and Ghosts, And concerning the Vampires of Hungary, Bohemia, Moravia, and Silesia* (London: M. Cooper, 1759), 233–4, https://books.google.com.au/books?id=CM1CAQAAMAAJ.

[41] Calmet, *Dissertations*, 233.

[42] Wright, *Vampires and Vampirism*, 29.

[43] Wright, *Vampires and Vampirism*, 20–35.

episcopal excommunication and after death are found with their bodies 'not loosed' (ἄλυτα)."[44]

Summers is openly derisive of the Greek over-reliance on the threat of excommunication as a means of ensuring the obedience of the laity, and he discusses, at some length, the relatively laxist (and therefore more merciful and humane) practices of the Roman Church with regard to excommunicants: "Finally canon law lays down that at the point of death or in danger of death, all reservations cease and all necessary jurisdiction is supplied by the Church. 'At the point of death,' says the Council of Trent (Session XIV, c. vii), 'in danger of death,' says the *Rituale Romanum*, any priest can absolve from all sins and censures, even if he be without the ordinary faculty of confessor or if he himself be excommunicated. He may even do this in the presence of another priest who is duly and canonically authorized, enjoying jurisdiction (Holy Office, 29th July, 1891)."[45]

Indeed, he quotes (and at great length) the little-known rite from the *Rituale Romanum* which allows any man in holy orders to lift a censure or writ of excommunication from the dead, and with or without the approval of a bishop.[46]

Calmet, in the end, is an unlikely intellectual ally for either Wright or Summers. Wright accepted supernatural claims about vampires and ghouls with little if any skepticism. Wright thought about vampires as the Theosophists thought about vampires: they were beings of occult origin that did their infernal work by night and preyed upon the living. Following the writings of Blavatsky, Franz Hartmann and the French Magnetists, Wright is more than willing to entertain theories of doubles and doubling, biomagnetic fields and "vibrations" to explain the phenomena of vampires and vampirism. It is this over-reliance upon the "psychical sciences" which helps drive Summers's own theological interventions on the subject of vampires, contra Wright.

For Summers, the "problem" of the vampire is a theological one. Vampires are diabolical in origin and the revenant is a parodic double of the risen Christ. "The Devil can effect no real resurrection of a dead person," Summers writes; "that is he cannot restore to life, for this is the power of God alone."[47] He then quotes Jesuit theologian, Martin Delrio, in Latin, and at great length.[48] Delrio is clear: Satan has no power over human life and lacks the capacity to do anything other than command a lesser demon to inhabit a human corpse. On this point, Summers and Calmet are in full agreement: "I lay it down, at first, as an indisputable principle, that to raise to life a person that is really dead, can be effected by the power of God. It is impossible for any man to restore life, either to himself or to another, without a visible miracle."[49]

It is here where Summers and Calmet part company. Calmet is agnostic on the

[44] Summers, *Vampire*, 91.
[45] Summers, *Vampire*, 88.
[46] Summers, *Vampire*, 101–102.
[47] Summers, *Vampire*, 213n64.
[48] Summers, *Vampire*, 213n64.
[49] Calmet, *Dissertations*, 184.

question of the very existence of vampires. That is a given. To carry matters further and attempt to create a full-blown "philosophy" of vampires would be improbable if not impossible, according to Calmet. Summers writes:

> Dom Calmet asks are the appearances of Vampires to be attributed to God, or to the souls of those who return or to the Devil? I answer that for the hauntings of a Vampire, three things are necessary: the Vampire, the Devil, and the Permission of Almighty God. Just as we know, for we learn this from the *Malleus Maleficarum*, that there are three necessary concomitants of witchcraft, and these are the Devil, a Witch, and the Permission of Almighty God (Part 1). So are these three necessary concomitants of Vampirism. Whether it be the Demon who is energizing the corpse or whether it be the dead man himself who by some dispensation of Divine Providence has returned is a particular which must be decided severally for each case. So much then for Dom Calmet's question, to whom are the appearances of Vampires to be attributed.[50]

Calmet avers that he cannot, in good conscience, attest to the reality of vampires. Whether they "exist" or not is of no consequence to him. His concerns are phenomenological: he was drawn to his subject not by any intrinsic interest in vampires, per se, but rather by the unequalled outbreak of reported vampirism cases in Slavic lands during the 1730s. As a theologian, and as someone sympathetic to the virtues of the Philosophes, Calmet felt the need to set matters aright: finding no miraculous or diabolical cause for the phenomenon, Calmet concludes that premature burial is the chief factor supporting belief in vampires:

> Nothing that relates to this subject has astonished me more than the accounts of the vampires of Hungary, Moravia, and Poland; of the Broucolacks of Greece; and of the bodies of excommunicated persons which are said never to rot. I thought myself obliged to give it all the attention I was capable of, and resolved to treat of it in a particular dissertation, distinct from that upon the apparitions of spirits. After having studied the point thoroughly, and got all the information relating to it that I could, I found that there was little in it which could be depended upon as certain. This consideration, joined to the advice of some judicious and respectable persons whom I consulted, made me abandon my design entirely, and quit a subject exposed to so many contradictions.
>
> But, considering the thing in another light, I resumed my pen, with a resolution of undeceiving the publick, if I found the common reports to be absolutely false, or of shewing that all that is advanced upon this subject is uncertain, and that one ought to be very cautious in deciding concerning these vampires [. . .] and concerning which people are still divided in their opinions, even in those countries which are the scene of their pretended return from the grave.[51]

Calmet concludes that vampires are often cataleptics who have been buried prematurely. They are also persons who have seemingly "died" as the result of

---

[50] Summers, *Vampire*, 174.
[51] Calmet, *Dissertations*, vi–vii.

some catastrophic event only to resuscitate, or be resuscitated, after their evident passing. The most unfortunate ones awaken to find themselves buried prematurely. Calmet postulates that those are the ones often seen and mistaken for vampires. Calmet notes (but only in passing) that vampire outbreaks often occur during or after local epidemics of disease. He surmises that the waves of reported deaths which take place during "vampire outbreaks" are most likely caused by diseases like consumption and not by vampire attacks. This is clearly a case of the *post hoc ergo propter hoc* fallacy at work.

Summers is unconvinced by Calmet's skepticism, and even goes so far as to dismiss the Benedictine's over-reliance on reason and the evidence of his senses as heterodox. But Summers's rejoinders to Calmet are less dependent on Catholic dogma than they are to Summers's curious credulity about spiritualism: "Moreover almost any séance will be sufficient reply to Dom Calmet's question."[52] Summers also quotes from *Modern Spiritism* (1904) by "Mr. T. [sic] Godfrey Raupert,"[53] which, in turn, alludes to "the late Leipzig Professor Zoellner's deeply interesting work *Transcendental Physics*"[54] as evidence of things unseen.

Zöllner was a prominent German scientist who, in 1875, embraced the truths of spiritualism after visiting William Crookes in England. He was among the first scientists to suggest that theories of the fourth dimension might explain, and justify belief in, the realm of spirits. In 1877, Zöllner invited the famously dubious spirit medium Henry Slade to conduct a séance under scientific "controls" which failed to catch Slade using simple feats of sleight of hand to produce "spirit writing" on previously clean chalkboards. This simple trick fooled Zöllner so thoroughly that when scientific colleagues questioned the reliability of his controls, he threatened to sue them. Both Harry Houdini and Chung Ling Soo (William Ellsworth Robinson) later proved that Slade was little more than a talented magician and contortionist who could write on slates using his toes.[55]

Summers also appeals to the existence of ectoplasm as the basis for his belief in

---

[52] Summers, *Vampire*, 175.

[53] Summers, *Vampire*, 175.

[54] J. Godfrey Raupert, *Modern Spiritism: A Critical Examination of Its Phenomena, Character, and Teaching in the Light of the Known Facts* (London: Sands, 1904), 36, quoted in Summers, *Vampire*, 175. [Although the edition is not specified, Raupert was probably referring to the first edition: Johann Carl Frederick Zöllner, *Transcendental Physics: An Account of Experimental Investigations, from the Scientific Treatises*, trans. Charles Carleton Massey (London: W. H. Harrison, 1880), originally published as *Die transcendentale Physik und die sogenannte Philosophie: eine deutsche Antwort auf eine "Sogenannte wissenshaftliche Frage"*, vol. 3 of *Wissenschaftliche abhandlungen* (Leipzig: L. Staackmann, 1879).—Ed.]

[55] David Phelps Abbott, *Behind the Scenes with the Mediums* (Chicago: Open Court, 1907), 191, https://archive.org/details/behindsceneswit03abbogoog; Joseph Jastrow, review of *Preliminary Report of the Commission Appointed by the University of Pennsylvania to Investigate Modern Spiritualism in Accordance with the Request of the Late Henry Seybert*, *Science* 10, no. 230 (July 1, 1887): 7–8, https://www.jstor.org/stable/1763929; and Christine Ferguson, review of *Invisible Hosts: Performing the Nineteenth-Century Spirit Medium's Autobiography*, by Elizabeth Schleber Lowry, *Aries* 18, no. 1 (2018): 141–4, https://doi.org/10.1163/15700593-01801008.

the ability of vampires to transmigrate from their graves. "Matter, then, can pass through matter and the séance answers Dom Calmet. We may, if we will, adopt the ectoplasmic theory to explain the mode whereby the Vampire issues from his grave, but although this is very probably true (in some instances at all events) it is not necessarily the only solution of the problem. According to Catholic theologians evil spirits, if permitted to materialize their invisible presence, to build up a tangible and active body, do not absolutely require the ectoplasm of some medium."[56]

Summers mentions ectoplasm several times in *The Vampire, His Kith and Kin*. His belief in spiritualist mediumship and its sham physical "manifestations" rendered him an outlier among Catholics, notably Fr. Herbert Thurston, S.J., a widely regarded Jesuit historian who was an expert on church dogmatics and liturgy. In the very same year that Summers published *The Vampire*, Sheed & Ward released Thurston's book, *Modern Spiritualism* (1928). Thurston and Summers carried on a quiet, running feud over a number of years. Even though Summers includes Thurston's *Month* article "Broucolaccas: A Study in Mediaeval Ghost Lore" (1897) in his book's bibliography,[57] he neglects to cite Thurston as a contemporary Catholic authority on the esoteric. And why? Likely because Thurston shared the skeptical attitude of Dom Calmet toward the very legends and folktales that Summers embraced as truth.

Thurston wrote a scathing review of three of Summers's books on witchcraft in *Studies*,[58] publicly challenging Summers to reveal the source of his holy orders. Summers never did. One may surmise that Summers disliked Thurston because he was a modernist and a friend of the Irish priest Fr. George Tyrrel, S.J., who was expelled from the Society of Jesus for his modernist convictions. Ironically, it was the very Bishop who received Summers into the Roman Catholic faith who placed Tyrrel under minor excommunication and then denied the priest burial in a Catholic cemetery. When word reached Bishop of Southwark Peter Emanuel Amigo that Tyrrel's friend Fr. Henri Brémond had publicly made the sign of the cross over his friend's grave, Brémond was suspended from the priesthood "a divinis" by Amigo, and for some time. Summers, like Tyrrel and Brémond, ran afoul of Bishop Amigo, too: Amigo interceded to forbid Summers from saying mass in the private oratory of one of his benefactors.[59]

In 1952, Herbert Thurston's *The Physical Phenomena of Mysticism* was posthumously published. In 1950 Summers's estate published a book by the very same name. In it, Summers again appealed to his own syncretistic blend of Catholicism and Spiritualism to explain miraculous events like the stigmata of the sanctified. Thurston's volume of the same title was reviewed favorably by the

---

[56] Summers, *Vampire*, 175.

[57] Summers, *Vampire*, 345.

[58] Thurston, "Diabolism," *Studies: An Irish Quarterly Review* 16, no. 63 (September 1927): 441–54, https://www.jstor.org/stable/30093800.

[59] Gerard P. O'Sullivan, "The Continuing Quest for Montague Summers," prologue to Summers, *Vampire*, xli.

eminent psychic researcher, E. J. Dingwall, who noted that Thurston's discussions of stigmata, levitation, bilocation and other such phenomena "is, to say the least, somewhat suggestive that many of the mediumistic phenomena regarded by psychical researchers as almost certainly fraudulent, are scarcely to be found among those recorded by hagiographers, materializations being confined, so it would seem, to the very curious cases of the alleged multiplication of food, which phenomena Thurston thinks cannot be lightly dismissed, although he agrees that the evidence is often inadequate to sustain them."[60]

This could easily be read as a swipe at Summers who accepted apparitional evidence without a qualm of conscience, doctrine, or good sound sense.

In many ways, Summers's position on vampires was closer to that of Wright than Summers (but not Wright) would have ever conceded. Summers's "philosophy of vampirism" mistook the muck and mire of spiritualism for a firm, evidentiary foundation for his own dogmatic convictions. Both writers appealed to Calmet as an intellectual precursor but neither writer could live with the informed ambivalence that shaped the learned Benedictine's approach.

BIBLIOGRAPHY

Abbott, David Phelps. *Behind the Scenes with the Mediums*. Chicago: Open Court: 1907. https://archive.org/details/behindsceneswit03abbogoog.

Altman, Michael J. "The Theosophical Quest for Occult Power." Chap. 5 in *Heathen, Hindoo, Hindu: American Representations of India, 1721–1893*. New York: Oxford University Press, 2017. https://www.doi.org/10.1093/acprof:oso/9780190654924.003.0005.

Ariès, Phillippe. *The Hour of Our Death: The Classic History of Western Attitudes Toward Death over the Last One Hundred Years*. Translated by Helen Weaver. New York: Random House, 1982. Originally published as *L'Homme devant la mort* (Paris: Éditions du Seuil, 1977).

Barber, Paul. *Vampires, Burial and Death: Folklore and Reality*. 1988. Reprint, New Haven, CT: Yale University Press, 2010.

Braude, Ann. *Radical Spirits: Spiritualism and Women's Rights in Nineteenth-Century America*. Bloomington: Indiana University Press, 2001.

Calderwood, Paul. *Freemasonry and the Press in the Twentieth Century: A National Newspaper Study of England and Wales*. Farnham, UK: Ashgate, 2013.

Calmet, Augustin. *Dissertations upon the Apparition of Angels, Dæmons, and Ghosts, And concerning the Vampires of Hungary, Bohemia, Moravia, and Silesia*. London: M. Cooper, 1759. https://books.google.com.au/books?id=CM1CAQAAMAAJ. Originally published as *Dissertations sur les apparitions des anges, des démons & des esprits, et sur les revenans et vampires de Hongrie, de Boheme, de Moravie, & de Silesie*. Paris: De Bure l'aîné, 1746.

Creighton, Jolene. "The Mysteries of Saturn." *Futurism*, December 10, 2013. https://futurism.com/the-mysteries-of-saturn-2.

Dingwall, E. J. Review of *Father Thurston: A Memoir*, by Joseph Crehan; *The Physical Phenomena of Mysticism*, by Herbert Thurston; and *Padre Pio Pietreleina*, by C. C.

---

[60] E. J. Dingwall, review of *Father Thurston: A Memoir*, by Joseph Crehan; *The Physical Phenomena of Mysticism*, by Herbert Thurston; *Padre Pio Pietreleina*, by C. C. Martindale, *Journal of the Society for Psychical Research* 36, no. 672 (November/December 1952): 720, https://archive.org/details/journalofsociety36soci.

Martindale. *Journal of the Society for Psychical Research* 36, no. 672 (November–December 1952): 718–23. https://archive.org/details/journalofsociety36soci.

Ferguson, Christine. Review of *Invisible Hosts: Performing the Nineteenth-Century Spirit Medium's Autobiography*, by Elizabeth Schleber Lowry. *Aries: Journal for the Society of Western Esotericism* 19, no. 1 (2018): 141–4. https://doi.org/10.1163/15700593-01801008.

———. "Conjuring the Market: Literature and Occult Populism at the *fin de siècle*." Review of *Popular Literature, Authorship and the Occult in Late Victorian Britain*, by Andrew McCann. *Journal of Victorian Culture* 20, no. 3 (September 2015): 435–8. https://doi.org/10.1080/13555502.2015.1058081.

Ferguson, Christine, and Andrew Radford, eds. *The Occult Imagination in Britain, 1875–1947*. London: Routledge, 2017.

Groom, Nick. "*Dracula*'s Pre-History." In *The Cambridge Companion to "Dracula,"* edited by Roger Luckhurst, 11–25. Cambridge: Cambridge University Press, 2017.

Huet, Marie-Hélène. "Deadly Fears: Dom Augustin Calmet's Vampires and the Rule Over Death." In "Faces of Monstrosity in Eighteenth-Century Thought," edited Andrew Curran, Robert P. Maccubbin, and David F. Morrill. Special issue, *Eighteenth-Century Life*, n.s., 21, no. 2 (May 1997): 222–32. Project Muse.

Jastrow, Joseph. Review of *Preliminary Report of the Commission Appointed by the University of Pennsylvania to Investigate Modern Spiritualism in Accordance with the Request of the Late Henry Seybert*. *Science* 10, no. 230 (July 1, 1887): 7–8. https://www.jstor.org/stable/1763929.

Kraft, Siv Ellen. "Theosophy, Gender and 'The New Woman.'" In *Handbook of the Theosophical Current*, edited by Olav Hammer and Mikael Rothstein, 357–74. Leiden: Brill, 2013. https://doi.org/10.1163/9789004235977.

Mayers, Simon, and John Belton. "The Life and Works of Dudley Wright." *Heredom* 23 (2015): 11–54.

Morrison, Mark S. "The Periodical Culture of the Occult Revival: Esoteric Wisdom, Modernity and Counter-Public Spheres." *Journal of Modern Literature* 31, no. 2 (Winter 2008): 1–22.

Olcott, H. S. "The Vampire." *The Theosophist* 12, no. 7 (April 1891): 385–93. http://www.iapsop.com/archive/materials/theosophist/theosophist_v12_n07_april_1891.pdf.

Oppenheimer, Janet. "Physics and Psychic Research in Victorian and Edwardian England." *Physics Today* 39, no. 5 (May 1986): 62–72. https://doi.org/10.1063/1.881027.

O'Sullivan, Gerard P. "The Continuing Quest for Montague Summers." Prologue to Summers, *Vampire*. xxviii–lxxii.

Partridge, Christopher. *Alternative Spiritualities, Sacralization, Popular Culture and Occulture*. Vol. 1 of *The Re-Enchantment of the West*. London: T & T Clark Publishers, 2006.

Prothero, Stephen. *Purified by Fire: A History of Cremation in America*. Berkeley: University of California Press, 2002.

Raupert, J. Godfrey. *Modern Spiritism: A Critical Examination of Its Phenomena, Character, and Teaching in the Light of the Known Facts*. London: Sands, 1904. https://archive.org/details/modernspiritismc00rauprich.

Scarborough, Dorothy. *The Supernatural in Modern English Fiction*. New York: G.P. Putnam's Sons, 1917. https://archive.org/details/supernaturalinm00scargoog.

Summers, Montague. *The Physical Phenomena of Mysticism: With Especial Reference the Stigmata, Divine and Diabolic*. New York: Barnes & Noble, [1950]. https://archive.org/details/physicalphenomen007373mbp.

———. *The Vampire, His Kith and Kin: A Critical Edition*. Edited by John Edgar Browning. Berkeley, CA: Apocryphile Press, 2011.

Taylor, James. *Occult Novels as Theosophical Propaganda*. Wheaton, IL: Theosophical

Publishing House, 1932.

Thurston, Herbert. "Diabolism." *Studies: An Irish Quarterly Review* 16, no. 63 (September 1927): 441–54. https://www.jstor.org/stable/30093800.

Vuillaume, Christophe. "Dom Augustin Calmet, exegete." *American Benedictine Review* 68, no. 1 (March 2017): 57–72.

Wright, Dudley. *The Eleusinian Mysteries & Rites.* London: Theosophical Publishing House; Denver: "The Square & Compass," 1919.

———. "A Living Vampire." *Occult Review,* July 1910, 45–47. http://www.iapsop.com/archive /materials/occult_review/occult_review_v12_n1_jul_1910.pdf.

———. *Vampires and Vampirism.* London: William Rider and Son, 1914. https://archive.org/de tails/b24876549.

Is Montague Summers Still Relevant to Vampire Studies?

Niels K. Petersen
Independent scholar, Denmark

Summers, Montague. *The Vampire, His Kith and Kin: A Critical Edition*. Edited by John Edgar Browning.

Berkeley, CA: Apocryphile Press, 2011. Pp. lxxviii + 433. ISBN 978-1-937002-17-6. Paperback, US$29.95.

We have grown so accustomed to the omnipresence of books, films and TV series about vampires that it must come as a surprise to learn that very few books had been published on the subject until about fifty years ago. In fact, the first full-length study of vampires written in English, Dudley Wright's *Vampires and Vampirism* (1914), was published just over a century ago.

Another British author with an interest in the supernatural, Montague Summers, found that "it were not an easy task to find a more insipid olio than *Vampires and Vampirism*,"[1] and decided to write not one, but two volumes on the subject. "It may, I think, not unfairly be claimed," he wrote in the introduction to the first of these volumes, *The Vampire, His Kith and Kin* (1928), "that the present work is the first serious study in English of the Vampire, and kindred traditions from a general, as well as from a theological and philosophical point of view."[2]

At the time, Summers had become known for two volumes on witchcraft, *The History of Witchcraft and Demonology* (1926) and *The Geography of Witchcraft* (1927), which were founded on his firm belief in witchcraft as a true force prevalent even in modern society. In his posthumously published autobiography, he recalled public reception of the former: "A veritable bombshell exploded amid the anti-christian and nihilist rabblement [. . .] the edition sold out in two or three days. Within less than a week copies were at a premium. Men awoke to the danger still energizing and active in their midst. The evil which many had hardly suspected, deeming it either a mere historical question, long dead and gone, of no interest save to the antiquarian, or else altogether fabled, was shown to be very much alive, potent in politics, potent in society, corrupting the arts, a festering, leprous disease and decay."[3]

With the publication of *The Vampire, His Kith and Kin*, and its companion volume, *The Vampire in Europe* (1929), he stated a similar belief in vampires: "Cases of vampirism may be said to be in our time a rare occult phenomenon. Yet whether

---

[1] Summers, *The Vampire, His Kith and Kin: A Critical Edition*, ed. John Edgar Browning (Berkeley, CA: Apocryphile Press, 2011), xi. All subsequent citations refer to this edition.

[2] Summers, *Vampire*, xii.

[3] *The Galanty Show: An Autobiography of Montague Summers* (London: Cecil Woolf, 1980), 156.

we are justified in supposing that they are less frequent to-day than in past centuries I am far from certain. One thing is plain:—not that they do not occur but that they are carefully hushed up and stifled."[4]

Summers religious affiliation remains a conundrum, but his view appears to be that of a Catholic informed by Spiritualism and other occult movements of his era. He found evidence for vampirism in spiritualist phenomena, not because he was an advocate of Spiritualism, but because he believed in the forces behind it. The Catholic Church condemns Spiritism, he writes, "not because she disbelieves in it, but because she believes in it so thoroughly, because she knows what is the real nature of the moving forces, however skilfully they may disguise themselves, however quick and subtle their shifts and turns, the intelligences which inform and direct the whole."[5] He himself goes one step further by stating that "modern Spiritism is merely witchcraft revived"[6] and "nothing else than demoniality in masquerade."[7] At the same time, Summers was a devoted reader of Gothic literature, seeking out and enjoying gothic novels, penny dreadfuls and ghost stories. However paradoxical it may appear, this duality between the Summers who revels in the horrors of the fictional supernatural while at the same time warning his fellow man against the reality of the forces working behind the supernatural, appears integral to his interest in the subject.

As apt at compiling material on witchcraft and vampires as Gothic fiction, Summers' work in many respects appears to be both a continuation of and an update of seventeenth and eighteenth century authors like Christian Friedrich Garmann and Augustin Calmet.[8] On the one hand he collects and discusses the *miracula* and *mirabilia mortuorum* like the Baroque scholars, while on the other he maintains an orthodox belief in Catholic—or perhaps rather quasi-Catholic— dogma regarding true miracles and the workings of the Devil and demons.

Thus, he had little time for sceptics like the Catholic Archbishop of Trani, Giuseppe Davanzati, whose conclusion of *Dissertazione sopra i vampiri* (1774) in Summers' view "cannot be securely maintained," because "to-day it will very generally be agreed that his line of argument is at least perilous. Nor can we accept 'Che l'apparizione de' Vampiri non sia altro che paro effetto di Fantasia.' The truth lies something deeper than that as Leone Allacci so well knew."[9] Allacci—or Leo Allatios—is certainly one of Summers' heroes. Born on the Greek island of Chios, Allatios left Greece as a child and became a devout Roman Catholic. In Summers'

---

[4] Summers, *The Vampire in Europe: A Critical Edition*, ed. John Edgar Browning (Berkeley, CA: Apocryphile Press, 2014), x–xi. All subsequent citations refer to this edition.

[5] Summers, *The History of Witchcraft and Demonology* (London: Kegan Paul, Trench, Trubner, 1926), 268.

[6] Summers, *History of Witchcraft and Demonology*, 269.

[7] *Galanty Show*, 157.

[8] Garmann, *De miraculis mortuorum* (Leipzig, 1670); and Calmet, *Dissertation sur les apparitions des anges, des demons & des esprit et sur les revenans et vampires de Hongrie, de Boheme, de Moravie & de Silesie* (Paris: De Bure L'Aîné, 1746).

[9] Summers, *Vampire*, 25.

words, Allatios "had no hesitation about declaring his own views, and he thoroughly believed in the vampire. He says, and says with perfect truth: "It is the height of folly to attempt to deny that such bodies are not infrequently found in their graves incorrupt and that by use of them the Devil, if God permit him, devises most horrible complots and schemes to the hurt and harm of mankind."[10]

It is easy to see a mirror of Summers himself in the Roman Catholic, who declares his own views about the reality of witchcraft and vampirism.

Students of Greek beliefs in vampires and revenants will seek out Karen Hartnup's study of Allatios' work, 'On the Beliefs of the Greeks': Leo Allatios and Popular Orthodoxy (2004). Hartnup's approach to Allatios' text is that of the modern historian, whose ambition is to understand it in its cultural context. Although Summers had assumed Allatios approached the beliefs and practices of the common people in Greece as an insider, Hartnup contends that he actually approached the subject as a Roman Catholic arguing for ecumenism.[11] Accordingly, Allatios' interpretation of revenants not only differed from that of the Orthodox clergy, but was influenced by his Catholicism. In fact, his representation of the popular beliefs were clearly affected by the aim of his work, as according to Hartnup, "it was necessary for Allatios to conflate the two revenants [the *vrykolakas* and the *tympaniaos*] in order to make them conform to western expectations of purgatorial spirits, walking the streets, warning relatives of the fate that would befall them if they did not repent of their sins during their lifetime."[12] Hartnup concludes that "Allatios' interpretation of the *tympaniaos* and the *vrykolakas* therefore cannot be taken at face value. He was more interested in using popular beliefs to bridge the gap between Orthodox and Catholic doctrinal positions than in investigating them for their own sake. The popular beliefs were employed in the service of his ecumenical project."[13]

Summers on the other hand does take Allatios at face value and sees in him a believer in the reality of vampires. Unlike the scholars of our day, Summers is not particularly interested in studying beliefs in their cultural context, because, ultimately, his context is that of his own belief in the underlying forces, which permeate and transcend history and culture. Consequently, he can define—today we would probably say, *construct*—a true vampire according to his vision.

Summers differentiates this true vampire from other notions about what a vampire might be by writing vampire with a capital V. This Vampire is "a dead body re-animated with an awful life, who issues from his tomb to prey upon the living by sucking their blood which lends him new vitality and fresh energies."[14] But "although his foul lust and horrid propensities be truly demoniacal and of

---

[10] Summers, *Vampire*, 32.

[11] Hartnup, 'On the Beliefs of the Greeks': Leo Allatios and Popular Orthodoxy (Leiden: Brill, 2004), 2–3.

[12] Hartnup, 'On the Beliefs of the Greeks', 235.

[13] Hartnup, 'On the Beliefs of the Greeks', 235–6.

[14] Summers, *Vampire*, 29.

hell,"[15] he is "neither ghost nor demon."[16] Afterall, "A demon has no body, although for purposes of his own he may energize, assume, or seem to assume a body, but it is not his real and proper body."[17] Yet "Neither may the vampire be called a ghost or phantom, strictly speaking, for an apparition is intangible".[18] Corporeality then is a *sine qua non* of the vampire:

> The true vampire is corporeal.
> The vampire has a body, and it is his own body. He is neither dead nor alive; but living in death. He is an abnormality; the androgyne in the phantom world; a pariah among the fiends.[19]

Furthermore, the Vampire is not a thing, an "it," the Vampire is a person, a "he." Summers adds "the Vampire is the actual person, energized with some horrible mystical life in death who visits the victims".[20] He who becomes a vampire is someone "who has led a life of more than ordinary immorality and unbridled wickedness; a man of foul, gross and selfish passions, of evil ambitions, delighting in cruelty and blood."[21] He may, for example, be someone who is "believed to have devoted himself during his life to the practice of Black Magic".[22]

Summers even describes the Vampire's features in rather specific terms:

> A Vampire is generally described as being exceedingly gaunt and lean with a hideous countenance and eyes wherein are glinting the red fire of perdition. When, however, he has satiated his lust for warm human blood his body becomes horribly puffed and bloated, as though he were some great leech gorged and replete to bursting. Cold as ice, or it may be fevered and burning as a hot coal, the skin is deathly pale, but the lips are very full and rich, blub and red; the teeth white and gleaming, and the canine teeth wherewith he bites deep into the neck of the prey to suck thence the vital streams which re-animate his body and invigorate all his forces appear notably sharp and pointed."[23]

Similarly, the Vampire's bloodsucking is described almost lyrically in terms of an embrace and kisses: "The vampire is, as we have said, generally believed to embrace his victim who has been thrown into a trance-like sleep, and after greedily kissing the throat suddenly to bite deep into the jugular vein and absorb the warm crimson blood."[24]

---

[15] Summers, *Vampire*, 2.
[16] Summers, *Vampire*, 1.
[17] Summers, *Vampire*, 2.
[18] Summers, *Vampire*, 2.
[19] Summers, *Vampire*, 6.
[20] Summers, *Vampire*, 178–9.
[21] Summers, *Vampire*, 77.
[22] Summers, *Vampire*, 78.
[23] Summers, *Vampire*, 179.
[24] Summers, *Vampire*, 184.

Despite stressing these characteristics of the true Vampire throughout the book, Summers appears to accept other uses of the word vampire (with a diminutive *v*), however remote they may appear to be from his strict definition of a true Vampire. Thus, he talks of "a spiritual vampire," because "Blood is the vital essence, and even without any actual sucking of blood there is a vampire who can—consciously, or perhaps unconsciously—support his life and re-energize his frame by drawing upon the vitality of others. He may be called a spiritual vampire, or as he has been dubbed a 'psychic sponge.'"[25] He even accepts the popular use of the word as a description of a German mass murderer: "Certainly in the extended sense of the word, as it is now so commonly used, Fritz Haarmann was a vampire in every particular."[26]

He actually appears to loosen his grip on the precise requirements for true Vampirism when he compiles examples of vampires and similar entities from antiquity and from Asia and Africa. Arguing by use of analogy and similarities,[27] he includes various spirits and demons that hardly fall into his strict definition of a Vampire. Even then, he does not hesitate in employing this multifaceted material as documentation for the "terrible truth" of Vampirism with a capital V: "By a comparison of the beliefs in these many lands, in ancient Assyria, in old Mexico, in China, India and Melanesia, although details differ, but yet not to any marked degree, it will be seen that the superstition and the tradition of the Vampire prevail to an extraordinary extent, and it is hard to believe that a phenomenon which has had so complete a hold over nations both old and young, in all parts of the world, at all times of history, has not some underlying and terrible truth however rare this may be in its more remarkable manifestations."[28]

Through employing a high degree of flexibility with the application of the term "vampire" or "Vampire," Summers comes full circle, and we are back at the underlying and terrible truth behind the vampire tradition.

But what of this underlying truth? Summers rejects various rationalist explanations, like those relating vampire beliefs to catalepsy and premature burial, as he finds that such incidents may have influenced or promoted the belief in vampires, but that they are not the origin of it: "I would rather emphasize that the tradition goes far deeper and contains far more dark and scathful reality than this."[29]

Unlike Calmet, he is not confounded by the rationalistic knot which Calmet could not untie: "Dom Calmet in his famous work more than once emphasized that his great difficulty in accepting the tradition of the vampire, that is to say the vampire proper and not a mere malignant phantom, lies in the fact that it is physically impossible for a dead body to leave its grave since (he argues) if it has

---

[25] Summers, *Vampire*, 133–4.

[26] Summers, *Vampire*, 193.

[27] Summers, *Vampire*, 239–40.

[28] Summers, *Vampire*, 267–8.

[29] Summers, *Vampire*, 48.

corporeity it cannot have subtilty, that is to say the power of passing through material objects."[30]

So how can Summers, while insisting on the corporeality of the Vampire, untie this knot? First, without referring to any specific source, he claims that the Vampire graves were actually not totally undisturbed: "Where careful investigation was made it was generally found that there were discovered four or five little holes or tunnels, not much larger indeed than a man's finger which pierced through the earth to a very considerable depth."[31]

Secondly, he returns to what he has learned from Spiritualism, stating that "this one little detail" of holes in the ground points to an explanation based on the Spiritualist séance. Here materialization takes place, "where physical forms are solidly built up and disintegrated again within an exceedingly short space of time. This is done by some power or entity which awails itself of the body of the passive medium and utilizes the ectoplasm which it can draw thence."[32]

Furthermore, during séances a medium may become extremely exhausted and show symptoms similar to those of a Vampire's victim: "It is extremely significant, and one might say even more significant that these are the very symptoms exhibited by those who have been attacked by a Vampire."[33]

Despite stressing the corporeality of the Vampire, Summers nevertheless introduces ectoplasm, astral forms and other ways in which "energy" can be transformed from "bodily energy" into "psychic energy" and vice versa:

> The body of the Vampire under certain conditions acquires subtilty and therefore it is able to pass through material objects, but in order to ensure not only its vitality but the permanence of this subtile quality it must draw this energy, no doubt very often in an ectoplasmic form, from its victim, as well as what is necessary for its rejuvenescence. The continual demand which a Vampire makes both physically and spiritually upon its victims must speedily result in the death of these persons, who being infected with the poison will in their turn visit others upon whom they will prey.[34]

Spiritualism, however, not only provided Summers with these subtler means of explaining Vampirism in terms of the extraction and transformation of bodily and spiritual "energy," but itself posed a threat to those participating in séances, because "It certainly seems a possibility, and something more than a possibility, that vampiric entities may be on the watch and active to avail themselves of the chances to use the ectoplasmic emanations of mediums at séances, and this certainly constitutes a very formidable danger."[35]

---

[30] Summers, *Vampire*, 193.
[31] Summers, *Vampire*, 194.
[32] Summers, *Vampire*, 194.
[33] Summers, *Vampire*, 195.
[34] Summers, *Vampire*, 196.
[35] Summers, *Vampire*, 197.

What is the reader of the twenty first century to make of this? Summers unties a knot by introducing new and undefined concepts drawn from Spiritualism—the root of Summers' truth behind both witchcraft and Vampirism. Although in vogue at the time, Spiritualism is hardly ever heard of today. Apart from the rare Spiritualist reader or a reader who nurtures some other kind of "occult" notion, the modern reader will, I think, find that Summers' at the same time very precise and rather loose notions about both Vampires and vampires, both Vampirism and vampirism, makes for a framework far too dilapidated for serious study of the subject.

One might argue that the reader can disregard Summers' outlandish beliefs, but the fact is that Summers' position regarding the terrible truth behind the Vampire is integral to his approach to the subject and consequently pervades the book. Still, one can try peeling off his "occult" ideas to use the book as a resource of information and texts on vampires and related subjects.

However, although his collection of material is impressive, it is very much of its time, long before academic research of the past few decades into the witch persecutions and their background in early modern beliefs. Thus, *The Vampire, His Kith and Kin* is from a time when very little was known about the archival material that is the subject of research these days, in the case of both witchcraft and vampirism. Summers could not have dreamed of the accessibility of archives and libraries that we have in today's globalized and digitalized world, where almost any book on a subject like vampires can be read or purchased online.

This is notable when Summers deals with vampire cases in Serbia in the 1720s and 1730s. In recounting the famous incidents in Medvedja in the winter of 1731–2, he relied on Herbert Mayo's *On the Truths Contained in Popular Superstitions*, 2nd ed. (1851). Mayo himself no doubt read about vampires when he was staying in Germany, but when writing about the incident, chose to embellish his account with a fictional story about Arnod Paole and his betrothed, Nina.[36] Summers reproduced this fictionalization in *The Vampire in Europe*,[37] while incidentally choosing to rename Arnod as Arnold. Furthermore, in *The Vampire, His Kith and Kin* he moves the location to Belgrade,[38] although Mayo clearly refers to "Meduegna, near Belgrade."[39]

Other sources used by Summers reflect what he had access to, e.g. Henry More's *An Antidote against Atheism*, while a modern reader should look up earlier sources and more recent research. In the case of the revenants found in More's book, one might study the work of Karen Lambrecht.[40]

---

[36] Mayo, *On the Truths Contained in Popular Superstitions: With an Account of Mesmerism*, 2nd ed. (Edinburgh: William Blackwood and Sons, 1851), 23–24, https://books.google.dk/books?id=rmwXAQAAMAAJ.

[37] Summers, *Vampire in Europe*, 151–6.

[38] Summers, *Vampire in Europe*, 175–6.

[39] Mayo, *On the Truths*, 29.

[40] Lambrecht, *Hexenverfolgung und Zaubereiprozesse in den schlesischen Territorien* (Cologne: Böhlau Verlag, 1995), 395.

Certainly, Summers cannot be blamed for not being aware of the information we have today. He really did make an incredible effort in supplying the reader with a wealth of material, but ninety years on, Summers' books can no longer be considered as go-to resources for source material. One need only to compare his two volumes on vampires with recent collections compiled by Klaus Hamberger, Gilles Banderier and Álvaro García Marín[41] to see, that both *The Vampire, His Kith and Kin* and *The Vampire in Europe* are outdated resources of material on vampires.

As for Summers' style, the twenty first century reader will probably find his prose almost as eccentric and old-fashioned as his approach, and fewer and fewer readers will probably find the frequent and often lengthy quotes in Latin, Greek and other languages without translation an asset.

Looking back on the literature on vampires of the past half century, it is patent Montague Summers had an incredible influence on those who wrote books on vampires in English, and why not? No one else had supplied anything similar to his two volumes on vampires in the English language since Henry Christmas' translation of Calmet in the mid nineteenth century,[42] so anyone in the English-speaking parts of the world interested in reading about vampires would eventually have wound up with Summers' books.

Although reprinted by University Books in 1960s, the volumes were hard to come by when I got interested in the subject in the late 1970s. Reading vampire studies of this decade from Anthony Masters, Raymond T. McNally and Radu Florescu, Leonard Wolf and Basil Copper,[43] despite some critical comments,[44] show Summers was considered *the* authoritative resource on vampires. Unfortunately, while *The Vampire in Europe* was reprinted in 1980, it was only during the 1990s onwards that reprints of *The Vampire, His Kith and Kin* began appearing again. Nowadays both books are readily available as reprints and online.

In the meantime, new resources and approaches to the subject matter have increasingly replaced Summers' work, relegating his books on witchcraft, vampires and werewolves to items of cultural history, perhaps even footnotes, rather than

---

[41] Hamberger, *Mortuus non mordet: Kommentierte Dokumentation zum Vampirismus, 1689– 1791* (Vienna: Turia + Kant, 1992); Banderier, *Les vampires: Aux origines du mythe* (Grenoble: Éditions Jérôme Millon, 2015); and García Marín, *Historias del vampire gregio* (Madrid: Consejo Superior de Investigaciones Científicas, 2017).

[42] Augustine Calmet, *The Phantom World: or, The Philosophy of Spirits, Apparitions, &c.*, ed. Henry Christmas, 2 vols. (London: Richard Bentley, 1850). Originally published as *Traité sur les apparitions des esprits, et sur les vampires, ou les revenans de Hongrie, de Moravie, & c.*, 2 vols. (Paris: Chez Debure l'aîné, 1751).

[43] Masters, *The Natural History of the Vampire* (London: Rupert Hart-Davis 1972); McNally and Florescu, *In Search of Dracula: A True History of Dracula and Vampire Legends* (Greenwich, CT: New York Graphic Society, 1972); Wolf, *A Dream of Dracula: In Search of the Living Dead* (Boston: Little, Brown, 1972); and Copper, *The Vampire: In Legend, Fact and Art* (London: Robert Hale, 1973).

[44] For example, McNally and Florescu note that "although serious," *The Vampire, His Kith and Kin*, "fails to distinguish between significant and insignificant details," *In Search of Dracula*, 214.

viable resources for research. That is, of course, what happens in the natural course of research and scholarly developments.

One needs only see what is published on the subject of vampires today to notice a new era of vampire studies. Historical sources are investigated, imprecise legends are questioned and refuted, and the borderline between fact and fiction becomes more clear-cut. As in the case of Margaret Murray's books on witchcraft, Summers' books lose their relevance and will probably be read by fewer and fewer people. Essentially, why should we bother to read Summers' translation of the *Malleus Maleficarum* in the twenty-first century, when academic translations based on recent research are available?[45] And come to think of it, maybe there was a reason in the first place that, while Margaret Murray was translated into several languages, Montague Summers has hardly ever been?[46]

Although it is hard to overestimate the influence of Summers' books on many people with an interest in vampires, there appears to be a sense of nostalgia related to their appreciation of his work. I certainly find it hard to think that younger readers who have been influenced by *Buffy the Vampire Slayer* and *Twilight*, will have much time for Summers' warnings against the threat from Spiritualism. Were Summers alive today, he would probably have been worried about our modern materialism and about how young people embrace the vampire of popular culture. But, given his fascination for Gothic literature, I wonder if he would himself have embraced the twenty-first century Gothic?

He certainly did have a keen eye for the fascination of the vampire. In a comprehensive chapter on the Vampire theme in literature, the first of its kind in English, he is quite critical of Bram Stoker's *Dracula*, but still finds that it is "a book of unwonted interest and fascination" due to "the choice of subject"[47]. Almost prophetical of the innumerous fictional vampires to come, he attributes the success of a rather indifferent play based on *Dracula* to "the fascination of the theme": "Consciously or unconsciously it is realized that the vampire tradition contains far more truth than the ordinary individual cares to appreciate and acknowledge."[48]

If he were alive today, we should expect him to still warn us against the forces underlying the Vampire legend. Faced with those us of, who, like myself, object to such notions and only seek to understand the belief in its cultural context, Montague Summers would, however, probably still comment: "To the feather-fool and lobcock, the pseudo-scientist and materialist, these deeper and obscurer things

---

[45] P.G. Maxwell-Stuart, ed., *The Malleus Maleficarum* (Manchester: Manchester University Press, 2007) features these comments on the blurb: "The only previous translation into English, that by Montague Summers produced in 1928, is full of inaccuracies. It is written in a style almost unreadable nowadays, and is unfortunately coloured by his personal agenda."

[46] For a recent assessment of both Murray and Summers, *see* Juliette Wood, "The Reality of Witch Cults Reasserted: Fertility and Satanism," in *Palgrave Advances in Witchcraft Historiography*, ed. Jonathan Barry and Owen Davies (Houndsmills: Palgrave Macmillan, 2007), 69–89.

[47] Summers, *Vampire*, 335.

[48] Summers, *Vampire*, 337.

must, of course, appear a grandam's tale. *Inconsulti abeunt sedemque odere Sibyllae.*"[49]

BIBLIOGRAPHY

Copper, Basil. *The Vampire: In Legend, Fact and Art*. London: Robert Hale, 1973.

Hartnup, Karen. *'On the Beliefs of the Greeks': Leo Allatios and Popular Orthodoxy*. Leiden: Brill, 2004.

Lambrecht, Karen. *Hexenverfolgung und Zaubereiprozesse in den schlesischen Territorien*. Cologne: Böhlau Verlag, 1995.

Masters, Anthony. *The Natural History of the Vampire*. London: Rupert Hart-Davis 1972.

Maxwell-Stuart, P. G., ed. *The Malleus Maleficarum*. Manchester: Manchester University Press, 2007.

Mayo, Herbert. *On the Truths Contained in Popular Superstitions: With an Account of Mesmerism*. 2nd ed. Edinburgh: William Blackwood and Sons, 1851. https://books.google.dk/books?id=rmwXAQAAMAAJ.

McNally, Raymond T., and Radu Florescu. *In Search of Dracula: A True History of Dracula and Vampire Legends*. Greenwich, CT: New York Graphic Society, 1972.

Summers, Montague. *The Galanty Show: An Autobiography of Montague Summers*. London: Cecil Woolf, 1980.

———. *The History of Witchcraft and Demonology*. London: Kegan Paul, Trench, Trubner, 1926.

———. *The Vampire, His Kith and Kin: A Critical Edition*. Edited by John Edgar Browning. Berkeley, CA: Apocryphile Press, 2011.

———. *The Vampire in Europe: A Critical Edition*. Edited by John Edgar Browning. Berkeley, CA: Apocryphile Press, 2014.

Virgil. *The Æneid of Virgil*. Translated by E. Fairfax-Taylor. 1907. Reprint, London: J. M. Dent; New York: E. P. Dutton, 1915. https://archive.org/details/aeneidofvirgiltr00virgoft.

Wolf, Leonard. *A Dream of Dracula: In Search of the Living Dead*. Boston: Little, Brown, 1972.

Wood, Juliette. "The Reality of Witch Cults Reasserted: Fertility and Satanism." In *Palgrave Advances in Witchcraft Historiography*, edited by Jonathan Barry and Owen Davies, 69–89. Houndsmills: Palgrave Macmillan, 2007.

---

[49] Summers, *Vampire in Europe*, ix. The Latin quote is from book III of Virgil's *Aeneid*. In English, it reads "Untaught the votaries leave, the Sibyl's cave to curse." *The Æneid of Virgil*, trans. E. Fairfax-Taylor (1907; repr., London: J. M. Dent; New York: E. P. Dutton, 1915), 75, https://archive.org/details/aeneidofvirgiltr00virguoft.

Bohn, Thomas M. *Der Vampir: Ein europäischer Mythos*.

Cologne: Böhlau Verlag, 2016. Pp. 368. ISBN 978-3-412-50180-8. Hardback, €26.

EDITOR'S NOTE *This review has been slightly revised from the original published in Spiegelungen 12 [66], no. 2 (2017): 83–85. Translated from German into English by the author. Of further interest, between the time Ruthner's translated review was solicited and published here, Bohn's book was published in English as* The Vampire: Origins of a European Myth, *trans. Francis Ipgrave (New York: Berghahn, 2019).*

> Worum [. . .] gehts es [. . .] in diesem Buch überhaupt? Es behandelt im Wesentlichen Störungen des friedlichen Abschieds der Lebenden von den Toten und die daraus erwachsenden Konsequenzen. Beide haben ihr Ursachen bzw. Manifestationen in zwischenmenschlichen Konflikten, die durch den Tod nicht gelöst wurden, oder im Ausbruch rätselhafter Krankheiten [. . .]. (11).

> (What [. . .] is this book [. . .] about anyway? It essentially deals with disturbances of the peaceful farewell of the living from the dead and the resulting consequences. Both have their causes and manifestations in interpersonal conflicts not resolved by death, or in the outbreak of mysterious diseases [. . .].)

Thomas M. Bohn's book on the "historical" vampire(s) is the rare epitome of a knowledgeable, critical and non-speculative monograph on the subject matter; it is not popular non-fiction, but still a very readable piece of academic writing. The merits of this work also lie in the demystification of the dark myth of the undead bloodsucker, whose historical origin is correctly located in the Ottoman Balkans and not in Transylvania (the latter being a half-false genealogy created by the Anglo-Irish author Bram Stoker). Neither do the roots of vampirism here necessarily go back thousands of years into the past, as is often claimed by speculative esoterics and gentleman scholars. The vampire as we know it is not a brainchild of Antiquity, but rather of Enlightenment (albeit with a prehistory), begotten by the existing (military) borders between Occident and Orient, i.e. the cultural contact between "Reason" and "superstition," and the alleged gap between "civilization" and "barbarism." Ultimately, this makes vampirism an "imperiale Kategorie" (imperial category), as Bohn rightly states (17), into which the colonization of East Central Europe and the Balkans, as well as latent xenophobia vis-à-vis this region, is inscribed.

In clearly put chapters, the author reconstructs the quasi-mythical formation of the central and (south) Eastern European vampire narrative (a "dispositive" in the sense of Michel Foucault), behind which the old belief in the *revenant* from the early days of burial may be suspected as an all-continental belief. In this more realistic genealogy of the monster in question, the occidental *Wiedergänger* of the Middle Ages (31–55) and the "shroud eaters" of the Great Plague of the early modern period (56–80) are placed next to the "Vampir im Orient" (vampire from the Orient): the *Upyr* or *Upiór* of the Kievan *Rus'* (81–90) and the *Vrykolakas* among the Ottoman Greeks (90–108).

In a next step, Bohn focuses on the "Entdeckung der Vampire" (Discovery of the vampire) (109–123), when two spectacular incidents rocked the Habsburg-occupied Western Balkans after the Turkish Wars and spread like wildfire into Europe: the living dead of Kisiljevo in 1725 and of Medvedja in 1732, who scared the Serbian villagers out of their dwellings and provoked a fact-finding mission by the Austrian military, whose reports have been kept in Viennese state archives ever since. It was those "X-Files" of early Enlightenment that gave the bloodsucker its name (which did not exist previously in any known language); and within months, the vampire epidemic in 1732 spread into contemporary theology, philosophy, and medicine causing controversy, until the case was closed in the mid-1700s up to the exhumation of the Balkan fiend by European romanticism in literature around 1800.

Bohn completes his splendid study with sketches of the relevant popular beliefs ("dämonische Gestalten" [demonic figures] in East / Central Europe, pp. 159–99, as well as the "verlorene Seelen im Donau-Balkan-Raum" [lost souls in the Danube-Balkan region], pp. 200–272), before he touches on vampire narratives in Eastern Europe and abroad after World War 2 (273–83), and on vampire stereotyping in Germany (273–87). In this rather cursory treatment of an interesting topic, unfortunately the last Romanian vampire case known of remains unmentioned, which took place in 2003 with so much media attention that the story found its way even into the *Edmonton Journal* in Canada, for instance.[1] Reflections on the social function of the folklore vampire—providing a local "scapegoat" in times of crisis—complete the book. This hypothesis is not really new, as the Hungarian historian Gábor Klániczay[2] already claimed in the 1980s that the vampire had served as an explanatory model of popular belief for traumatic incidents within communities, replacing witchcraft as an explanatory pattern in the South-East of the Continent in the 18th century. Bohn now extends this functional spectrum by ascribing three social functions to the vampire:

> Zum einen eröffnete er die Möglichkeit, Botschaften aus dem Jenseits zu empfangen. Zum anderen verhieß er als konkretes Feindbild einen Konsens stiftenden Ausweg aus irrationalen Gefahren [. . .]. Schließlich und vor allem diente er der Entlarvung von Störenfrieden und der Marginalisierung bzw. Eliminierung von Sündenböcken. Als anthropologische Grundkonstante für das Erscheinen der Verstorbenen in den Träumen und der Phantasie der Lebenden ist dabei das Nachwirken des schlechten Gewissens respektive die Bewältigung von Schuld infolge sozialer oder zwischenmenschlicher Konflikte festzuhalten. (294–5)

---

[1] Matthew Schofield, "Vampires: An Ancient Terror Lives On," *Edmonton Journal*, April 7, 2004, 15, Newspapers.com.

[2] Klaniczay, "Decline of Witches and Rise of Vampires in 18th Century Habsburg Monarchy," *Ethnologia Europaea* 17, no. 2 (1987): 165–80.

(On the one hand, it kept the possibility of receiving messages from the hereafter open. On the other hand, the vampire was a promising bogeyman, providing a concrete way out of irrational dangers [. . .]. Finally, and above all, it served to expose villains and facilitated the marginalization or elimination of scapegoats. The anthropological basis for this appearance of the deceased in dreams and the imagination of the living is the after-effect of bad conscience and/or the handling of guilt as a result of social or interpersonal conflicts.)

However, as already mentioned, the big advantage of Bohn's book is that here a very skilled and learned scholar of East European history has been busy putting together findings from the various cultures of Central, Eastern and South Eastern Europe convincingly in order to tease out the greater picture. Moreover, it is the rare case of a historian being able of and open towards (comparative) cultural studies, taking into account, for instance, the "imperial factor," and abstaining from wacky speculation like the annoying "vampire archaeology" of recent years that spotted vampires in almost every graveyard. Also stringent, for example, is Bohn's observation that the Serbian village vampires and the other revenants are not necessarily bloodsuckers.

Thus, in the footsteps of the oeuvre of the prolific French Medievalist, Claude Lecouteux, from the 1980s, a formidable new standard work has been published. This is also the reason why one gladly pardons minimal—and, in view of the abundance of materials, inevitable—shortcomings since they just inspire further investigation: e.g. the analysis of how much the vampire (and especially its/his/her name!) is due to the quasi-*colonial* cultural contact between "superstitious" Balkan residents and "enlightened" Europeans from the centre and the west of the Continent. Hindsight shows that this encounter was a case of extremely productive intercultural misunderstanding, as our lasting fascination with the vampire and the ongoing—and sometimes xenophobic—(re)production of images of the living Self and the undead Other by the cultural industries demonstrate, which Bohn unfortunately has excluded from his considerations as well as the Serbian legend of Sava Savanović. On these topics, however, there are already excellent studies available, like Norine Dresser's *American Vampires: Fans, Victims, Practitioners* (1989) or Tomislav Z. Longinović's *Vampire Nation: Violence as Cultural Imaginary* (2011). Bohn excels in filling other important gaps in Vampire Studies for good.

Clemens Ruthner

Trinity College Dublin, Ireland

BIBLIOGRAPHY

Klaniczay, Gábor. "Decline of Witches and Rise of Vampires in 18th Century Habsburg Monarchy." *Ethnologia Europaea* 17, no. 2 (1987): 165–80.

Schofield, Matthew. "Vampires: An Ancient Terror Lives On." *Edmonton Journal*, April 7, 2004, 15. Newspapers.com.

D'Agostino, Thomas. *A History of Vampires in New England.*

Charleston, SC: Haunted America, 2010. Pp. 143. ISBN 978-1-59629-998-6. Paperback, US$16.99.

After acknowledgements and introduction, this book consists of the following, unnumbered chapters: "A Brief History of Tuberculosis," "Life, Death and Superstition in Early New England," "Vampires in New England," "Tuberculosis in the Twentieth Century" and "Other Strange Exorcisms and Interesting Legends." The back matter consists of a bibliography, index, and brief biography, "About the Author."

In *A History of Vampires in New England*, Thomas D'Agostino summarizes stories of New Englanders who, desperate to stop the spread of consumption (pulmonary tuberculosis) that was overwhelming their communities during the late eighteenth and throughout the nineteenth century, performed a ritual (D'Agostino terms them "exorcisms" [10]) that characteristically entailed exhuming the corpses of family members. Let me begin by explaining why I think the word *history* in the book's title is misleading. D'Agostino comes down on the side of what I term "soft" history, modeled on the journalistic distinction between "hard" news and "soft" news.[1] In soft history, as in soft news, facts are subordinated to narrative vividness and interest. Stories that can be improved, get improved. What "improved" means, of course, depends on one's perspective. Historians probably would not consider a narrative improved if it moved away from accepted historical fact (hard history). Certain audiences—and, by extension, writers—however, might forego complete accuracy and nuanced analysis in favor of narrative with a predisposed slant.

We are in an age where entertainment has seeped into nearly every cultural system—including journalism, history, science, education, politics, and religion—so D'Agostino's narrative approach certainly is not novel,[2] nor unexpected, in light of his specialized pursuit. In the book's "About the Author" section, D'Agostino is described as "one of the region's most well-known writers and investigators of the paranormal. [. . .] As founders of the Paranormal United Research Society [PURS], Tom and his wife, Arlene, have been extensively studying and investigating paranormal accounts for over twenty-eight years." (143) An Internet directory listing paranormal societies describes the specialties of the purs, founded in Putnam, Connecticut in 1982, as "Photo, EVP [Electronic Voice Phenomena], Video, Dowsing, Tarot Cards to field questions, Intelligent rational investigations using many years of experience, historical knowledge and keen sense of awareness,"[3] while the society's goal "is to help our clients with their paranormal issues and at

---

[1] Gaye Tuchman, *Making News: A Study in the Construction of Reality* (New York: Free Press, 1978), see esp. 46–47, 98–99.

[2] Diane E. Goldstein, Sylvia Ann Grider, and Jeannie Banks Thomas, "The Commodification of Belief," chap. 6 in *Haunting Experiences: Ghosts in Contemporary Folklore* (Logan: Utah State University Press, 2007).

[3] "Paranormal United Research Society," ParanormalSocieties.com, accessed November 21, 2018, http://paranormalsocieties.com/view_society.cfm?id=510.

the same time, solve the mysterious puzzle we call the fascinating world of the paranormal."[4] If we accept the Gallup Poll's most recent findings on paranormal beliefs, the audience for paranormal discourse must be substantial, as David W. Moore's summary of this 2005 poll states: "About three in four Americans profess at least one paranormal belief, according to a recent Gallup survey. The most popular is extrasensory perception (ESP), mentioned by 41%, followed closely by belief in haunted houses (37%)."[5] Thus, it is within the frame of a paranormal paradigm that *A History of Vampires in New England* is best understood. Paranormal research, as opposed to empirical scientific inquiry, is based on speculation drawn from anecdotal testimony, most often in the form of personal-experience narratives. Subjectivity, and thus credibility, is built into this approach.

Unfortunately, the book's narratives are too often inaccurate, exaggerated, or only marginally relevant to the book's nominal focus on vampires. Lack of historical documentation is evident in the second and third chapters ("A Brief History of Tuberculosis" and "Life, Death and Superstition in Early New England"). The sparse information on tuberculosis, given with no attribution save to a local veterinarian whom D'Agostino presumably interviewed, does not seem to have been selected or organized to show its relevance to vampires. D'Agostino provides some pertinent information in the third chapter, but a lack of documentation compromises his conclusions. For example, when addressing life expectancy in the eighteenth and nineteenth centuries, D'Agostino writes, "Wealthy women rarely tended to their own chores and therefore were subject to an early death due to lack of physical exercise" (15–16). Then he asserts that "farmers were known to live much longer due to the rigorous daily tasks of tending to their homesteads." (16) In place of published statistics or reliable evidence, D'Agostino cites rural gravestones that he has seen, concluding that "the self-sufficient families either died very young of disease [. . .] or lived to be very old" (16).

The heart of the book is the fourth chapter, where D'Agostino discusses eighteen New England vampire cases. Some of the factual errors in these narratives are due to incomplete data or simply not paying attention to detail.

Exemplifying the latter is D'Agostino's assertion that Mercy Brown's brother, Edwin, contracted consumption *after* he returned to Rhode Island in 1892, even though two sentences earlier D'Agostino had written that Edwin traveled to Colorado Springs because he was ill (111). Contemporary published sources were clear that Edwin went to Colorado expressly in the hope that he could regain his health and fight off consumption. For example, the *Pawtuxet Valley Gleaner* included the following statement from a member of Edwin's community: "Our young fellow townsman, Eddie Brown, who has been tarrying at Colorado Springs about two years in pursuit of health, but without success except temporarily at times, has

---

[4] "Paranormal United Research Society," ParanormalSocieties.com.

[5] Moore, "Three in Four Americans Believe in Paranormal," Gallup, June 16, 2005, https://news.gallup.com/poll/16915/three-four-americans-believe-paranormal.aspx.

returned to R.I. accompanied by his wife, she having been with him a good part of the tie to nurse and cheer him. They remained abroad until it became evident he could derive no more benefit there and then sadly and gladly started for their old home in Exeter."[6] Regarding Rachel Harris Burton, the suspected vampire who was exhumed in Manchester, Vermont in 1793, D'Agostino writes that "many unmarked graves are still believed to be in the green, including that of Rachel" (50). Yet, her finely engraved tombstone is plainly visible in the Factory Point Cemetery, in Manchester Center.

The case of the Rose family, which D'Agostino situates in South Kingstown/Exeter, Rhode Island, in 1874 (99–102) is a good example of D'Agostino relying on inaccurate published accounts. My research showed that previously published references to this case were in error regarding both the date and the name of the newspaper in which the exhumation was reported: it was not the *Providence Journal* in 1874, but the *Providence Evening Press* of September 4, 1872. Knowing this allowed me to identify the correct Rose family, thus leading to my detailed account of the event, which was not published until after D'Agostino's book appeared.[7] Criticizing an author for not knowing then what is known now may seem uncharitable. But this instance illustrates what is evident throughout the book: D'Agostino usually is content to accept, without further examination, information that has already been researched and published.

Other factual errors or historical exaggerations take us back to the paranormal paradigm, which concedes credibility to speculation and subjectivity, and grants narrative authority to popular culture. Of the case from Saco, Maine, ca. 1852–1862, D'Agostino writes, "It appears that once, while the residents slept, there were some who were reported to be roaming the night, sucking the life out of their loved ones" (89). And, when discussing the 1854 Jewett City, Connecticut case, he asserts: "Scores of families began digging up their loved ones for fear that one of them may be returning in the dark of night to take them all to the grave" (93). No credible historical evidence asserts that anyone in Saco or Jewett City, or even New England, believed that corpses actually left the grave at night and sucked the life out of the living. This kind of narrative embellishment simply plays to the popular vampire image. In his discussion of Nancy Young's 1827 exhumation in Foster, Rhode Island, D'Agostino describes his investigative visit to the cemetery with his wife and a friend from the New England Ghost Project. I think the following passage captures the spirit (if you will pardon the pun) of D'Agostino's approach:

With permission from the owner of the land, we visited the small cemetery and looked at the gravestones, which were all of the same style. We began to try some EVP (electronic voice phenomena) recordings. The area was quiet, being mostly farmland off the beaten path, so we figured the tranquil setting might be the right combination for receiving a few answers from the other side. Could we actually get

---

[6] "Exeter Hill and Vicinity," *Pawtuxet Valley Gleaner*, March 25, 1892, 5.

[7] Michael E. Bell, *Food for the Dead: On the Trail of New England's Vampires* (New York: Carroll & Graf, 2001; Middletown, CT: Wesleyan University Press, 2011), xix–xxv.

some answers about what happened so many years ago? What if we had firsthand information from those who were present in 1827? It may sound a bit farfetched, but that is the purpose of EVP work, to get answers and information that helps in paranormal cases. Yes, we treated even the vampire cases with a bit of a paranormal edge. After all, there could still be lingering energy. Unfortunately, there were no voices captured on the recorder (80).

In his final chapter, "Other Strange Exorcisms and Interesting Legends," D'Agostino stretches vampire relevance to include eight stories of witches, ghosts, and other vengeful revenants, asserting that "some interesting and lesser-known legends of witches [. . .] have traces of the vampire legend within them" (128). These traces, however, are based on vampire beliefs that did not travel from Europe to become established in the New England tradition, including the ability to shape-shift (128) and driving a stake through the heart of the corpse (131).

D'Agostino closes his book with a commonplace of this genre of writing, leaving ajar the door between two worlds: "In conclusion, there is no doubt that New England is full of strange facts and folklore in regard to witches, werewolves, demons and vampires. No wonder our ancestors and early settlers took precautions against things they could not see. What did they see back then that we do not today? Perhaps it is sitting right beside us on the bus or subway or walking past us on the street" (135).

Imagining that some mysterious, supernatural threat is still at large, liable to strike at any moment, obviously packs more thrills than descriptions of events resolved long ago. Even as narratives, supernatural encounters are powerful and captivating: they bring the past into the present; audiences are prompted to reflect on, perhaps even share, their own apparently inexplicable experiences. Paranormal narratives stimulate debate about what lies beyond our reach, compelling us to explore the margins of experience. Even if paranormal beliefs and narratives cannot be affirmed as metaphysical or historical facts, they provide social and psychological benefits to those who engage in them. If you value these qualities and are not resolutely invested in hard history, then you may enjoy *A History of New England's Vampires*. With the foregoing in mind, I suggest that perhaps a more accurate (and less misleading) title for D'Agostino's book might have been something like, *A Paranormalist's View of New England's Vampires*.

Michael E. Bell
Independent scholar, USA

BIBLIOGRAPHY

Bell, Michael E. *Food for the Dead: On the Trail of New England's Vampires*. Middletown, CT: Wesleyan University Press, 2011. First published 2001 by Carroll & Graf (New York).
Goldstein, Diane E., Sylvia Ann Grider, and Jeannie Banks Thomas. "The Commodification of Belief." Chap. 6 in *Haunting Experiences: Ghosts in Contemporary Folklore*. Logan: Utah State University Press, 2007.
Moore, David W. "Three in Four Americans Believe in Paranormal." Gallup, June 16, 2005. https://news.gallup.com/poll/16915/three-four-americans-believe-paranormal.aspx.

ParanormalSocieties.com. "Paranormal United Research Society." Accessed November 21, 2018. http://paranormalsocieties.com/view_society.cfm?id=510.

Pawtuxet Valley Gleaner. "Exeter Hill and Vicinity." March 25, 1892, 5.

Tuchman, Gaye. *Making News: A Study in the Construction of Reality*. New York: Free Press, 1978.

Meehan, Paul. *The Vampire in Science Fiction Film and Literature.*

Jefferson, NC: McFarland, 2015. Pp. 230. ISBN 978-0-7864-7487-5. Paperback, US$35.

Paul Meehan's *The Vampire in Science Fiction Film and Literature* is a highly detailed monograph examining the vampire as a figure of science fiction rather than fantasy. His brief "Introduction" states that the goal of the book is to investigate the metamorphosis of the vampire from a magical, religious being to the popular figure of genre literature and film. Meehan notes that the popular vampire's fictional debut in English is concurrent to the beginnings of the science fiction tradition itself, as John Polidori was present with Mary Shelley at Lord Byron's famous literary party during the summer of 1816 that culminated in a challenge to write ghost stories. While Shelley wrote the novel that would become *Frankenstein*, Polidori wrote a short story that would eventually be called "The Vampyre." Both works would find themselves the progenitors of genres and tropes that would prove influential for centuries, and Meehan does an excellent job in tracing and connecting how these works inform the idea of the vampire in science fiction.

The book is divided into two parts: "Part One: Origins" consists of two chapters that provide a concise yet extensive overview of the vampire, its probable origins, and its depiction in popular fiction. "The Scientific Origins of the Vampire Myth" briefly connects the folkloric revenant with various theories to explain its origins, from genetic disorders such as porphyria and anemia to a catalog of diseases including Bubonic plague (Meehan notes that the term *nosferatu* is thought to derive from *nosophorus*, the Greek word for "plague carrier" (p. 13) rabies, and syphilis. Somnambulism and mesmerism are also discussed as possible explanations for "vampiric sleep." The second chapter, "The Science Fiction Vampire in Literature," proceeds to examine fictional vampires from Polidori to H.G. Wells, Richard Matheson, Brian Aldiss, and Robert Zelazny. Meehan's tight focus on vampires as science fiction rather than fantasy lends itself to an intriguing introduction to and overview of authors who may be less familiar to some readers, including Tanith Lee (who, despite having written several novels about vampires, is often neglected in the scholarship) and George Alec Effinger, among numerous others. The emphasis on genre divides also means that the more familiar romantic vampires of Anne Rice and Stephenie Meyer are acknowledged briefly and then disregarded in favor of examples from the sf and horror traditions.

"Part Two: The Films" takes up the better part of the book with its five chapters. "Plagues of Blood" examines numerous films where the conceit of vampirism is inextricably linked with disease, from the classic *Nosferatu* (1922) to the more recent *Daybreakers* (2010). In particular, the chapter looks at a number of lesser-known movies such as *The Bat People* (1974), *Rabid* (1977), *Nightwing* (1979), and *Bats* (1999) that link vampires (and vampire bats) to rabies and other bloodborne diseases. Curiously, though *The Hunger* (1983) is analyzed in this vein, the classic reading of that film as a parable of HIV/AIDS anxiety is not mentioned. The protagonists of these films are usually heroic doctors and scientists earnestly trying to make the world a better place and/or save the human race from extinction. "Mad Scientists and Vampires" considers the inversion of this trope, in which vampirism stems not from natural causes but from scientific experiments and medical intervention gone wrong. The vast majority of films examined here are shlock-horror fests from the 1930s through the 1960s, including *The Vampire Bat* (1933), *The Return of Doctor X* (1939) with its infamously miscast Humphrey Bogart, *The Quatermass Xperiment* (1954) and so on. While the majority of these films are American, Meehan includes a brief excursion into European cinema as he discusses *Atom Age Vampire* (1960) and dips into Korean horror with *Thirst* (2009). Both chapters function as compelling surveys of their respective tropes.

"The Psychic Dimension" is almost a digression, discussing psychic vampires rather than literal, or blood-drinking, vampires. Meehan argues that the trope has its origins in Stoker's *Dracula* as the eponymous character evinces telepathic and mesmeric powers not seen in earlier works. He then turns to cinema, analyzing examples of psychic control in such films as *The Cabinet of Doctor Caligari* (1919), *Svengali* (1931), *L'Atalante* (1932), *The Climax* (1944), and a slew of films in the 1950s and 1960s as public fascination with hypnosis grew into a fad. "Vampires vs. High Technology" briefly surveys films from *Dracula* (1931) to *Priest* (2011), with earlier entries featuring the titular count or his relatives facing the modern technology of the 1930s and 1940s, and latter films such as *The Blade Trilogy* (1998–2004) and the *Underworld* franchise (2003–2012) positing vampires—and werewolves—as genetically similar to humans but a species of their own; both franchises also feature hybrid-vampires as major characters with unique abilities. Both of these chapters look at films that have been under-represented in the scholarship; a brief examination of Guillermo del Toro's first film, *Cronos* (1992), is particularly welcome given that del Toro is more often discussed in the context of his better-known vampire works like *Blade II* (2002) and *The Strain* (2009).

"Bloodsuckers from Outer Space" analyzes films in which the vampires, or vampire-like creatures, are aliens. Meehan examines a number of cheesy mid-century films like *The Thing from Another World* (1951) and *Plan 9 from Outer Space* (1959), the problematic classic *Lifeforce* (1985), and discusses the 2005 remake of *War of the Worlds* at length as it restored the vampiric aliens of Wells' novel. The brief "Epilogue: The Vampires We Need" posits the possibilities of future vampires in science fiction, noting both burgeoning interest in stories set in alternative histories (like *Abraham Lincoln, Vampire Hunter* [2012]) and superhero franchises. He concludes that "The future may bring android vampires, nanotech vampires, genetically-engineered vampires, virtual-reality vampires, or other science fiction vamps that are currently beyond our level of technological comprehension" (211). It is noteworthy that Meehan does not dismiss the vampire trend as being "over" as far too many think-pieces have recently done. Finally, the "Filmography" at the end of the book lists the sixty-four films referenced the book which meet Meehan's definition of the vampire in science fiction. The list includes titles, major credits, run time, and media format. It is also in alphabetical rather than chronological order. It is a useful list within these constraints, but I think a more expansive listing would be more useful to the reader.

A particular strength of this volume is the sheer variety of texts examined; there were a number of titles I had simply never heard of that were welcome new entrees after a surfeit of "From *Dracula* to *Twilight*" analyses in the past decade. However, because so many of these films are lesser-known, Meehan dedicates expansive and possibly excessive space to summarizing characters and plots, sacrificing study for description. The book is also light on scholarly engagement, with only a handful of academic texts referenced or utilized. As such, the book is useful as a reference but not necessarily as a study on the topic. That said, *The Vampire in Science Fiction Film and Literature* is a readable and fascinating work and will likely be of interest to scholars.

Cait Coker
University of Illinois at Urbana-Champaign, USA

Melton, J. Gordon, and Alysa Hornick, comps. *The Vampire in Folklore, History, Literature, Film, and Television: A Comprehensive Bibliography.*

Jefferson, NC: McFarland, 2015. Pp. 380. ISBN 978-0-7864-9936-6. Paperback, US$35.

J. Gordon Melton, author of several reference works on vampires, notably three editions of *The Vampire Book: The Encyclopedia of the Undead*, collaborates with Alysa Hornick, an authority on Joss Whedon's productions such as *Buffy the Vampire Slayer* and *Angel*, to create this monumental compilation. Before acquiring this book, the prospective reader should be aware that it does not include a filmography or a bibliography of vampire fiction. (The latter will appear as a second volume planned for future publication.) Rather, the present volume cites secondary works of all lengths, in English, about the media named in the title. The time span covered by this bibliography ranges from 1800 through 2013. The body of the work contains 6,018 entries, numbered for convenient reference.

Melton's Introduction explains the origins of this volume, describes and analyzes the format of the citations, and finally devotes six pages to "The Scope of the Work" in two major areas. First, he tackles the definitional problem, "What is a vampire?" Beginning with the standard dictionary definition, he expands on it by discussing several of the many types of folkloric and literary vampires that deviate from the basic concept of a reanimated, blood-drinking corpse. After mentioning a few of the widely varied creatures in world folklore that fall under the general category of "vampire," he briefly surveys the transformations undergone by that concept in literature and other media from the early nineteenth century to the present. The second heading under "The Scope of the Work" deals with "Practical Considerations": What types of works are included in the bibliography? Although the main focus is on printed material, the blurred line that now exists between print and electronic media is acknowledged, and Internet-only journals are indexed. Ephemera such as newspaper articles and book and movie reviews (as opposed to longer, more substantive essays on similar topics) are excluded. In addition, as noted later, some peripheral topics, e.g., vampire bats and serial killers, have such a vast body of literature devoted to them that only a "sampling" of relevant texts can be included.

The next section, "Vampire Studies: A Brief Overview," begins with the official investigations and reports on alleged vampire cases in Eastern Europe in the eighteenth century. The essay then comments on late-nineteenth-century studies of vampirism by psychologists, spiritualists, and occultists. After a discussion of Montague Summers' seminal but eccentric books, a broad survey of post-1970 academic and popular nonfiction on vampirism follows, with particular reference to the rise of the "good guy vampire" and "conflicted vampire" in fiction and film, phenomena that contributed to increasing scholarly interest in the vampire as portrayed in popular culture. At a length of four pages, this essay provides a far from exhaustive or in-depth treatment, but then, as the title indicates, it does not claim to do that. A "Vampire Timeline" from 1800 through 2013 follows, with emphasis on literature, stage drama, films, and television. Other items of interest, such as awards, also appear here. Many entries include brief notes elaborating on their significance.

The main body of the text is divided into nine major parts: Vampires and Vampirism: General Sources (including bibliographies), Folklore and History, Literature, Vampires on Stage and Screen, Vampires on Television, Vampires in Music and Art, The Metaphorical Vampire, The Contemporary Vampire Subculture (including a subsection for cookbooks, of which there are a surprising number), and Juvenilia. Each part and subsection is preceded by a short introduction, usually consisting of a paragraph or two, although the introductory remarks on *Buffy the Vampire Slayer / Angel* and comic books amount in each case to essays of about three pages. Each of the nine parts has subdivisions, the number varying according to topic. Many prominent figures and works, such as Vlad Tepes, Elizabeth Bathory, *Dracula*, the *Twilight* series, and *Buffy the Vampire Slayer*, have their own subdivisions. The longest subsection under "Literature," not surprisingly, covers materials related to Bram Stoker and *Dracula*.

Part IX, "Juvenilia" (in the sense of books written for, not by, children and adolescents), comprises a wide range of nonfiction for young readers about vampires and related topics (e.g., vampire bats) in folklore, history, literature, film, and television. Here what I consider an error in classification conveys a misleading impression. "Juvenilia" is subdivided into "Children's Books" and "Pseudo-Documentaries." The latter items, although the introductory note characterizes the intended reader as "usually a teenager" (350), include many works clearly intended for adults. By "pseudo-documentaries," the editors mean publications "[E]xisting in the space between fiction and non-fiction" (350), books of mock information and advice that "assume the reality of vampires" (350) and counsel the reader on how to deal with such creatures. Since guidebooks including but not limited to *Vampire Seduction Handbook*, *The Vampire Relationship Guide*, *How to Get a Date with a Vampire*, and *The Vampire Is Just Not That into You* are directed at an adult audience (having read the last two, I can confirm their intended readership), the entire subsection should not, in my opinion, be subsumed under "Juvenilia."

The book concludes with three appendices constituting checklists of the twenty-five top-grossing vampire films, vampire television series from 1960 through 2010, and major academic conferences on *Buffy the Vampire Slayer* as well as a handful of general vampire-themed conferences. An index lists authors of works cited in the text, along with a few titles in lieu of author names for anonymous entries. This feature compensates for the fact that works by a single writer are often distributed among several different categories, so that the index performs a vital function for the reader in search of all items written by a particular author. Melton and Hornick wisely choose to index by entry number rather than page number, making exact references easy to find. Throughout the book, running headers facilitate quick searches for topics, with the part title on the left-hand page and the subsection on the right.

Like any other reference book, this work is not quite perfect. Nits can be picked. For example: in the Vampire Timeline, Lord Byron's poem "The Giaour" is said to include "the hero's encounter with a vampire" (15); actually, the hero is threatened with the possibility of his becoming a vampire after death. A. E. Van Vogt's "Asylum" (1942) hardly qualifies as "the first story about an alien vampire" (16); "Shambleau" (1933), by C. L. Moore, and *Sinister Barrier* (1939), by Eric Frank Russell, immediately come to mind. Moreover, Van Vogt's name is misspelled in the Timeline (16). Later, novelist Laurell K. Hamilton's first name is misspelled several times (59, 110). *Prism of the Night* (1991), by Katherine Ramsland, is inaccurately cited as *Prism in the Night* (130). In the preface to the subsection for stage drama, Charles Nodier's last name is rendered as "Nordier" (135), and Hamilton Deane appears as "Hamilton Dean" (135). The book would have benefited from another round of proofreading.

On the whole, however, this bibliography makes available the fruits of years of research and admirably fulfills the promise of the term "Comprehensive" in the book's subtitle. It should become an indispensable reference for specialists in all areas of vampire studies. Fortunately, the price of this trade paperback is modest enough (in comparison to most academic publications) to allow scholars to purchase personal copies rather than depending on library access.

Margaret L. Carter
Independent scholar, USA

Murphy, Ronald, Jr. *On Vampires*.

Bideford, UK: CFZ Press, 2017. Pp. 140. ISBN 978-1-909488-51-9. Paperback, £10. Originally published as On Vampires: Unearthing the Legends and Folklore of These Creatures of the Night *(Self-pub., CreateSpace, 2017).*

A writer must first and foremost keep his or her audience in mind: who am I writing for? A lay audience? Scholars and academics? Those with a passing interest in the "unexplained"? When beginning writers ask for advice on starting books (or any other endeavor from a podcast to a film), one of the first questions I ask is: why? What are *you* going to bring to it? Why are *you* writing it? Why should a reader pick up *your* book, out of dozens or hundreds out there on the same topic? What makes your book different from all the rest? Are you doing original research, or describing your own experiences, or re-analyzing information in a fresh, new way? What is the reader of your book going to get that they can't get skimming Wikipedia or buying the next book featured on Amazon.com?

I thought of this when reading *On Vampires* by Ronald Murphy, Jr. *On Vampires*, like Murphy's other books with the same theme—*On Mermaids* (2016), *On Ghosts: The Spirit World Throughout History* (2016), *On Wildman: Tracking Bigfoot Through History* (2016; 2018), and so on—seems to be a personal, idiosyncratic look at his personal musings on the topic, supplemented by some research. Which is fine, but it leaves the book in sort of a "neither fish nor fowl" state: it's not really comprehensive enough to be authoritative and academic, so it doesn't have the scope of, say, Paul Barber's *Vampires, Burial, and Death: Folklore and Reality* (1988), or Matthew Beresford's *From Demons to Dracula: The Creation of the Modern Vampire Myth* (2008). (Theresa Cheung's *The Element Encyclopedia of Vampires: An A-Z of the Undead* [2009], though heavily plagiarized and liberally cribbed from superficial internet sources,[1] is a reasonably comprehensive overview.) But at the same time, it's marginally more scholarly and objective than gonzo-marinated books by Nick Redfern, for example.

Murphy is prone to flourishes such as "Let us ponder [. . .]" and "Grab a comfy seat and settle in [. . .]" and reminds me of the colorful friend of yours from down the street who has a longstanding interest in the occult or unexplained, and holds court at parties with tales of the goblin universe and his thoughts about the dark denizens therein. Nobody—including those of us familiar with the subject—really wants to spoil the fun by challenging him on occasional sketchy claims or logic, so we all happily listen, nod, and enjoy his tale.

Murphy offers an accounting of his approach: "looking through the lens of Jungian psychology, I am left with the fundamental conclusion that hidden animals not only exist to this very day but inform us of how we view the world" (114). This is all well and good, but Jungian approaches traditionally have a very poor track record of success in finding, cataloguing, and verifying unknown animals, to say nothing of less corporeal quarry such as vampires and ghosts. We can ponder archetypes all day, but such musings bring us no closer to confirming the existence of the vampires and other cryptids Murphy seeks; that will be done—and has been done—through field investigation, genetic analysis, zoological study, and so on. I

---

[1] Benjamin Radford, "Investigating Plagiarism in New Age Books," Online Extras, *Skeptical Inquirer*, June 20, 2013, https://skepticalinquirer.org/exclusive/investigating_plagiarism_in_new_age_books.

don't question Murphy's knowledge or sincerity, just the fruitfulness of his approach.

As Murphy noted in his introduction to *On Ghosts*, "I am a researcher and I want to be able to have my findings scrutinized by the scientific community so all of us in the paranormal field will get the respect which we deserve."[2] This admirable goal is unfortunately at odds with many of Murphy's points, which are often highly speculative. In one section he ruminates about the idea that vampire bats may have played a role in the popular conception of the anthropomorphic vampire. All well and good, but for example over the course of two pages (115–16) he goes further and further out on conjectural limbs: "Could it be that large bats were at one time witnessed in human settlements and day's [*sic*] later people started bleeding [. . .]?," "Could it be that an unknown bat was responsible for those and other periodic plagues?," "could this theoretical bat have been personified in the grotesque guise of a person?," "Could this strange, flying conjectured ape-like creature, a chimera of man and beast, be part of the pantomime of shadows witnessed during sleep paralysis, a dimly recalled image of a predator that swooped in and fed off the blood of mankind? Could this ape that flew on leathery wings, if it did indeed exist, so impact ancient human lives that its retention has burned itself into our collective memoires [*sic*]?" And so on; you get the idea.

In this and other sections it's less what Murphy has learned and researched about vampires than what he imagines could *possibly* be, with little recourse to what the evidence shows (he begins by discussing the Ebola virus in West Africa and connecting it with bats [115], though of course vampire bats don't exist in Africa, their range being limited to the Americas). With an open mind and/or enough qualifiers, anything is possible. In science the question is not what's *possible* but instead what's most plausible given the available evidence.

There are more than a few unfortunate typographical errors (the third paragraph of the book referenced "Crytpids";[3] *Twilight* author Stephenie Meyer's name is misspelled [p. 136]; *tenets* is mistaken for *tenants*, and so on). These are not fatal, of course—and I'm sympathetic as I know that CFZ Press hardly has a huge editorial staff—but such mistakes should have been caught prior to publication, especially in a slim book of 140 pages. The book would have been more useful (to scholars and researchers, anyway) if it had an index. It isn't essential but lack even of a simple table of contents is more baffling.

Many of the book's passages have inconsistent, inadequate, or non-existent references. On several occasions I read a fascinating passage and looked in vain for a reference, either finding none or a passing in-text mention but no corresponding citation in the bibliography. On page 93, for example, we find the phrase

2 Murphy, *On Ghosts: The Spirit World Throughout History* (self-pub, CreateSpace, 2016), 12.

3 Jen Devillier, foreword to *On Vampires*, by Ronald Murphy Jr. (Bideford, UK: CFZ Press, 2017), 5.

"According to *RoadsideAmerica.com*, 'until the 20th century, tuberculosis was thought to be caused by vampires in Rhode Island.'" Readers interested in following up on this bit of curiosa (or, perhaps, verifying it) will be in for a frustrating experience. Murphy provides no author, no date, no title, no URL, or any further reference in the bibliography—just the name of a website.

It's as if Murphy is determined to make the contents of his book as difficult to access as possible, which is unfortunate, as there's some interesting material within. Murphy is at his best—and in his element—when grounded in historical context, especially in the social and religious aspects of the Middle Ages. He reveals somewhat lesser-known early vampire stories such as "Carmilla" (1871–2), a Gothic novella that predates Stoker's classic by a quarter-century. His discussions about Lilith are enlightening, as is his review of the Lamia and the Victorian era notions of vampires.

In the last chapter he surveys various entities—some more clearly vampiric than others—found in folklore from around the world, devoting a paragraph or two of citation-free (and occasionally superficial) discussion (he seems unaware of considerable research done on Puerto Rico's *chupacabra*, for example) to each. Murphy adopts an overly inclusive "kitchen sink" approach to the book, delving into subjects such as the famous 1855 "Devil's footprints" found in Dover; the Jersey Devil; Wendigo, and other entities whose connections to vampires is tenuous at best. This serves to somewhat dilute the focus of the book, and one wished for more of Murphy's cogent historical analysis.

Benjamin Radford
Committee for Skeptical Inquiry, USA

BIBLIOGRAPHY

Devillier, Jen. Foreword. In Murphy, *On Vampires*, 5–6.
Murphy, Ronald, Jr. *On Ghosts: The Spirit World Throughout History*. Self-published, CreateSpace, 2016.
Radford, Benjamin. "Investigating Plagiarism in New Age Books." Online Extras. *Skeptical Inquirer*, June 20, 2013. https://sketpicalinquirer.org/exclusive/investigating_plagiarism_in_new_age_books.

Sherman, Aubrey. *Vampires: The Myths, Legends, & Lore.*

Avon, MA: Adams Media, 2014. Pp. 224. ISBN 978-1-4405-8076-5. Hardcover, US$16.99.

Vampires is freelance writer Aubrey Sherman's sanguineous contribution to Adams Media's Myths, Legends, & Lore series which encompasses entries on mermaids, wizards, fairies, and various other tenants of the collective imagination. A broad, introductory survey of the vampire in folklore, history, and popular culture, Sherman's book is an acknowledged condensation of Barb Karg, Arjean Spaite, and Rick Sutherland's *The Everything Vampire Book: From Vlad the Impaler to the Vampire Lestat—a History of Vampires in Literature, Film, and Legend* (2009), sporting more carry-friendly dimensions (5.5 x 7.5 inches) than its larger predecessor. Though intended as light overview as opposed to incisive commentary, *Vampires* has faults that preclude recommendation even for those with modest expectations.

Sherman organizes her material in broad thematic and geographic categories. These include introductory chapters on vampiric origins and attributes, followed by several chapters on regional folklore, then treatments of various media (including literature, film, television, and gaming), and closing with profiles of notable historical vampires (such as Peter Plogojowitz and Erzsébet Báthory), blood-driven serial killers, the diverse place of "vampires today," and the traits of successful vampire hunters. Though seemingly conventional, this schema invites confusion in its execution. For example, Sherman's material on historic vampires would probably be better placed in the regional sections. Specifically, Arnod Paole is probably best understood as a Slavic vampire, the Alnwick vampire as a UK exemplar, Johannes Cuntze as a Central European figure, and so forth. This is also a concern in the chapters on undead characteristics and vampire hunting. Many of the attributes and vulnerabilities that Sherman applies to ostensibly folkloric vampires in general are only applicable in regional contexts—or in pop culture. To wit, though vampirism is often contagious in traditional tales, the "maker" concept that Sherman describes (11) is not nearly as ubiquitous outside of recent fiction as she implies. Likewise, Sherman gives forced exposure to sunlight as one of the "best methods of catching vampires" (198) without specifying that this is almost exclusively a twentieth-century convention with little antecedent in folklore. Though these misconceptions may be widespread in popular ideas about vampires in folklore and fiction, it is disappointing to see mistakes like these published without qualification.

Though Sherman's prose is readable, there is inconsistent effort to tie concepts together; in places, the book reads like a set of encyclopedia entries arranged to an outline without the usual transitions. Some casual readers might like this just fine, but others will find it difficult to engage the book. For example, the pop culture chapter on gaming, though adequate in describing the role-playing games from TSR and White Wolf, only addresses video games by giving a list of titles (omitting the long-time favorite *Castlevania*, for some reason), and vampiric music barely gets a paragraph shoehorned into the "Vampires Today" chapter. Bram Stoker himself gets a brief biography in the literature chapter (which incorrectly identifies him as Henry Irving's stage manager at the Lyceum Theatre as opposed to the business manager), but, perhaps unique to all surveys of the vampire motif, *Dracula*'s plot is never summarized anywhere—only alluded to in bits scattered about. Granted, the book's brevity precludes any real depth for any topic, but the meager attention given to so many tentpoles of vampire culture is disheartening, nonetheless. As with most popular books, Sherman cites sources only occasionally. There is a bibliography, but its use is not always apparent. The bibliography also omits the essential works of Michael E. Bell and Jan L. Perkowski, which does not speak well of its research process.

The summary nature of the text also raises the related problems of context and clarity, such as when Sherman conflates Bulgarian religious belief with the *vampir* of Hungarian folklore, then implies that the latter was effectively the prototypical European vampire (50); suffice to say that Bulgaria and Hungary are strikingly distinct along religious and linguistic lines, and that the Hungarian word was not used until after the advent of vampire fiction in Western Europe.[1] Likewise, the drive to summarize complex material leads to odd perambulations like citing an 1810 printing of a 1734 manuscript to show that the word "vampire" entered English in the late 1600s (10) or declaring that the Greek Orthodox Church addressed *vrykolakas* belief in the first century CE (45), which religious historians will tell you is something of a temporal impossibility. In an odd turn, Sherman gives sexual sadists Fritz Haarmann and Peter Kürten disproportionate attention; by word count, Kürten gets more attention than Bram Stoker. Inexplicably, Sherman includes explicit details of Haarmann and Kürten's pathology that would likely be censored on most social media. Given the book's tone and reading level, which is otherwise appropriate for young readers, this is borderline irresponsible.

Sherman does have her good points here and there. She informs the reader up front that "the majority of vampires aren't pristine, white-skinned, radiant beings. Most are reanimated corpses in various states of disarray and decay." (11) She casts a critical eye at the supposedly antique "vampire kits" that have popped up in recent years, her treatment of those who consider themselves "real vampires" is fair and open-minded, and the book's modular style allows for diverse topics in minimal space, even if some only get a bare mention. It is obvious that this is not a long-fraught labor of love, but rather a freelance assignment that, given the diversity of the subject, lends itself to omissions and gaffes more than most.

Though I cannot recommend this book to anyone but a resolute completest, reading through Sherman's perfunctory survey provides serendipitous lessons in critical thinking and the limits of one's knowledge. For example, she obliquely states that the Greek term *vrykolakas* is derived from South Slavic "descriptions of wearers of wolf pelts." (46) Since this was the familiar etymology of the Serbo-Croatian *vukodlak*, I was tempted to dismiss Sherman's note as an error; some quick research corrected my own lack of erudition.[2] Likewise, I had not read medieval chronicler William of Newburgh for years, and Sherman's problems with his biography (she dates the end of his *Historia* as both 1098 and the correct 1198 [143]) drove me back to William's beloved writings on English history and legend. Paradoxically, reading through a book of such questionable accuracy exercises skills that might otherwise fall neglected, providing an unexpected lesson in the nature of knowledge.

Stu Burns
Independent scholar, USA

---

[1] Katharina M. Wilson, "The History of the Word *Vampire*" in *The Vampire: A Casebook*, ed. Alan Dundes (Madison: University of Wisconsin Press, 1998), 5, 8.

[2] John Cuthbert Lawson, *Modern Greek Folklore and Ancient Greek Religion: A Study in Survivals* (Cambridge: Cambridge University Press, 1910), 377.

BIBLIOGRAPHY

Lawson, John Cuthbert. *Modern Greek Folklore and Ancient Greek Religion: A Study in Survivals*. Cambridge: Cambridge University Press, 1910.
Wilson, Katharina M. "The History of the Word *Vampire*." In *The Vampire: A Casebook*, edited by Alan Dundes, 3–11. Madison: University of Wisconsin Press, 1998. Originally published as "The History of the Word 'Vampire.'" *Journal of the History of Ideas* 46, no. 4 (October–December 1985): 577–83.

Books received by prospective reviewers in arrangement with the Editor, author or publisher. Inclusion on this list does not guarantee review.

Crandle, Marita Woywod. *New Orleans Vampires: History and Legend*. Charleston, SC: Haunted America, 2017. Pp. 128. ISBN 978-1-4671-3742-3. Paperback, $21.99.

Frayling, Christopher. *Vampyres: Genesis and Resurrection from Count Dracula to Vampirella*. London: Thames & Hudson, 2016. Pp. 464. ISBN 978-0-500-25221-5. Hardcover, £19.95.

Fredriksson, Cecilia. *Vampirist: A Book about Real Vampires*. [Eskilstuna]: Makaber, 2018. Pp. 215. ISBN 978-1-84583-139-4. Paperback, $9.99. Originally published as *Vampyrist: En bok om riktiga vampyrer* ([Eskilstuna]: Makaber, 2017).

Guarneri, Michael. *Vampires in Italian Cinema, 1956–1975*. Edinburgh: Edinburgh University Press, 2020. Pp. viii + 224. ISBN 978 1 4744 5813 9. Webready PDF, £75.

Hovi, Tuomas. *Finding Heritage Through Fiction in Dracula Tourism*. Helsinki: Suomalainen Tiedeakatemia/Academia Scientiarum Fennica, 2016. Pp. 253. ISBN 978-951-41-1122-8. Hardcover, €35.

Le Fanu, Joseph Sheridan. *Carmilla: A Critical Edition*. Edited and with an introduction by Kathleen Costello-Sullivan. New York: Syracuse University Press, 2013. Pp. xxvi + 168. ISBN 978-0-8156-3311-2. Paperback, $19.95.

Stoker, Dacre. *Stoker on Stoker: Dracula Revealed; Notes and Background to the Writing of "Dracula"*. 2019. Reprint, Canterbury: Telos Publishing, 2020. Pp. 108. ISBN 978-1-84583-139-4. Paperback, £10.99.

Swiderski, Richard. *A Plague of the Imagination: Cruentation, the Night Visitor and the Names of the Vampire*. Self-published, Kindle Direct Publishing, 2019. Pp. 371. ISBN 9781795343718. Paperback, $15.95.

Unterholzner, Bernhard. *Die Erfindung des Vampirs: Mythenbildung zwischen populären Erzählungen vom Bösen und wissenschaftlicher Forschung*. Wiesbaden: Harrassowitz Verlag, 2019. Pp. 372. ISBN 978-3-477-19892-9. E-book (pdf), €49,90.

Open Graves, Open Minds Present: 'Some Curious Disquiet': Polidori, the Byronic Vampire, and Its Progeny; A Symposium for the Bicentenary of *The Vampyre*

Keats House, Hampstead, UK, April 6–7, 2019

Since the project began in 2010, Open Graves, Open Minds (OGOM) has been integral to the cultural shift in attitudes and pedagogies relating to the study of vampiric literature. OGOM's inaugural vampire conference, Open Graves, Open Minds: Vampires and the Undead in Modern Culture, on April 16–17, 2010 sought to bring the vampire home, as it were, after a spike in American vampire fiction following the success of Stephenie Meyer's *Twilight* (2005). Since then, Dr. Sam George (University of Hertfordshire) and Dr. Bill Hughes (OGOM) have expanded the project into an MA course on vampire literature, an edited collection,[1] and several more conferences, the most recent of which was 'Some Curious Disquiet': Polidori, the Byronic Vampire, and Its Progeny.

The symposium, held on April 6–7, 2019 at Keats House, Hampstead, celebrated the bicentenary of John William Polidori's *The Vampyre* (1819)—a short work of prose fiction derived from the same Geneva ghost story competition that produced Mary Shelley's *Frankenstein* (1818), and representing the first appearance of the vampire in English prose fiction. The two-day conference was varied in its approach, interrogating issues spanning from the text's original context right up to its contemporary resonance in cinematic vampire movies and TV series. Following registration and a welcome talk by Dr. George, conference attendees were treated to a guided tour of Keats House. Through this, the house was able to be used not only as a beautiful and evocative setting for the conference, but also a historical place transporting us back to the Romantic era in which *The Vampyre* was written. Keats House had displayed a second edition of *The Vampyre* especially for the conference, and the programme had been cleverly designed to mimic an early binding of the text. Sections of the tour that addressed Keats' untimely death from tuberculosis served as precursors to papers such as Marcus Sedgwick's, which would discuss the links forged between the disease and vampirism.

The papers were organised chronologically, beginning with "The Bloody Horde of Vampires in the Villa Diodati" by Prof. Nick Groom (University of Exeter). Prof. Groom began with an overview of eighteenth-century reports of vampires and some of the more disturbing preventative measures undertaken to keep them away, providing a fascinating introduction and grounding the mythology that we have subsequently come to associate with vampires to this day. Moving on to the nineteenth century, Prof. Groom discussed the emergence of the vampiric figure in

---

[1] Papers from the inaugural conference were published in Sam George and Bill Hughes, eds., *Open Graves, Open Minds: Representations of Vampires and the Undead from the Enlightenment to the Present Day* (Manchester: Manchester University Press, 2013).

poetry through Robert Southey's *Thalaba the Destroyer* (1801) and Lord Byron's *The Giaour* (1813), leading us to that fated evening at the Villa Diodati. Here the paper took an unexpected turn in demonstrating an unequivocal semantic link between vampirism and descriptive elements of Mary Shelley's *Frankenstein*. Quotations from both the novel and Shelley's letters were used to evidence a proliferation of references to bloodshed, blood sucking, blood curdling, and vampires more explicitly, resulting in a new interpretation of *Frankenstein* as a text that utilises vampiric metaphor. Dr. Ivan Phillips (University of Hertfordshire) followed with a paper entitled "'In Their Nocturnal Orgies': Polidori's *The Vampyre* and the Many Inventions of Special Effects," leading with a discussion of the importance of Lord Ruthven's gaze, in which he commented that words drawn from the semantic field of vision occur roughly every two to four sentences. He went on to talk about the importance of the vampire's image, and the effects used to depict this on stage and in film, asserting that the aesthetic focus in vampiric narratives originated with Polidori's Lord Ruthven—a character who is himself difficult to visually perceive and one whose gaze seems to pierce victims more frequently than his fangs do.Following a coffee break, during which guests were treated to "Vampyre cupcakes," Dr. Hughes, one of the conference's organisers, presented a paper on "Rebellion, Treachery, and Glamour: Lady Caroline Lamb's *Glenarvon* and the Progress of the Byronic Vampire." *Glenarvon* (1816) scandalously recounts the tale of Lady Caroline Lamb's affair with Lord Byron through the characters of Calantha and Lord Ruthven. Despite the pseudonyms, readers were left with no doubt as to the true identities of Lamb's characters, and the scandal that the book subsequently initiated rendered her a social outcast. In adopting the same name for his vampire, Polidori was able to transfer traits of Lamb's Ruthven to his own in the mind of the reader, while simultaneously asserting that his vampire was similarly based on Lord Byron.

Dr. George, another organiser, presented "Phantasmagoria and Spectriana: The Legacy of Polidori's Vampyre from Theatricals to Vampire Slaying Kits" and talked of *The Vampyre*'s afterlife through adaptations such as Cyprien Bérard's novel, J. R. Planché's dramatizations, and the effects used in *Phantasmagoria*. Through these examples, leading on nicely from Dr. Phillips' earlier paper, Dr. George discussed stage effects such as the "vampire trap" and props such as the "vampire slaying kit," one of which was on display at the conference.

Novelist and critic, Marcus Sedgwick, in his paper entitled "Sexual Contagions: Vampirism and Tuberculosis," explained the ways in which consumption came to be seen as a mysterious and fashionable disease and one whose visual symptoms bared striking similarities to those associated with vampirism. Through an analysis of medical dissertations that Polidori may have been aware of when completing his doctorate, Sedgwick drew parallels between the illness and the figure of the vampire. He went on to provide evidence suggesting that Percy Shelley may have had consumption, and that Lord Byron had commented that he hoped to die of consumption so that women would comment on how interesting he looked while dying! He ended with an extremely apt quote from John Murray's *A Treatise on*

Pulmonary Consumption (1830)—a medical paper which explicitly compares consumption to vampirism.[2]

Prof. William Hughes (Bath Spa University) was scheduled to give a talk entitled "'To Fill My Heart with Deeper Crimson': Physiology and the Fictional Vampire". This talk, however, was unfortunately cancelled.

Prof. Gina Whisker (University of Brighton) followed with her paper entitled "From Polidori's Holiday Escapes: Florence Marryatt's *The Blood of the Vampire*, Sarah Smith's 'The Red Storm Comes', and Moira Buffini/Neil Jordan's *Byzantium*." These texts were linked through their shared setting of a supposedly relaxing seaside town. Marryatt's novel, published in the same year as Stoker's *Dracula* (1897), features a psychic vampire whose foreignness and exoticism is seen as a part of her sexual appeal; the sexuality of the vampire is further explored through "When the Red Storm Comes" (1993); and the division of vampiric gender roles is evident in *Byzantium* (2013).

The next paper was "'Now My Clothes are Right Again': Byronic Vampires in the Long 1960s," presented by Prof. Catherine Spooner (Lancaster University). Prof. Spooner interrogated the many Byron biographies of the long 1960s; Byronic links in ostensibly the first 1960s vampire novel, Simon Raven's *Doctors Wear Scarlet* (1960); vampiric dandyism in Jane Gaskell's *The Shiny Narrow Grin* (1964); and the return of stereotypical vampire fashion in *Adam Adamant Lives!*, a British TV series that ran from 1966 to 1967. Her paper shed light on a comparatively under-researched era of vampire literature and demonstrated the impact of 1960s works on vampire literature today.

Saturday ended with a keynote paper by Sir Christopher Frayling, in which he traced the development of vampire studies, sharing his own personal memories of his time at the Villa Diodati when filming for *Nightmare: The Birth of Horror* (1996), and his experiences researching vampire literature prior to its emergence as a literary field of study. His paper was titled "Polidori Revisited" and, as such, many accepted truths about Polidori were brought into question. His apparent death by suicide was interrogated in light of evidence suggesting that he may have died of a head injury that he had suffered some time prior. This, along with other inaccuracies highlighted in the keynote presentation, served to illustrate that there is still work to be done in this area and that vampires have more to offer us yet.

Sunday began with a tour of Highgate Cemetery. Conference attendees were accompanied by Peter Mills and Stephen Sowerby, who had tailored their tour to their guests' vampiric interests. We visited the graves of the Rossettis, learned of

---

[2] "Consumption, like the vampire, while it drinks up the vital stream, fans with its wing the hopes that flutter in the hectic breast; the transparent colours that flit on the features like those of the rainbow on the cloud, are equally evanescent, and leave its darkness more deeply shaded." Murray, *A Treatise on Pulmonary Consumption; Its Prevention and Remedy* (London: Whittaker, Treacher and Arnot, 1830), 3, https://wellcomecollection.org/works/tvk8 s7r6.

the "Highgate Vampire" hoax, and were given a comprehensive history of the cemetery, its occupants, and its origins as a means to combat body-snatching from overfilled city graveyards.

Upon our return to Keats House, Dr. Stacey Abbot (University of Roehampton) presented a paper entitled "'I Walk and the Past Walks with Me': Rewriting Polidori's Vampyre in *Byzantium*." Leading on nicely from Prof. Whisker's earlier assertions, Dr. Abbott discussed the ways in which *Byzantium* can be seen to channel earlier vampiric characters from a predominantly female perspective. For instance, Anne Rice's Louis and Lestat are mirrored through the characters of Eleanor and Clara. Names are also used to provide links to Polidori and other works of canonical vampire fiction. Dr. Sorcha Ní Fhlainn (Manchester Metropolitan University) followed this up with "'The Vulgar Fictions of a Demented Irishman': Postmodern Vampirism in the Cinema of Neil Jordan," in which she discussed *Byzantium* as a companion piece to *Interview with the Vampire*, tracing the similarities and modifications made by Jordan during the process of adaptation. Storytelling was identified as a key theme, along with Irish culture.

Daisy Butcher (University of Hertfordshire) then presented on "The Legacy of Romanticism's Female Fiends: *Christabel*, 'Carmilla', 'Luella Miller', and the Psychic Vampire," tracing the lineage of the female vampire starting with Geraldine in Samuel Taylor Coleridge's *Christabel* (1816), which established many of the recurring metaphors and imagery seen in later works. Butcher argued that psychic vampires, such as Harriet Brandt, Luella Miller, and Carmilla, share many character traits and evoke sympathy for the female vampire as, to some extent, they are shown to be unable to control their parasitic nature. The female vampire's languidness is also considered to be vital to her depiction as it conceals her true monstrosity. Dr. Sue Chaplin (Leeds Beckett University) was scheduled to open the next panel with her paper on "Polidori and the Postmillennial Vampire," however this paper was cancelled. Following another round of coffee and cupcakes, Dr. Kaja Franck (University of Hertfordshire) discussed more contemporary vampires in her paper entitled "'The Deadly Hue of His Face': The Genesis of the Vampiric Gentleman and His Deadly Beauty; or, How Lord Ruthven Became Edward Cullen." She began by discussing Buffy's Angel as a modern Byronic vampire and commented that both contemporary and Romantic vampires tend to be depicted as visually beautiful sexual objects. This assertion was reinforced by several quotations from *The Vampyre* and *Twilight* which, despite their temporal disparity, bared clear similarities. The importance of the gaze was further illustrated, and gender roles were seen to be opposed in the two narratives, with Bella looking upon Edward in the same way that Aubrey gazes upon Ianthe.

Dr. Jillian Wingfield (University of Hertfordshire) then presented on "Vampensteins: The Conjunction of the Undead and Reanimated in Twenty-first-century Fiction," discussing the ways in which vampire fiction has found itself repeatedly linked with emerging scientific developments. Octavia Butler's *Fledgling* (2005) was used as an example of this as the vampire is seen to be rationalised through scientific allusions. *The Vampyre* and *Frankenstein* are linked through their shared conception story and, even now, vampires and science continue to be intertwined.

Dr. Xavier Aldana Reyes (Manchester Metropolitan University) ended the conference with his paper on "Vampiros: On the Spanish Vampire." Dr. Aldana Reyes provided a fascinating insight into the vampires of Spanish Gothic fiction, giving a comprehensive report on the various Spanish texts/films influenced by canonical British vampires (particularly Dracula and Carmilla), interspersed with video clips to provide visual points of comparison. Emilia Pardo Bazán's *Vampiro* (1901) was the first literary Spanish vampire, and drew heavily on themes from Polidori's *The Vampyre*, however the social anxieties addressed in vampire fiction in Spain following this tended to be more political.

The conference was a huge success, prompting excellent questions and animated discussions between attendees and speakers. Some attendees live-tweeted at the event, and their comments can be viewed under the hashtag "#OGOMVampyre200." The scope of these papers served to demonstrate that the field of vampire studies is as un-dead as ever, with many more discussions to be had and much more research to be conducted.

Eleanor Bryan
University of Lincoln, UK

BIBLIOGRAPHY

George, Sam, and Bill Hughes, eds. *Open Graves, Open Minds: Representations of Vampires and the Undead from the Enlightenment to the Present Day*. Manchester: Manchester University Press, 2013.

Murray, John. *A Treatise on Pulmonary Consumption; Its Prevention and Remedy*. London: Whittaker, Treacher and Arnot, 1830. https://wellcomecollection.org/works/tvk8s7r6.

Vampire Studies, 2019 National PCA Meetings and Events, National Conference of the Popular Culture Association/American Culture Association

Wardman Park Marriott, Washington, DC, April 17–20, 2019

For forty-nine years, the National Conference of the Popular Culture Association/American Culture Association (PCA) has drawn American and international scholars to an American city each year. Across four days, starting at 8 a.m. and ending at 10 p.m., and with continuous panels throughout, attending scholars share papers, attend film screenings and creative readings, and engage in enthusiastic and thoughtful dialogue with one another. PCA encompasses well over a hundred subject areas, each with its own track of programming; such areas include, variously, Animation, Comics and Comic Art, Fan Culture and Theory, Horror, Libraries, Science Fiction and Fantasy, Tolkien Studies, and more. Since 2007, the Vampire Studies area has had a regular program at the conference, usually spread over at least two days. Founded by Mary Findlay, initially as The Vampire in Popular Film and Literature area, the current co-chairs of the group are

Prof. Lisa Nevarez (Siena College) and Prof. U. Melissa Anyiwo (Curry College). This year's organizational team also included Amanda Hobson (Indiana State University) as Social Media Coordinator, William Tringali (University of Illinois at Urbana-Champaign)[1] as Graduate Coordinator, and Dr. Vicky Gilpin (Millikin University; Harvard; Cerro Gordo) as Events Coordinator.

This year's meetings were held over April 17–20, 2019 at Wardman Park Marriott Washington, DC, and included three film screenings,[2] ten paper panels with two discussion roundtables, and an optional attendee dinner outing. Given that the full print copy of the PCA program was only available for purchase,[3] Prof. Anyiwo and Prof. Nevarez privately printed a four-page brochure detailing the dates, topics, and presenters for Vampire Studies area attendees.[4]

The business meeting kicked off the Vampire Studies sessions proper on April 18. Hosted by Prof. Anyiwo and Prof. Nevarez, this yearly session allows for the chairs to collect feedback and for the attendees to suggest ideas for future programming. This year's topics for discussion included: suggestions for next year's film and television screenings and suggestions for an optional book club, in which members read a selected text in advance and discuss it in depth at an open meeting (in which any attendee may participate) next year. Also discussed were the possibilities of starting a buddy or mentoring program for graduate students and first-year attendees, ideas for future roundtables, and discussions of where best to share Calls for Papers and related material.

Opening April 19 was the Crime & Justice[5] panel, consisting of a joint presentation by Prof. Anyiwo and Prof. Rebecca Allen Paynich[6] (Curry College). Their paper "Vigilantes or Villains? Perceptions of Crime and Justice in the *Blade &*

---

[1] At the time of the conference, Tringali was in his final semester of a Masters in Library and Information Science at the University of Illinois at Urbana-Champaign. He is now a librarian at Emory University.

[2] George Romero's *Creepshow* (1982), co-sponsored by the Gothic, Horror, Stephen King, and the Vampire Studies areas, on April 17; Joel Schumacher's *The Lost Boys* (1987); and Joss Whedon's "Once More with Feeling" episode of *Buffy the Vampire Slayer* (aired November 6, 2001, on UPN), both on April 20.

[3] A web app, with varying levels of successful functionality, has been in use since 2016 instead, alongside a heavily abbreviated print program that names only sessions and locations, rather than presenters and paper titles.

[4] There are some discrepancies between the PCA program, *National Conference of the Popular Culture Association/American Culture Association, April 17–20, 2019, Marriott Wardman Park Hotel, Washington, D.C.* (N.p.: Wiley, 2019), https://pcaaca.org/sities/default/files/pca_201 9_conference_program_digital_v5.1.pdf, and the brochure, *Popular Culture Association National Conference, April 2019: Vampire Studies; Full Schedule*, [2019], https://www.facebook.co m/download/preview/461069584621142. These will be noted throughout the report for historical interest, but the titles used in the brochure are the "official" versions used throughout this report. Subsequent footnotes relating to the PCA program and brochure are my own.—Ed.

[5] "Crime & Punishment." *National Conference*, 94.

[6] Incorrectly listed as Rebecca L. Paynich in *National Conference*, 215, 351.

Underworld Series" analyzed the two series, which ran for nearly two decades in total. Prof. Anyiwo and Prof. Paynich discussed the two series in terms of how minorities of all genders are represented as, variously, victim, offender, and vigilante, and how this is contrasted with the roles of their white male counterparts. This analysis focused on informal social control, justice, and vigilantism in the series. Prof. Anyiwo's and Prof. Paynich's work sparked critical conversations on the way race and gender affect the portrayal of the figure of the vampire in these two texts, especially when contrasted with more mainstream white male vampires. Scheduled presentations by Dr. Sarah Farrell[7] (University of Texas at Arlington), "Batman: The Disguise of the Modern Day Dracula"; Jasmina Kuenzli (Texas A&M University), "Driving a Stake Through the Heart of Slavery: *Abraham Lincoln: Vampire Hunter* and Civil War Memory"; and Prof. Natalie Kate Wilson (California State University San Marcos), "Rape Culture Sucks: The Female Vampire Avenger in *A Girl Walks Home Alone at Night, Byzantium, Avenged,* and *The Passage"* did not take place.

Next was the Gaming panel with presentations by William Tringali and Samuel Stinson (Shepherd University). Tringali's presentation, "Building Vampiric Morality: Constructing 'Good and Evil' in Vampire RPGs," examined the morality systems of two vampire video games: *Vampire the Masquerade: Bloodlines* (2004) and *Vampyr* (2018). Tringali examined how "moral content signifiers" built and defined the acceptability or unacceptability of in-game actions. Stinson, in a video essay titled "When It Sucks, It Really Sucks: Multimodal Affordances and Failed Suture in Gamic and Filmic Representations of *Bram Stoker's Dracula,"* examined how Bram Stoker's novel *Dracula* was adapted and evaluated by the 1992 film *Bram Stoker's Dracula,* the 1993 video game *Bram Stoker's Dracula,* and said game's review by Angry Video Game Nerd (James Rolfe), in 2007.[8] Tringali's and Stinson's panel further hosted discussions of how gaming could move beyond binary systems of "good" and "bad" player behavior, and whether assigning moral "points" systems potentially undermined player agency. A scheduled presentation by Dr. Brian Allen Santana (Shepherd University), "*Vampire: The Masquerade*: Fantasy and Roleplaying in an Age of Consent," did not take place.

The panel (Ancient) Monstrous Women[9] had Dr. Gregory N. Daugherty (Randolph-Macon College) presenting on "Cleopatra the *Fatale Monstrum"* and freelance writer Nancy Schumann presenting "Pardon My Bite: Vampire Women Who Kill Children from Ancient Folklore to Post-Modern Literature." Dr. Daugherty, a trained classicist who specializes on the iconography of Queen Cleopatra, overviewed several decades of the figure's appearances in popular culture before settling into an extended analysis of Anne Rice's duology of novels

---

[7] Incorrectly listed as "Ferrell" in *Popular Culture Association National Conference,* 1.

[8] First uploaded to GameTrailers.com (site discontinued) on October 14, 2008, the episode is available on YouTube. Cinemassacre, "Dracula - Angry Video Game Nerd - Episode 57," YouTube Video, 11:57, October 2, 2009, https://youtu.be/sDR8HKC9wgl. — Ed.

[9] "Monstrous Women." *National Conference,* 238.

The Mummy, or Ramses the Damned (1989) and *Ramses the Damned: The Passion of Cleopatra* (2017). Cleopatra in these texts is a psychic, rather than blood-drinking, vampire who haunts characters in the twenty-first century. Schumann's paper also drew on the intersections of the historical and the popular, analyzing the mythic figures of Lilith and the Lamia to analyze vampiric mothers in Joseph Sheridan Le Fanu's "Carmilla" (1871–2) and Anne Rice's characters of Claudia, Mekare and Maharet from her Vampire Chronicles, and how these figures contrast with "über-mothers" like *Twilight*'s Bella or *The Vampire Diaries'* Elena. Discussion afterwards focused on the problems of systemic injustice and gender, especially with motherhood and the perceptions of "good" and "bad" mothers in the context of child death, and especially how these historic patterns hold true in contemporary culture. A scheduled presentation by independent scholars Sofia Gieysztor and Michael Gilbert, "Years Are Only Skin-Deep: How Vampire Romances Refute Popular Excuses for Ageism," did not take place.

The Vampire Genders & Sexualities[10] panel also had two speakers, with Amanda Hobson presenting on "It's Not Just Subtext: An Exploration of Contemporary Queer Vampire Fictions" and Cain Edward Miller (Southern Methodist University) speaking on "Compensatory Masculinities and 'Otherness' in The Transfiguration." Hobson briefly examined a number of contemporary texts, including Otava Heikkilä's *Letters for Lucardo* graphic novel series (2017–current) and Audre's Revenge Film Collective's forthcoming film *Bitten, A Tragedy*. Miller's paper was an extended analysis of a single film, Michael O'Shea's *The Transfiguration* (2016), in which the teenager Milo adopts a vampiric persona—one that is specifically queer *vis-à-vis* deadly hookups in public restrooms and raced through Milo's African-Americanness—is set against conventional violent masculinity in contemporary America. Both papers balance the question of queer behavior with queer identity in the tradition of fictional vampires—a tradition that is becoming problematic in our current cultural moment where open queerness can be both socially acceptable but still socially penalized. A scheduled presentation by independent scholar Hannah Louise Miller, "*Twilight* and Conversations about Trauma," did not take place.

The World Vampires Roundtable[11] was chaired by Dr. James Aubrey with Dr. Vincent Piturro, Dr. Wendolyn Weber and Charles Hoge (all Metropolitan State University of Denver) as presenters. The group were there to talk about their forthcoming edited book *World Vampire Films* (McFarland, 2021)[12] and touched on the films *Let the Right One In* (2008), *Byzantium* (2013), *Only Lovers Left Alive* (2014), and *What We Do in the Shadows* (2014). Once the floor was opened up to all attendees, discussion ranged freely to reference how American shows like *Buffy* and *Angel* were edited or aired much later in foreign markets, the popularity of the

---

[10] "Genders & Sexualities." *National Conference*, 249.

[11] "World Vampires." *National Conference*, 259.

[12] Published as James Aubrey, ed., *Vampire Films Around the World: Essays on the Cinematic Undead of Sixteen Cultures* (Jefferson, NC: McFarland, 2020).—Ed.

western vampire in Korean and Chinese television dramas, and to recommend additional films like *A Girl Walks Alone at Night* (2014), among others.

The Vampires in Diverse Spaces panel opened with Dr. Gilpin's piece "Fangs for the Education: Vampires Teaching Teachers," which examined how vampire educational theory has changed in the past decade. Prof. Maureen-Claude LaPerriere (University of Quebec at Trois-Rivières) examined the Québécois vampire in the 2004 film *Éternelle*, in her presentation, "'The More Labour It Sucks': The Vampire as Parasite in Québec," arguing that the vampire presented has a much more Marxist metaphorical value than the mainstream vampire. Léna Remy-Kovach (University of Freiburg) presented "Reversing the Tropes in Drew Hayden Taylor's *Night Wanderer*: Colonial Vampirism and Land as Redemption," which examined the figure of the vampire as a manifestation of British colonialism, transferring the popular culture status of "savage" from Indigenous person to settler. Finally, Prof. Bertena Varney's (Southcentral Kentucky Community & Technical College) "Interview with Vampires: A Look into the World of 'Real' Vampires" discussed Prof. Varney's research, gathered through a number of interviews since 2005, into people living the "real life" vampire lifestyle. Coming from the fields of education, North American Indigenous literatures, and sociology, these presentations truly exemplify the diversity of spaces the figure of the vampire can be found in modern life: as a tool for learning in the classroom, as method for exploring Canada's colonial legacy, and even our own reality. These presentations not only spark fascinating understandings of how the figure of the vampire can be approached, but how deeply interdisciplinary Vampire Studies is as an area.

On April 20, the "Vampires on Film"[13] panel saw research from Duncan Hubber (Federation University Australia), Dr. James Robert Pate (Shepherd University), and Caden Parker Berry (Lee University). Hubber's presentation "Italian Feasts: Devouring the National Body in Deodato's *Cannibal Holocaust*" argued the Italian found-footage film involving cannibalism makes cannibals out of its own audience in their hunger for gore. Dr. Pate's "Vampiric Absences: The Decentering Vampire Narratives of Dreyer's *Vampyre* [sic] and Brite's 'His Mouth Will Taste of Wormwood'" discusses the abstracted and anthropomorphized vampires of those texts as complicating binaries often present in vampiric media. Finally, Berry's presentation "Nosferatu: A Symphony of Inspiration" discussed and argued the influence of F. W. Murnau's *Nosferatu, eine Symphonie des Grauens* (1922) on vampiric media. Each of these papers deals with vampiric film and interpretation. Dr. Pate's and Berry's pieces examined how the vampire itself has been reinterpreted by different artists, allowing for different readings of the vampire, while Hubber's piece argues that *Cannibal Holocaust* forces audiences to reinterpret themselves as cannibal.

The Vampires on TV[14] panel had three speakers: Jenna Guitar (University of

---

[13] "Cinematic Vampires." *National Conference*, 311.

[14] "Vampires on Television." *National Conference*, 314. The PCA program incorrectly lists Bertena Varney as the session chair (314); Guitar was actually the session chair.

Rhode Island) spoke on "*Angel* 20 Years Later: Convergence Culture and the Return of the Undead," providing a brief retrospective of the show alongside a queer reading of its text, as well as how the series leaves on in licensed comic books (including a forthcoming reboot) and in fan fiction. Dr. Leah Richards (LaGuardia Community College, CUNY) presented "'I Don't Kill Children, But I Could Make Him a Blood Relative': Vampires and Anti-Vaxxers in *American Horror Story: Hotel*," in which she provided an extended analysis of the show's vampirism as a literal disease that can be communicated (or not) via exposure, which culminates in an accidental, and preventable, outbreak of vampires. Aleksandra Tarasova's (Russian State University for the Humanities) presentation, "Domestication of the Vampire in the Joseon Era: The Korean TV series *The Scholar Who Walks the Night*." The 2015 series follows vampire/vampire hunter Kim Sung-yeol and focuses on the relationship between said vampire and the daughter of a disgraced nobleman. Dr. Tatiana Prorokova (University of Vienna) spoke on "The Ecohorror of *The Strain*: Plant Vampires and Climate Change as a Holocaust" in which she analyzed how the show's WWII narratives, especially the threat of the nuclear bomb, echoes its presentation of climatological catastrophe. Both papers addressed the explicit politics of their individual texts at length, demonstrating the most up-to-date cultural anxieties that vampires can personify.

"Coffin Talk: 'Once More with Feeling' and the Legacy of *Angel*" was the finale for the area and took place during the last time slot of the conference. Following a screening of the beloved *Buffy* musical episode, a roundtable consisting of Prof. Anyiwo, Prof. Nevarez, Guitar, Hobson, and Cait Coker (University of Illinois at Urbana-Champaign) discussed the twentieth anniversary of *Buffy*'s spin-off, *Angel*. Group discussion touched on how well (or in some cases, how poorly) the show had aged, and considered its debut season from 1999–2000 as prefiguring the resurgence of the popular vampire hero in other TV series such as *Moonlight* (2007–2008), *The Vampire Diaries* (2009–2017), and so on. Attendees also analyzed the show's use and attitudes towards race and queerness (which likewise aged problematically). In general, the attendees were willing to overlook the show's weaknesses for the nostalgia factor: as problematic as it could be, there simply was nothing else like it on air at the time.

After the conference, the organizational team shared notable "awards" with attendees and presenters. Though Jim Aubrey was honored for attending all sessions in person with a bottle of wine before the final film screening, the other awards were shared with the group via email. "Most Publishable Paper" was awarded to Jenna Guitar. Duncan Hubber won "Best 'Out of the Coffin' Paper." Newcomers, Cain Edward Miller and Cadan Parker Berry, won, respectively, "Best Emerging Scholar" and "Best Fledgling/Undergraduate Scholar." "Best Werewolf-Among-the-Vampires" was given to Rebecca Allen Paynich. "Most Original Content" was awarded to both Leah Richards and Léna Remy-Kovach. And the "Lorne Award for Most Unique Delivery" went to William Tringali.

Over the past decade, the Vampire Studies area has waxed and waned dramatically. During the height of the "Twi-craze" between 2009–2011, there were over fifty sessions throughout the conference. More recent years have had less than a dozen sessions, so the 2019 meeting marked what is hopefully the start of another upturn in presenter population and attendance. Nonetheless, the sustained presence and size of the area is still notable, and with the core organizational team and other regular attendees, the longevity of the area is still assured.

Cait Coker
University of Illinois at Urbana-Champaign, USA

William Tringali
Emory University, USA

Response to "Etymologies of *vampire* with *pirъ* 'a feast,'" by Kamil Stachowski (I)

The article under review[1] is an addendum to an earlier paper published by Kamil Stachowski and Olaf Stachowski which provided a useful summary of the etymologies of the word "vampire" proposed over the years.[2] The earlier paper concluded that an "oriental," i.e. Turkic origin for the word was "most probable."[3] The specific proposal was that a Turkic word for "witch, evil spirit" which appears in Tatar as *ubyr* and in Chuvash as *vubăr*, was borrowed into Slavic languages twice, once into Southern Slavic, giving rise to, e.g., Polish *wampir* and a second time into Eastern Slavic, producing Russian *upyr'* and Polish *upiór*.[4]

While this theory addresses the issue of the Slavic forms with initial *w-*, it presents some other significant difficulties. First, the notion of two separate borrowings during different historical periods but with the same non-trivial semantic shift, while not absolutely impossible, is hardly elegant.

Second, the issue of a Turkic voiced bilabial stop being borrowed into Slavic as a voiceless stop is not exactly the typical process. For example, the Old East Slavic epic poem *The Tale of Prince Igor's Campaign* (late twelfth century) gives an account of a failed raid by a Kievan Rus' prince against the "Polovtsians" or Cumans, a Kipchak people of the Pontic-Caspian steppe. Among the Turkic words which show up in this early document is the ethnonym Шельбиры *Sheljbiry* which clearly preserves a Turkic *b* as a Slavic *b*.[5]

Finally, the inserted bilabial nasal *-m-* in *wampir* and other Slavic forms remains unaccounted for.

It should be noted in passing that the initial *vu-* of Chuvash *vubăr* is the result of a regular sound change in which all word-initial rounded vowels were prefixed with a labial on-glide.[6] Thus the number "three" in Chuvash is *viş* as opposed to Turkish *üç*, "ten" is *vun* as opposed to Turkish *on* and "thirty" is *vătăr* as opposed to Turkish *otuz*. Foreign words borrowed into Chuvash would naturally be given

---

[1] Kamil Stachowski, "Etymologies of *vampire* with *pirъ* 'a feast,'" *Journal of Vampire Studies* 1, no. 1 (2020): 5–18.

[2] Stachowski and Stachowski, "Possibly Oriental Elements in Slavonic Folklore. Upiór ~ wampir," in *Essays in the History of Languages and Linguistics: Dedicated to Marek Stachowski on the Occasion of His 60th Birthday*, ed. Michał Németh, Barbara Podolak, and Mateusz Urban (Kraków: Księgarnia Akademicka, 2017), 643–93.

[3] Stachowski and Stachowski, "*Upiór ~ wampir*," 664, 683.

[4] Stachowski and Stachowski, "*Upiór ~ wampir*," 668–72.

[5] J. Dyneley Prince, "Tatar Material in Old Russian," *Proceedings of the American Philosophical Society* 58, no. 1 (1919): 86, https://www.jstor.org/stable/984481.

[6] Peter B. Golden, *Studies on the Peoples and Cultures of the Eurasian Steppes*, ed. Cătălin Hriban (Bucharest: Editura Academiei Române; Brăila: Editura Istros a Muzeului Brăilei, 2011), 239.

the same treatment, since it would have been impossible to pronounce an initial rounded vowel.[7] A similar example from another language family comes from Celtic, where Welsh -*w*- cannot occur at the beginning of a word except after *g*-. Thus, the inherited word for "men" became *gwŷr* instead of *wŷr* (cf. Latin *viri*, Irish *fir*). Borrowed words were treated the same way, so that Latin *vinum* "wine" became Welsh *gwin*.[8] For other examples we need look no farther than Modern English, which permits the velar nasal phoneme /*ng*/ only in the middle and at the end of a word.[9] When word-initial /*ng*/ comes into English from languages which do not share this limitation, English speakers tend to substitute a simple alveolar nasal, thus the Vietnamese name *Nguyen* is pronounced "Nwen."

In the current article, the author provides a justifiable critique of the etymology proposed by Bruce McClelland in *Slayers and Their Vampires: A Cultural History of Killing the Dead* (2006), but, as I indicated in my previous comments,[10] Stachowski is too quick to dismiss the possibility of a native Slavic source for the vampire word based on the Slavic root meaning "to drink." In principle there is no overriding reason to prefer a Turkic as opposed to a native Slavic source for the concept of a spirit of the recently deceased seeking to harm living humans. The concept of the vengeful ghost is widespread, if not universal, and figures prominently in Norse folklore. Scandinavian influence among the Kievan Rus' was significant during the Rurik dynasty (AD 862–1610),[11] so the figure of the *draugr* was no doubt a familiar one. *Draugar* were believed to be reanimated corpses with superhuman strength and the ability to shape-shift into a variety of animal forms.[12] A living person killed by a draugr could in turn become one himself (as occurs in the *Eyrbyggja Saga*).[13] The point here is that there is no reason to look to a non-Indo-European culture as a source for the characteristics that were later assimilated into the Slavic vampire legend.

---

[7] For the principle of phonemic substitution *see* Lyle Campbell, *Historical Linguistics: An Introduction* (Cambridge, MA: MIT Press, 1999), 65–68.

[8] Kenneth Hurlstone Jackson, *Language and History in Early Britain: A Chronological Survey of the Brittonic Languages, First to Twelfth Century A.D.* (Edinburgh: Edinburgh University Press, 1953), 390–3.

[9] Heidi Harley, *English Words: A Linguistic Introduction* (Oxford: Blackwell Publishing, 2006), 61.

[10] Dilts, email message to Anthony Hogg, July 30, 2018; repr., "Re: Vampire Etymology Article," *Journal of Vampire Studies* 1, no. 1 (2020): 130–1. Subsequent citations refer to *JVS* version.

[11] The *Primary Chronicle*, written during the twelfth century, describes the role of the Varangians (Scandinavian mercenaries) initially establishing the kingdom of the Rus' as well as reestablishing Vladimir the Great after his exile. Samuel Hazard Cross and Olgerd P. Sherbowitz-Wetzor, trans., *The Russian Primary Chronicle: Laurentian Text* (Cambridge, MA: Mediaeval Academy of America, [1953]), 59–60, 91.

[12] Jesse Byock, trans., *Grettir's Saga* (Oxford: Oxford University Press, 2009), xxi–xxii.

[13] William Morris and Eiríkr Magnússon, trans., *The Story of the Ere-Dwellers (Eyrbyggja Saga): with The Story of the Heath Slayings (Heiðarvíga saga)* (London: Bernard Quaritch, 1892), 137, https://archive.org/details/sagalibrary01magngoog.

If *upyr"* is of native Slavic extraction and is related to the word for "feast," what would be its semantic development? The Russian word *pir* "feast, banquet" is ultimately derived from the Indo-European root *peh_3- "to drink" (as are Latin *potio* and Greek *pósis*, both meaning "a drink").[14] The root appears in Proto-Slavic as *$p\bar{o}i$- : *$p\bar{\imath}$-[15] and Russian *pir* is from Proto-Slavic *$pirъ$, Old East Slavic *pirъ* (*pirŭ*), with a suffix derived from Indo-European *-ro-, typically an adjectival formation.[16] Thus the original meaning would have been "having to do with or intended for drinking."

A feast or banquet would have been a place where drinking took place, especially the ritualized consumption of intoxicating beverages. The associated meaning "libation" has obvious connections with the same semantic sphere. The use of a substantivized adjective to denote a "drinking place" is familiar from British English, where the word *pub*, short for *public*, is used to refer to a "public house" where alcoholic beverages are sold.

The prefix *u*- "away"[17] also functions as a preposition with the meaning "from" or "at." Its meaning in combination with "pir" could refer to something performed at a feast or taken from the drinking place, a meaning consistent with "libation."

The "soft" final consonant of *upir'* suggests the presence of the derivational suffix *-ь in Proto-Slavic, an ending typically used to produce nouns from adjectives. Thus *upir'* could be the personification of a feast or libation. A parallel example can be found in the Roman pantheon, where *Liber Pater*, along with his female counterpart *Libera*, are the deities of viticulture, wine and wine consumption. While Liber Pater is often translated "the Free Father,"[18] the name is more properly derived from *libare* the Roman word for pouring out a libation, ultimately from the Indo-European root *lei*- "to flow."[19] Note that Liber contains the same adjectival *-ro- ending as *pir*.

In ancient times, the cultural value associated with "drunkenness" did not carry the same negative connotations and implications of personal weakness that it does in the modern world.[20] Drunkenness was a form of "divine madness," an

---

[14] J. P. Mallory and D. Q. Adams, *The Oxford Introduction to Proto-Indo-European and the Proto-Indo-European World* (Oxford: Oxford University Press, 2006), 98.

[15] Rick Derksen, *Etymological Dictionary of the Slavic Inherited Lexicon* (Leiden: Brill, 2008), 401–402.

[16] Mallory and Adams, *Introduction to Proto-Indo-European*, 57; *pirъ* is cited by Reinhold Trautmann, *Baltisches-slavisches Wörterbuch* (1923; repr., Göttingen: Vandenhoeck & Ruprecht, 1970), 228; the reconstructed form is based on derivational rules presented by Horace G. Lunt, *Old Church Slavonic Grammar*, 7th rev. ed. (Berlin: De Gruyter Mouton, 2001), 192ff.

[17] Proto-Slavic *u*-, OCS *u*-, Russian *u*-, cf. Derksen, *Etymological Dictionary*, 506.

[18] John F. Miller, "Ovid's Liberalia," in *Ovid's "Fasti": Historical Readings at Its Bimillennium*, ed. Geraldine Herbert-Brown (Oxford: Oxford University Press, 2002), 219n62.

[19] Ovid, *Fasti*, trans. and ed. A. J. Boyle and R. D. Woodard (London: Penguin Books, 2004), 76; and William Morris, ed., *American Heritage Dictionary* (Boston: Houghton-Mifflin, 1975), 1526, for root *lei-.

[20] In a Slavic context, the Danish twelfth/thirteenth century historian, Saxo Grammaticus,

inspiration from the immortal beings whose spiritual essence was imbued in the beverage. Drinking parties were times of creativity, an opportunity to honor the gods.[21] Thus poets in Vedic India, consumed *soma* before beginning to recite their inspired accounts of the deeds of Indra, Varuna, Rudra and their companions.[22] The Bacchantes and Maenads and other followers of Dionysos abandoned all vestiges of civilization, dressed in animal skins and took to the woods to celebrate their rites, which involved intoxicating drink and ecstatic dance.[23] *Liber Pater's* springtime fertility festival of the *Liberalia* was a similar event, although the focus was on the youth of the community, who underwent a rite of passage which involved offering cakes, pouring libations and crowning a giant phallus with a wreath of flowers.[24]

The notion of "libation" or the ritual offering of alcoholic drinks, oil or honey poured out to deities, ancestors and spirits of the dead, is virtually universal. It has been practiced throughout history—by the Ancient Egyptians, Ancient Israelites, Ancient Greeks and Romans,[25] and its practice continues to this day from Siberia and Asia to South America.[26] In my previous comments, I noted that the Germanic word for "god" is most likely derived from the past participle a verb meaning "to pour or libate" and thus literally means "the libated one, the one for whom the libation is poured."[27] *Upir'* could originally have had a similar meaning.

If the AD 1047 attestation of *upyr'* in the *Book of Prophets* colophon is a misattribution, as shown by Sjöberg, then *The Sermon of St. Gregory* is the earliest example of the word. The *Sermon* is dated by Boris Rybakov to beginning of twelfth

---

described a feast presented in honor of one of the gods in which it was the participants' sacred duty to "violate sobriety" (i.e. get drunk) to observe the local custom. Alfred Holder, ed., *Saxonis Grammatici Gesta Danorum* (Strassburg: Karl J. Trübner, 1886), 566, lines 24–25, https://hdl.handle.net/2027/mdp.39015030075710.

[21] Giovanni Pico de Mirandola, *Oration on the Dignity of Man: De hominis dignitate*, trans. Charles Wallis (self-pub., CreateSpace, 2014), 12; and Plato, *The Symposium*, trans. Christopher Gill (1999; repr., London: Penguin Books, 2003), 52–53.

[22] *Rig-Veda*, bk. 8, hymn 48, verses 1 and 3, for example. "We have drunk the Soma; we have become immortal; we have gone to the light; we have found the gods." Wendy O' Flaherty Doniger, trans. *The Rig Veda: An Anthology* (London: Penguin Books, 1981), 134.

[23] The rite is described in Euripides, *The Bacchae and Other Plays*, trans. John Davie (London: Penguin Books, 2005), 145–7.

[24] Miller, "Ovid's Liberalia," 201.

[25] *See* Utterance 685 in R. O. Faulkner, trans., *Ancient Egyptian Pyramid Texts* (Oxford: Clarendon Press, 1969; Stilwell, KS: Digireads.com, 2007), 295; Genesis 35:14; and Walter Burkert, *Greek Religion: Archaic and Classical*, trans. John Raffan (Cambridge, MA: Harvard University Press, 1985; Malden, MA: Blackwell Publishing, 1991), 70–73. Citation refers to the Blackwell edition.

[26] Dmitry Ermakov, *Bø and Bön: Ancient Shamanic Traditions of Siberia and Tibet in Their Relation to the Teachings of a Central Asian Buddha* (2008; repr., Kathmandu: Vajra Publications, 2010), 421–428; and William H. D. Adams, *The Land of the Incas and the City of the Sun: The Story of Francisco Pizarro and the Conquest of Peru* (Boston: Estes & Lauriat, 1885; Neuilly sur Seine: Ulan Press, 2012), 98.

[27] Dilts, "Re: Vampire Etymology Article," 130–1.

century but by N. M. Gal'kovskii to end of thirteenth or beginning of fourteenth.[28] According to a translation provided by Stella Rock, the relevant passage reads: "These Slavs also began to hold rites to *rod* and *rozhanitsy*, at first Perun was their god and before that they held rites to *upiry* [vampires?] and *bereginy* [river-bank spirits?]. By holy baptism they rejected Perun and accepted Christ as God. But now also on the outskirts they pray to him, to the accursed god Perun, and Khors, and Mokosh and *vily*, and this they do in secret and they cannot give this up."[29]

Rod and Rozhnitsky are the primordial divine couple and can be compared to Saturn and Ops in the Roman tradition or Kronos and Rhea in the Greek pantheon.[30] Perun is the Slavic equivalent of Jupiter or Zeus, the god of thunder and lightning.[31] The Bereginy are nature spirits or nymphs associated with riverbanks.[32] Khors, or Xors-Dazhbog, is a male fertility god.[33] Mokosh is an earth goddess and Vily or Vila are female mountain spirits who control the winds.[34] In this context, it seems justifiable to assume that *upiry* refers to another variety of divinity or nature spirit who must be appeased with sacrifices and offerings. The author of the sermon seems to indicate that *upiry* belong to an early cult which predates the worship of Perun, perhaps similar to the Vanir group of gods in Norse tradition who are in competition with the Aesir, the principal and more recent pantheon.[35]

According to Jan Máchal, the ancient tradition of holding feasts and festivals in honor of deceased ancestors survived in some Slavic countries until the early twentieth century. Three times a year the souls of the dead were invited to join the living for a sumptuous meal during which plates of food were set aside and libations poured for them. Máchal described variations of these celebrations practiced in White Russia, Russia and Bulgaria, where the Orthodox Church was more tolerant of such observances than the Roman Catholic Church elsewhere in the Slavic world.[36]

How would an ancestral spirit normally appeased by libation become identified with a harmful undead being frequenting graveyards and attacking the living?

---

[28] Stella Rock, *Popular Religion in Russia: 'Double Belief' and the Making of an Academic Myth* (London: Routledge, 2007), 26.

[29] Rock, *Popular Religion in Russia*, 28. Notes in parentheses are Rock's.

[30] Mike Dixon-Kennedy, *Encyclopedia of Russian and Slavic Myth and Legend* (Santa Barbara, CA: ABC-CLIO, 1998), 233.

[31] Dixon-Kennedy, *Russian and Slavic Myth and Legend*, 217–18.

[32] Theresa Bane, *Encyclopedia of Fairies in World Folklore and Mythology* (Jefferson, NC: McFarland, 2013), 55.

[33] Constantine L. Borissoff, "Non-Iranian Origin of the Eastern Slavonic God *Xŭrsǔ/Xors*," *Studia Mythologica Slavica* 17 (2014): 36, https://www.researchgate.net/publication/270904956.

[34] Dixon-Kennedy, *Russian and Slavic Myth*, 194; and Bane, *Encyclopedia of Fairies*, 338.

[35] John Lindow, *Norse Mythology: A Guide to Gods, Heroes, Rituals, and Beliefs* (Santa Barbara, CA: ABC-CLIO, 2001; Oxford: Oxford University Press, 2002), 311–12. The comparison to the Vanir group of gods is my own.

[36] Máchal, "Slavic Mythology," in *Mythology of All Races*, ed. Louis Herbert Gray, vol. 3 (Boston: Marshall Jones, 1918), 233–9, https://archive.org/details/mythologyofall03gray.

Exaggeration of the vices of one's opponents is not a tactic invented by modern politicians. After Christianization of the Slavs, all pagan divinities, along with those faithful to them, were considered "accursed" and demonic.[37] According to *The Russian Primary Chronicle*, Vseslav of Polotsk (ca. 1039–1101 AD), one of the last pagan rulers among the Kievan Rus', was conceived by sorcery and was born with a caul on his head.[38] For this reason, he gained a reputation as a great magician with supernatural abilities to shape-shift and divine the future.[39] As recently as 2005 he was depicted on a commemorative Belarusian coin running in the shape of a wolf alongside his portrait in human form.[40] Lycanthropy was apparently among the abilities granted by the old gods to their worshippers.

Like the draugar of Norse tradition, the Slavic dead may not always have rested quietly after burial. In the Icelandic *Eyrbyggja Saga*, for example, Thorolf Halt-Foot dies while engaged in a grudge with one of his neighbors, and not long after he has been laid to rest, a herdsman is found dead near Thorolf's burial mound, "and he was all coal-blue, and every bone in him was broken."[41] The cattle were either killed or fled from the area. After this, Thorolf began walking all over the valley, killing many residents and frightening away the rest. Finally, Thorolf's son and his household servants open his tomb, finding Thorolf "all undecayed and most evil to look on."[42] With much difficulty they transport him to a new location for reburial and build a wall around his tomb "so high that none might come thereover but fowl flying."[43] Sometime later, after the death of his son, Thorolf begins walking again, and his tomb is opened a second time revealing that he is still "unrotten, and as like to a fiend as like could be, blue as hell, and big as a neat."[44] The brave locals pry the body up with wooden levers, roll it down to the seaside and burn it "to cold coals," casting the ashes out to sea.[45]

Given the linguistic difficulties of the Chuvash and Tatar word for "witch" and the ubiquity of the archetype of the bloodthirsty revenant, it seems extremely difficult to identify a compelling motive for the importation of the lexeme or the concept of the vampire from a Turkic cultural milieu. The Turkic words for "witch," if related at all, could just as easily have been borrowed from Slavic into Tatar and Chuvash, or into Tatar and from Tatar into Chuvash. Reborrowing from Chuvash with a slight semantic shift could account for the Slavic forms with initial

---

[37] Rock, *Popular Religion in Russia*, 30.

[38] Cross and Sherbowitz-Wetzor, *Russian Primary Chronicle*, 139.

[39] Leonard A. Magnus, ed. and trans., *The Tale of the Armament of Igor, A.D. 1185: A Russian Historical Epic* (London: Oxford University Press, 1915), 19, https://archive.org/details /taleofarmamentof00magnuoft.

[40] National Bank of the Republic of Belarus, reverse side of silver Vseslav Polotsky coin, https://commons.wikimedia.org/wiki/File:Usiaslau_sr_2005.gif.

[41] Morris and Magnússon, *Story of the Ere-Dwellers*, 89.

[42] Morris and Magnússon, *Story of the Ere-Dwellers*, 91.

[43] Morris and Magnússon, *Story of the Ere-Dwellers*, 92.

[44] Morris and Magnússon, *Story of the Ere-Dwellers*, 172.

[45] Morris and Magnússon, *Story of the Ere-Dwellers*, 172.

"w-" as in Polish *wampir* "vampire, ghoul" alongside *upiór* "ghost, phantom." The intrusive nasal remains unexplained in either case.

Michael Dilts
Independent scholar, USA

BIBLIOGRAPHY

Adams, William H. D. *The Land of the Incas and the City of the Sun: The Story of Francisco Pizarro and the conquest of Peru*. Neuilly sur Seine: Ulan Press, 2012. First published 1885 by Estes & Lauriat (Boston).

Bane, Theresa. *Encyclopedia of Fairies in World Folklore and Mythology*. Jefferson, NC: McFarland, 2013.

Borissoff, Constantine L. "Non-Iranian Origin of the Eastern Slavonic God *Xŭrsŭ/Xors*." *Studia Mythologica Slavica* 17 (2014): 9–36. https://www.researchgate.net/publication/2709 04956.

Burkert, Walter. *Greek Religion: Archaic and Classical*. Translated by John Raffas. Malden, MA: Blackwell Publishing, 1991. First published 1985 by Harvard University Press (Cambridge, MA). Originally published as *Griechische Religion der archaischen und klassischen Epoche* (Stuttgart: Kohlhammer, 1977).

Byock, Jesse, trans. *Grettir's Saga*. Oxford: Oxford University Press, 2009.

Campbell, Lyle. *Historical Linguistics: An Introduction*. Cambridge, MA: MIT Press, 1999.

Cross, Samuel Hazard, and Olgerd P. Sherbowitz-Wetzor, trans. *The Russian Primary Chronicle: Laurentian Text*. Cambridge, MA: Mediaeval Academy of America, [1953].

Derksen, Rick. *Etymological Dictionary of the Slavic Inherited Lexicon*. Leiden: Brill, 2008.

Dilts, Michael. "Re: Vampire Etymology Article." *Journal of Vampire Studies* 1, no. 1 (2020): 130–1.

Dixon-Kennedy, Mike. *Encyclopedia of Russian and Slavic Myth and Legend*. Santa Barbara, CA: ABC-CLIO, 1998.

Euripides. *The Bacchae and Other Plays*. Translated by John Davie. London: Penguin Books, 2005.

Ermakov, Dmitry. *Bø and Bön: Ancient Shamanic Traditions of Siberia and Tibet in Their Relation to the Teachings of a Central Asian Buddha*. 2008. Reprint, Kathmandu: Vajra Publications, 2010.

Faulkner, R. O., trans. *Ancient Egyptian Pyramid Texts*. Stilwell, KS: Digireads.com, 2007. First published 1969 by Clarendon Press (Oxford).

Golden, Peter B. *Studies on the Peoples and Cultures of the Eurasian Steppes*. Edited by Cătălin Hriban. Bucharest: Editura Academiei Române; Brăila: Editura Istros a Muzeului Brăilei, 2011.

Harley, Heidi. *English Words: A Linguistic Introduction*. Oxford: Blackwell Publishing, 2006.

Holder, Alfred, ed. *Saxonis Grammatici Gesta Danorvm*. Strassburg: Karl J. Trübner, 1886. https://archive.org/details/saxonisgrammati01saxogoog.

Jackson, Kenneth Hurlstone. *Language and History in Early Britain: A Chronological Survey of the Brittonic Languages, First to Twelfth Century A.D.* Edinburgh: Edinburgh University Press, 1953.

Lindow, John. *Norse Mythology: A Guide to Gods, Heroes, Rituals, and Beliefs*. Oxford University Press, 2002. First published 2001 by ABC-CLIO (Santa Barbara, CA).

Lunt, Horace G. *Old Church Slavonic Grammar*. 7th rev. ed. Berlin: De Gruyter Mouton, 2001.

Máchal, Jan. "Slavic Mythology." In *Mythology of All Races*, edited by Louis Herbert Gray, 215–314. Vol. 3. Boston: Marshall Jones, 1918. https://archive.org/details/mythologyofall0

3gray.

Magnus, Leonard A., ed. and trans. *The Tale of the Armament of Igor. A.D. 1185: A Russian Historical Epic*. London: Oxford University Press, 1915. https://archive.org/details/taleofarmamentof00magnuoft.

Mallory, J. P., and D. Q. Adams. *The Oxford Introduction to Proto-Indo-European and the Proto-Indo-European World*. Oxford: Oxford University Press, 2006.

Miller, John F. "Ovid's Liberalia." In *Ovid's "Fasti": Historical Readings at Its Bimillennium*, edited by Geraldine Herbert-Brown, 199–224. Oxford: Oxford University Press, 2002.

Morris, William, ed. *American Heritage Dictionary*. Boston: Houghton-Mifflin, 1975.

Morris, William, and Eiríkr Magnússon, trans. *The Story of the Ere-Dwellers (Eyrbyggja Saga): with The Story of the Heath Slayings (Heiðarvíga saga)*. London: Bernard Quaritch, 1892. https://archive.org/details/sagalibrary01magnoog.

National Bank of the Republic of Belarus. Reverse side of silver Vseslav Polotsky coin. https://commons.wikimedia.org/wiki/File:Usiaslau_sr_2005.gif.

O' Flaherty Doniger, Wendy, trans. *The Rig Veda: An Anthology*. London: Penguin Books, 1981.

Ovid. *Fasti*. Translated and edited with an introduction and notes by A. J. Boyle and R. D. Woodard. London: Penguin Books, 2004.

Pico della Mirandola, Giovanni. *Oration on the Dignity of Man: De hominis dignitate*. Translated by Charles Wallis. Self-published, CreateSpace, 2014.

Plato. *The Symposium*. Translated by Christopher Gill. 1999. Reprint, London: Penguin Books, 2003.

Prince, J. Dyneley. "Tatar Material in Old Russian." *Proceedings of the American Philosophical Society* 58, no. 1 (1919): 74–88. https://www.jstor.org/stable/984481.

Rock, Stella. *Popular Religion in Russia: 'Double Belief' and the Making of an Academic Myth*. London: Routledge, 2007.

Stachowski, Kamil. "Etymologies of *vampire* with *pirъ* 'a feast.'" *Journal of Vampire Studies* 1, no. 1 (2020): 5–20.

Stachowski, Kamil, and Olaf Stachowski. "Possibly Oriental Elements in Slavonic Folklore. Upiór ~ wampir." In *Essays in the History of Languages and Linguistics: Dedicated to Marek Stachowski on the Occasion of His 60th Birthday*, 643–93, edited by Michał Németh, Barbara Podolak, and Mateusz Urban. Kraków: Księgarnia Akademicka, 2017.

Trautmann, Reinhold. *Baltisches-slavisches Wörterbuch*. 1923. Reprint, Göttingen: Vandenhoeck & Ruprecht, 1970.

Response to "Etymologies of *vampire* with *pirъ* 'a feast,'" by Kamil Stachowski (II)

The eminent historian of religions, Bruce Lincoln, on multiple occasions and always light-heartedly told me that publishing scholarship (especially in non-practical subjects like religion, anthropology, folklore, etc.) was like putting a message in a bottle and tossing it out into the sea: should it end up in someone's possession and prove useful, if only for the sake of confirmation or contradiction (cf. "starting a driftwood fire"), so much the better.

It is with that advice in mind that I am grateful to Kamil Stachowski for honoring me with a cogent critique of the etymology of the word "vampire" that had first been proposed,[1] albeit in more detailed form, in my dissertation, "Sacrifice, Scapegoat, Vampire: The Social and Religious Origins of the Bulgarian Folkloric Vampire" (1999). Unfortunately, his criticisms are aimed at a somewhat simplified (but not, in my opinion, incorrect) version of my reasoning: my only published discussion of the vampire etymology was inserted as a tangential appendix to my book *Slayers and Their Vampires: A Cultural History of Killing the Dead* (2006), which is directed primarily at the folklore of the "vampire slayer" (or: "seer") rather than at the origin of the vampire *per se*. I take responsibility for trying to slip that slimmed down version of my historical and linguistic reasoning into a book that was trying to remain scholarly while simultaneously trying to avoid being arcane. (Perhaps as a consequence of that effort, the book is still in print.)

It had not occurred to me in 2006 that the appendix would ever have been subjected to such rigorous analysis, but I don't know why it didn't: for the fact of the matter is that my very impulse, in 1991, to get a doctorate in Slavic Folklore was prompted by a long correspondence with Jan L. Perkowski at University of Virginia. The tenor of that earliest correspondence was my grumbling dissatisfaction with *his* discussion of the etymology of the term "vampire,"[2] for which I could find no coherent semantic basis. So, it may be the case that as the successive generations attempt to understand why the cultural notion of the vampire keeps rising from the dead, some of them will seek the reasons in the prehistory of the word itself — if possible.

And that is the hard part: we actually have so little usage of the term *vampir* (or, later, East Slavic *upyr'*) to work with that virtually all proposed etymologies suffer from at least one of two basic problems: (1) there is retrospective projection, in which contemporary notions of the vampire, replete with what are in fact very late and folkloric/literary attributes such as blood drinking, shapeshifting, undeadness, mistakenly become semantically explanatory. Thus, Max Vassmer[3] and others have taken the Slavic root *pir-*, which is cognate with many Indo-European descendant terms having to do with the meaning "drink," as referring to the vampiric inclination to drink blood;[4] or else (2) one has to scrounge around for words that either sound similar and therefore might be related, or else interpret phrases such

---

[1] Kamil Stachowski, "Etymologies of *vampire* with *pirъ* 'a feast,'" *Journal of Vampire Studies* 1, no. 1 (2020): 5–18.

[2] Perkowski, *The Darkling: A Treatise on Slavic Vampirism* (Columbus, OH: Slavica Publishers, 1989), 32–34.

[3] Vasmer, *Russisches etymologisches Wörterbuch*, vol. 1, pt. 2 (Heidelberg: C. Winter, 1950), s.v. Лихой.

[4] Proposed etymologies linking the word "vampire" to drinking (whether cognate with proposed Proto-Indo-European forms or later, such as Greek or Latin) are scattered but still discoverable. For example: Упырь, вампир < Gk. ἐμπίνω [ἐμ-πίνω] "to drink a lot, or greedily; to get drunk"; Lat. *uber* "udder, suckling; ubera ducere — to suck the breast; maternal breast." TrueView, "Вурдалаки, вампиры, упыри," *TrueView* (blog), October 30, 2012, https://trueview.livejournal.com/78891.html. Such associations, as well as those that derive the term from Turkish *uber*, seem phonologically unmotivated.

as *"pop upyr' likhij"* in the social and religious context of the Christianization of the Balkans, and hope for the best.

I am guilty of both, I suppose, at least in the sense that it is linguistically clear (to me) that the second component of Slavic "vamPIR" does indeed pertain to some variant of the PIE **peh-,* "drink." But I cannot be persuaded that the association with drinking initially had anything to do with drinking blood except in a ritual sense (e.g. Dionysian).[5] My indulgence in the second sin, in which I try to find the earliest written citations of the term we have and then examine the historical context in which it was used in order to infer what it might have meant in the absence of any other glosses, still seems reasonable to me, though I would never claim it to be conclusive, much less unarguable.

Until the word *vampir* began to be used folklorically, probably no earlier than the sixteenth century Macedonia, according to my research in the Bulgarian archives, it was not in common use, at least among those who could write. Since writing in Glagolitic and Cyrillic in the Balkans was initially the province of Christian proselytizers,[6] we must infer that the concept was not particularly significant to such people in the first period of its neologistic phase, however long that lasted. Furthermore, there do not seem to be any cognate forms that undergo "semantic drift."[7] That is, while the attributes of the thing designated by the term (referents) undergo change (from, say, pejorative or denigrative to symbolic), the word itself in its putative homeland does not seem to undergo any significant morphological enhancements (such as being generalized to the attributive [adjectival] or verbal).[8]

---

[5] "It is unlikely that the earliest meaning of the word *vampir* denoted anything supernatural. Rather, I suspect that the term generally designated someone who engaged in *pirštestvo*, that is, in ritual feasting, where sacrifice was performed and wine was drunk to excess and ritually poured out (as libation), sometimes mixed with blood." Bruce A. McClelland, *Slayers and Their Vampires: A Cultural History of Killing the Dead* (Ann Arbor: University of Michigan Press, 2006), 191.

[6] Broadly known. See, for example, Asya Pereltsvaig, "Old Church Slavonic Writing: Glagolitic vs. Cyrillic," *Languages of the World* (blog), January 4, 2015, https://www.languages oftheworld.info/writing-or-spelling/old-church-slavonic-writing-glagolitic-vs-cyrillic.html.

[7] See various discussions of semantic change or semantic split in the literature of both historical and sociological linguistics, particularly Henry Hoenigswald, *Language Change and Linguistic Reconstruction* (Chicago: University of Chicago Press, 1960), esp. ch. 7, "Reconstruction of Grammatical and Semantic Features" and "Semantic Change", 45–47; and Dell Hymes, ed. *Language in Culture and Society: A Reader in Linguistics and Anthropology* (New York: Harper & Row, 1964), esp. pt. 4, "Cultural Focus and Semantic Field."

[8] Michael Dilts' reference to (presumably Old Church Slavonic) *оупирити,* "become inebriated" does suggest some form of denominalization, but actually, the existence this form supports my hypothesis regarding Christian objections to drinking at sacrificial feasts and the potentially Dionysiac aspect of agrarian ritual sacrifice in the Balkans. Dilts, "Re: Vampire Etymology Article," *Journal of Vampire Studies* 1, no. 1 (2020): 131. There is the amusing issue of competing terms in Modern Russian, in which the word *вампир* is in semantic competition with *упырь,* but that is because the former term was actually borrowed

The lack of importance of this term is something that has not been adequately addressed. I might argue, in fact, that even within the Slavic lower demonology, the Balkans vampire (versus the "unquiet dead" in East Slavic folklore) does not play a major role. The interest in the vampire in contemporary Bulgaria, which now far surpasses the interest in the concept when active folklore about vampires was circulating there, as late as mid-twentieth century, is essentially based on the vampire's cinematic and literary popularity in Western Europe and the U.S. This relative insignificance is difficult to interpret in isolation, but it does suggest there wasn't anything conceptually remarkable about the term vampire, which eventually became symbolic (folkloric), but only through attrition of the initial referents. (That is, where it may have designated an attitude toward certain social groups with specific behavioral or ritual characteristics, when those groups were no longer a political threat, the term began to refer more generally to a certain theological status [namely, "excommunicate"]).

While I would of course welcome new or additional evidence that might supplant the analyses based on the scant citations we have available, Stachowski likewise does not bring any help to solving either of the two historical linguistic problems cited above.

I have alluded, in that regard, to my dissertation. I do not wish to pre-empt Stachowski's arguments here, and in any case I don't have time or space to address his individual objections, but there are a few places where I believe it might be best to just point the argument to my dissertation, the whole of which is devoted to looking at the religious history of the Balkans, as well as attitudes toward ritual sacrifice, afterlife, etc. in the folk religion of the Balkans Slavs, in order to provide a more cohesive rationale to support the admittedly thin-ice propositions of my etymology.

Stachowski summarizes his objections to not only mine, but also Perkowski's and Michael Dilts' etymological conjectures, in his Conclusions section. Let me quickly address a couple of them. First, he asserts that the morphological reasoning is problematic "primarily because it is not clear how *pirъ* 'feast' could turn into the name of a person or monster without the help of any suffix at all."[9] The gloss of *пиръ* as "feast" is itself problematic: as I have argued, in the context of both *pop upir' likhij* (which, let's face it, is East Slavic, so already an issue) and early polemics against the pagans, the concept of "feast" was bound to the notion of "sacrifice." As is spelled out much more thoroughly in my dissertation, there was enormous hostility toward Slavic animal sacrifice on the part of the Byzantine Orthodox Christians, for both theological reasons (viz. Christ is the only sacrifice necessary, and obviates further sacrificial killing) and socio-moral reasons ("Dionysian" [a term actually used by polemicists] sacrifices led to self-abandonment).

As long as I'm dealing with that overloaded/overcited citation, I ought to go

---

from French into Russian after it became primarily literary. Vasmer, *Russisches Etymologisches Wörterbuch*, s.v. вампир.

[9] Stachowski, "Etymologies of *vampire*," 16.

further into a discussion of *likhij*. This term, which in modern Russian may certainly have the sense of "evil," did not have that meaning a thousand years ago.[10] The term really has as its core a meaning closer to "cut off," hence "expendable, superfluous." It is related to Greek λείπω, which according to Liddell and Scott has meanings around such concepts as "left behind," "forsaken," also "to be wanting, lacking."[11] During discussions with Bulgarian lexicographer Sabina Pavlova in 1998, she stated that Old Slavic лих- in the Bulgarian Middle Ages and in this phrasal context, *could have* had an intentionally self-denigrating, that is, humbling if not humiliating, meaning (similar in nature to the more common "humble servant"). While there is no strong evidence for that assertion, virtually all the early senses of words with a similar root seem to center around ideas of something that is extraneous, cut off, superfluous, hence *separated from* the main object or organization. Even modern Bulgarian лихва, meaning "interest" (as in monetary interest), finds its semantic core in the idea that interest is a *separate* aspect of the main debt.

I realize I am on very unsteady ground here, but my point is that, given the absence of significant attestation of the word *vampir* in its earliest (to our knowledge) usage, we have no choice but to look for analogies and corollary or tangential evidence (such as, for example, the unexpected infrequency of the word's written use—unexpected, that is, if the word referred to something outstanding or unusual). Clearly, all such etymological conjectures for now must remain just that: hypothetical, conjectural, in the absence of a new supply of linguistic or anthropological evidence.

That is not to throw cold water on the efforts of Stachowski or the others (including myself) who keep up the noble effort to discern the essence of the vampire in its linguistic history. Each of us hypothesizers bring our own preconceptions and biases to a very small archaeological find. What we find there and what we claim we have found may in fact be different—a difference that is tolerable if we are all honest enough to acknowledge that for now, we have little choice but reconstructive speculation.

Bruce A. McClelland
Independent scholar, USA

BIBLIOGRAPHY

Dilts, Michael. "Re: Vampire Etymology Article." *Journal of Vampire Studies* 1, no. 1 (2020): 130–1.
Hoenigswald, Henry. *Language Change and Linguistic Reconstruction*. Chicago: University of Chicago Press, 1960.
Hymes, Dell, ed. *Language in Culture and Society: A Reader in Linguistics and Anthropology*. New York: Harper & Row, 1964.

---

[10] *See* note 2 above.

[11] "λείπω" q.v. LSJ: The Online Liddell-Scott-Jones Greek-English Lexicon, http://stephan us.tlg.uci.edu/lsj/#eid=1&context=lsj.

McClelland, Bruce A. [Bruce Alexander McClelland]. "Sacrifice, Scapegoat, Vampire: The Social and Religious Origins of the Bulgarian Folkloric Vampire." Ph.D. diss., University of Virginia, 1999.

———. *Slayers and Their Vampires: A Cultural History of Killing the Dead*. Ann Arbor: University of Michigan Press, 2006.

McClelland, Bruce Alexander. *See* McClelland, "Sacrifice, Scapegoat, Vampire."

Pereltsvaig, Asya. "Old Church Slavonic Writing: Glagolitic vs. Cyrillic." *Languages of the World* (blog), January 4, 2015. https://www.languagesoftheworld.info/writing-or-spelling/old-church-slavonic-writing-glagolitic-vs-cyrillic.html.

Perkowski, Jan L. *The Darkling: A Treatise on Slavic Vampirism*. Columbus, OH: Slavica Publishers, 1989.

Stachowski, Kamil. "Etymologies of vampire with *pirъ* 'a feast.'" *Journal of Vampire Studies* 1, no. 1 (2019): 5–20.

TrueView. "Вурдалаки, вампиры, упыри." *TrueView* (blog), October 30, 2012. https://trueview.livejournal.com/78891.html.

Vasmer, Max. *Russisches etymologisches Wörterbuch*. Vol. 1, pt. 2. Heidelberg: C. Winter, 1950.

Imperial Provisor Frombald's First Name—Discovered

Unlike regimental field surgeon Johann Flückinger—the well-known author of a 1732 report on vampires in the Serbian town of Medveđa[1]—and even his assistants in that particular inspection,[2] the first name of Imperial Provisor Frombald, the man who pioneered vampire reports from the Habsburg Military Frontier in Serbia with his 1725 piece on the town of Kisiljevo,[3] has never been revealed before.

Both the quick transmission of Frombald's report from Kisiljevo to Vienna, skipping the middle step of Belgrade, and the fact that only a copy of the original has been preserved[4]—apart from the version published in the *Wienerisches Diarium*,[5] presumably based on the original—might have been the key for this lack of information.[6] It is impossible to know whether the original document that Frombald, contrary to custom,[7] dispatched directly to the Aulic War Council in Vienna, and now seemingly lost forever, contained the author's full name or at least his personal signature.

While the copy kept in the Haus-, Hof- und Staatsarchiv in Vienna only mentions "*Herrn Frombald*" (Mr. Frombald) in its heading,[8] the article in the *Wienerisches Diarium* did not reveal at all the name of the author, referring to him as merely "Kayserl. [Kayserlich] Provisor in Gradisker District" (Imperial Provisor in the Gradisca District).[9] It is probable that, at this time, imperial officers were commonly identified just by the juxtaposition of their title and surname; or maybe Frombald, as well as the other district chiefs in the new acquired provinces—after

---

[1] Klaus Hamberger, *Mortuus non mordet: Dokumente zum Vampirismus, 1689–1791* (Vienna: Turia & Kant, 1992), 49–54.

[2] For example, Johann Friedrich Baumgarten or J. H. von Lindenfels; *see* Hamberger, *Mortuus non mordet*, 54.

[3] Hamberger, *Mortuus non mordet*, 43–45.

[4] [Frombald], *Copia des vom Herrn Frombald kayserlichen Cameral Provisore zu Gradiska im Königreich Servien erlasenen Briefs anno 1725. Die im Königreich Servien damals in Schwung gegangenen sogenannten vanpiri oder Blutsauger betreffend*, AT-OeStA/HHStA StAbt Türkei I/191, Konvolut 1725, fol. 25–26, Türkei I Turcica der Reichshofkanzlei/ des Hofkriegsrats, Haus-, Hof- und Staatsarchiv, Vienna.

[5] Frombald [Kayserl. Provisor in Gradisker District], "Copia eines Schreibens aus dem Gradisker District in Ungarn," *Wienerisches Diarium*, July 21, 1725, [11–12], http://anno.onb.ac.at/cgi-content/anno?aid=wrz&datum=17250721.

[6] For a detailed history of the transmission of the document, *see* Aribert Schroeder, *Vampirismus: Seine Entwicklung vom Thema zum Motiv* (Frankfurt: Akademische Verlagsgesellschaft, 1973), 42–45.

[7] *See* Adam Mezes, "Insecure Boundaries: Medical Experts and the Returning Dead on the Southern Habsburg Borderland" (master's thesis, Central European University, 2013), 30, www.etd.ceu.hu/2013/mezes_adam.pdf; and Schroeder, *Vampirismus*, 41–42.

[8] Frombald, *Copia des von Herrn Frombald*, 25r.

[9] Frombald, "Copia eines Schreibens," 45. All translations are my own.

all there were not so many as to lose track of them—was sufficiently known in the Viennese administration circles not to need his first name to be explicitly mentioned in official documents.

However, none of these were always the case. In November 2017, while in the Austrian Staatsarchiv seeking evidence for an obscure eighteenth-century vampire case,[10] I came across a couple of references to Frombald which *did* include his first name. They were buried in two entries of an understudied corpus: the protocol books of the Belgrade Administration between 1721 and 1738. This body of texts, which probably suffered important losses during the hasty flight of the Habsburg administration from Serbia in 1739 after the sudden defeat to the Ottoman Empire in the 1730s war for this territory, contains the recordings of the regular sessions held in Belgrade once or twice a month by the Central Administration of the Serbian Military Frontier. The gatherings of the Belgrade Habsburg High Command, usually presided by Duke Carl Alexander von Württemberg, the Governor of Serbia, would deal with the requests, complaints, and special or ordinary reports submitted by lower officers on the terrain, primarily district chiefs. The High Command issued, when possible, binding decisions on each particular question. While these documents were "returned" by the Austrian State to the Yugoslav Republic at some point in the 1960s or 1970s, the Vienna *Kriegsarchiv* (War Archive) still keeps two boxes with photocopies of all of them under the reference KA Terr Admin Belgrad 1 Akten 1721-1738 and KA Terr Admin Belgrad 2 Akten 1722-1738.

My main aim at looking at them was, as mentioned, to find some allusion to the Kragujevac case around the dates the report was likely written (see the article in this issue). Since the account talks about a request sent to Belgrade by Staniša Marković prior to the official visitation, I had the hope of finding it mentioned among the countless entries belonging to 1725, the date included in the published version of the report. Not having found any trace of such a request, however, I checked the previous registers in search of a confirmation of Staniša Marković's real existence and current position at this period. I found it in the section 3/1, as is explained in my article, in an entry that even proved his personal relationship with Frombald ("provisor zu Gradisca"[11]). But not only did I find this: I also discovered a number of scattered references to Frombald himself, who was apparently very active in 1724—the year before the Kisiljevo vampire case—considering the abundant requests, reports or even complaints he sent to Belgrade as the district chief of Gradisca. However, the spelling of his surname was remarkably inconsistent; even though the form "Frombald," as we got to know him, was the most frequent by far. In an entry from January 4, 1724, he is mentioned as "Frümbald,"[12] and several years later, in 1736, we find him as "Fromwaldt."[13]

---

[10] García Marín's findings will be published in the next issue.—Ed.

[11] Entry 79, 14 February 1724, Fascik. 3/1, Akten 1721-1738, Administration Belgrad, AT-OeStA/KA Terr Admin Belgrad 1, Kriegsarchiv, Vienna (hereafter cited as Akten 1721-1738).

[12] Entry 1, 4 January 1724, Fascik. 3/1, Akten 1721-1738, AT-OeStA/KA Terr Admin

Nonetheless, in two of the cases the reference to the *Provisor* of Gradisca was still more complete, including his full name: Ernst Frombald. Both are part of the section 3/2 of the first box, belonging to 1724. The first one bears the date of April 11, 1724, when a report "von dem Ernst Frombald" (by Ernst Frombald) was examined regarding a building owned by the Orthodox priests of the Ram and Gradisca district and used as a school.[14] A few months later, on July 20, 1724, the Belgrade Administration addressed "an den provisor Ernst Frombald"[15] (to the provisor [of Gradisca[16]] Ernst Frombald) concerning an issue almost indecipherable due to the especially tight handwriting in that part of the entry. Historians and experts in German palaeography of this period should be called upon to reveal the specific content of those entries.

I did not have the time to examine all the protocol books, so it is highly probable that not only are there are other uses of Frombald's first name, but also further information about his life, personality or career are still hiding in them. It is even likely that a thorough study of this corpus would render original and significant evidence about individuals involved in vampire cases in the Military Frontier in the third and fourth decade of the eighteenth century, or about unknown vampire cases or documents themselves. Be that as it may, the discovery of Frombald's first name, Ernst, fills a basic gap in scholarship and does a little justice for the poorly known author of the first official vampire report (at least from the Serbian Military Frontier), who was, after all, the man who allegedly introduced the word "vampire" in Western languages. More importantly, it might be the starting point for new researches on the origin, circumstances or death of this mysterious but essential figure to the field of vampire studies.

Álvaro García Marín
University of Málaga, Spain

BIBLIOGRAPHY

Akten 1721–1738. Administration Belgrad. Kriegsarchiv, Vienna.
Akten 1722–1738. Administration Belgrad. Kriegsarchiv, Vienna.
[Frombald, Ernst]. *Copia des vom Herrn Frombald kayserlichen Cameral Provisore zu Gradiska im Königreich Servien erlassenen Briefs anno 1725. Die im Königreich Servien damals in Schwung gegangenen sogenannten vanpiri oder Blutsauger betreffend.* HHStA StAbt Türkei I/191, Konvolut 1725, fol. 25–26. Türkei I Turcica der Reichshofkanzlei/ des Hofkriegsrats.

Belgrad 1.

[13] Entry [?], 5 November 1736, Fascik. [?], Akten 1722-1738, Administration Belgrad, AT-OeStA/KA Terr Admin Belgrad 2, Kriegsarchiv, Vienna. Unfortunately, I did not write down the entry or fascik information at the time of my visit to the archive.

[14] Entry 232, 11 April 1724, Fascik. 3/2, Akten 1721-1738, AT-OeStA/KA Terr Admin Belgrad 1.

[15] Entry 424, 20 July 1724, Fascik. 3/2, Akten 1721-1738, AT-OeStA/KA Terr Admin Belgrad 1.

[16] "Gradisca" is the heading in the margin that serves as a title or identification term for the whole entry.

Haus-, Hof- und Staatsarchiv, Vienna.

———— [Kayserl. Provisor in Gradisker District]. "Copia eines Schreibens aus dem Gradisker District in Ungarn." *Wienerisches Diarium,* July 21, 1725, [11–12]. http://anno.onb.ac.at/cgi -content/anno?aid=wrz&datum=17250721.

Hamberger, Klaus. *Mortuus non mordet: Dokumente zum Vampirismus, 1689–1791.* Vienna: Turia & Kant, 1992.

Kayserl. Provisor in Gradisker District. *See* Frombald, Ernst, "Copia eines Schreibens."

Mezes, Adam. "Insecure Boundaries: Medical Experts and the Returning Dead on the Southern Habsburg Borderland." Master's thesis, Central European University, 2013. www.etd.ceu.hu/201 3/mezes_adam.pdf.

Schroeder, Aribert. *Vampirismus: Seine Entwicklung vom Thema zum Motiv.* Frankfurt: Akademische Verlagsgesellschaft, 1973.

On Writing "'Blood Suckers Most Cruel:' The Vampire and the Bat in and Before Dracula"

In writing "'Blood Suckers Most Cruel': The Vampire and the Bat in and Before Dracula,"[1] I established that both the bat and the monster were referred to as "vampires" in the nineteenth century; that the vampire bat was thought to be much larger than it actually is; and that the metamorphosis of monster into bat and vice versa preceded Bram Stoker's *Dracula* (1897). The quote in the article's title refers to a designation Johann von Spix famously gave to the bat *Glossophaga soricina*—i.e. *Sanguisuga crudelissima*—one of many bats mistaken for the vampire bat in the nineteenth century.[2] Today they are collectively known as "false vampires."[3]

My interest in the subject grew from researching for the class pack I was preparing for a vampire class I wanted to teach at the Watkins College of Art, Design, and Film in Nashville, Tennessee. I found so much material on nineteenth century vampirism, I asked my supervisor if I could teach a class just on that time period. It was approved, but before I could start, I quit the faculty to take care of my 92-year-old mother-in-law—one of the best decisions I've ever made.

While I was caring for her, I continued to carry on with my studies. I was beginning to realize that the nineteenth century vampire was seriously understudied, that scholars had their tropes, or common places, to which they returned time and again. So, I continued with the class pack, which has now grown to some eight hundred entries. My research began with the presupposition that the word "vampire" referred only to the monster and that "vampire bat" was used for the animal; whenever I encountered the word, I interpreted it as a reference to the

---

[1] Kevin Dodd, "'Blood Suckers Most Cruel:' The Vampire and the Bat in and Before Dracula," *Athens Journal of Humanities & Arts* 6, no. 2 (April 2019): 107–32, https://doi.org/10.3 0958/ajha.6-2-1.

[2] Spix [Jean de Spix], *Simiarum et vespertilionum Brasiliensium species novae* [. . .] (Munich: Typis Francisci Seraphi Hybschmanni, 1823), 66–67, https://archive.org/details/simiarumetve spe00spix.

[3] Barbara French, "False Vampires and Other Carnivores," *Bats,* Summer 1997, http://ww w.batcon.org/resources/media-education/bats-magazine/bat_article/796.

undead.

Just a few months before my wonderful mother-in-law passed away in 2015, I was reading "A Human Vampire" (1894), an unsigned short story published in the *Mataura Ensign*,[4] when it occurred to me that the nineteenth century had two creatures named "vampire"—the monster and the bat. More often than not the bat was simply called "vampire." The realization had more to do with the title, which I had already encountered several times, than with the content of the tale, although it did touch on it. I returned to the previous articles with the same heading and found that several referred to the bat alone and not the monster. A human, not a bat vampire.

I re-read *Dracula* and discovered that Stoker himself never referenced the "vampire bat" but solely used "vampire." I also learned that several classic vampire stories which had been anthologized in vampire volumes—including William H. G. Kingston's "The Vampire; or, Pedro Pacheco and the Bruxa" (1863)[5] and Sabine Baring-Gould's "Margery of Quether" (1884)[6]—referred to the bat alone. It made sense of a number of satirical illustrations depicting a vampire bat with a human face hovering over or feasting on a prone man or woman[7]; they were not comparing the person with a vampire monster but a vampire bat.

I became fascinated with the bat. Before that point I had ignored all but a few articles on it, but now I included everything that I ran across and even created categories in my reader that dealt only with the bat between the sixteenth- and eighteenth century and then again in the nineteenth century—articles from naturalists, travelers, priests, and journalists. One of the first things I noticed was the size. It was, in the word of the period, "monstrous."[8] The blood-sucking bat, native only to Latin America, had been identified as huge ever since the first descriptions of the New World were published in the early sixteenth century and it remained so until the dawning of the nineteenth century.

However, the body of the common vampire bat (*Desmodus rotundus*) has a is only about 3 ½ inches with a wingspan of 14–16 inches; these dimensions class it as a microbat. Félix de Azara correctly identified its size 1801,[9] but even important

---

[4] "A Human Vampire," *Mataura Ensign,* October 5, 1894, 7, https://paperspast.natlib.govt.nz/newspapers/ME18941005.2.31.

[5] Kingston, "The Vampire; or, Pedro Pacheco and the Bruxa," *Vintage Vampire Stories,* ed. Robert Eighteen-Bisang and Richard Dalby (New York: Skyhorse Publishing, 2011), 9–18.

[6] Baring-Gould, "Margery of Quether," in *Vintage Vampire Stories,* ed. Robert Eighteen-Bisang and Richard Dalby (New York: Skyhorse Publishing, 2011), 59–103.

[7] For example, [John Tenniel], "The Irish 'Vampire,'" cartoon, *Punch, or The London Charivari,* October 24, 1885, 199, https://doi.org/10.11588/diglit.17759.17.

[8] "Attacked by Vampires," *Marshall County Republican,* February 26, 1876, 7, https://newspapers.library.in.gov/cgi-bin/indiana?a=d&d=MCR18740226.1.7; and Alfred H. Miles, ed., *Natural History in Anecdote: Illustrating the Nature, Habits, Manners and Customs of Animals, Birds, Fishes, Reptiles, Insects, etc., etc., etc.* (New York: Dodd, Mead, 1895), 37, https://archive.org/details/naturalhistoryin00mile.

[9] Azara [Félix d'Azara], *Essais sur l'histoire naturelle des quadrupedes de la province du*

nineteenth century naturalists, like Richard Schomburgk and Alfred Russel Wallace continued to report on larger bats as the vampire.[10] The writers who correctly drew attention to its diminutive dimensions often designated other large ones as vampires as well.[11]

I had already collected a few sources that predated Dracula's metamorphosis into a bat and vice versa, but their import suddenly came into focus with my study of the bat. With the growing influence of his story, the bat started to lose its designation of "vampire" and became "vampire bat." It was treated as merely an adjunct to the monster. The previous listings treated them the same way, presaging the change. I found two sources that list the bat among other critters into which the living-challenged can transform. In 1879 we read that "vampyre bats" are huge tropical bats named after the monster who is a dead man wandering the earth and performing mischievous deeds on the living "He lies as a corpse during the day; but at night, especially at full moon, he wanders about in the form of a dog, bat, &c, biting sleepers on the back or neck." [12] The following year, we are informed that "Die Vampyre nehmen die Gestalt von Katzen, Fröschen, Kröten, Fliegen, Spinnen oder Fledermäusen an" (Vampires take the form of cats, frogs, toads, flies, spiders, or bats).[13] In both cases the bat is not viewed as independent, but as subsidiary to the monster.

Then there's a story by the famous German writer Karl May.[14] Kara Ben Nemsi, while traveling in the Bulgarian Mountains, passes the night with a poor man, Kerpitchi, who is convinced his recently deceased daughter has become a vampire. She is said to turn into a bat, knock at his door, and go to her fiancé and suck the blood of her fiancé. He is slowly dying. Kara decides to stake out the place, despite Kerpitchi's warning that no one can behold a vampire and live. Kara discovers that the servant of Wlastan, her fiancé's father, has been poisoning him so he can inherit the estate.

Paraguay (Paris: Charles Pougens, 1801), 2:273–6, https://hdl.handle.net/2027/ucm.5324207340.

[10] Schomburgk, *Reisen in Britisch-Guiana in den Jahren 1840—1844* (Leipzig: J. J. Weber, 1847), 1:289, https://archive.org/details/reiseninbritisch01scho; and Wallace, *A Narrative of Travels on the Amazon and Rio Negro* [. . .] (London: Reeve, 1853), 449, https://archive.org/details/narrativeoftrah00wall. Both confused vampire bats with larger bats in the *Phyllostomidae* family.

[11] For example, Richard Lydekker, ed., *The Royal Natural History* (London: Frederick Warne, 1893–94), 1:299–306, https://archive.org/details/royalnaturalhist01lyderich.

[12] H. Courthope Bowen, ed., *Simple English Poems: English Literature for Junior Classes; In Four Parts*, pt. 2 (London: C. Kegan Paul, 1879), 42, Google Play Books.

[13] Edmund Veckenstedt [Edm. Veckenstedt], *Wendische Sagen, Märchen und abergläubische Gebräuche* (Graz: Leuschner & Lubensky, 1880), 354, https://archive.org/details/wendischesagenm01veckgoog (my translation).

[14] May, "Ein Vampir," in *Lasst die Toten ruhen: Deutsche Vampirgeschichten aus dem 19 Jahrhundert*, ed. Oliver Kotowski (Stolberg: Atlantis Verlag, 2012), 189–217. "Ein Vampir" is actually part of a novel, indeed the sixth chapter of *In den Schluchten des Balkan* (1892) from the Orient Cycle. The selection first appeared in the periodical *Deutscher Hausschatz*.

In this example the bat is primary; the body is inert; the bat is active. But Dracula does not follow this instance for the obvious reason that Dracula is the main character of the book, that he is interacting with the other characters in his human form from which he can turn into a bat, a wolf, mist, or particulate matter as the need arises.

So, the moment I had with the *Mataura Ensign* story spun off in three interrelated directions. First, I learned that the nineteenth century did not use the word "vampire" the same way we use it today. It was used equally for the monster and the bat. Second, I discovered that the nineteenth century bat was generally enormous in proportions and not the small creature we designate today. In fact, *Dracula* is the primary instance of the monster turning into a recognizable "vampire bat." Today if a monster turns into a bat it is *sui generis*, a unique specimen unlike the true vampire bat, a vampire-turned-into-a-bat not a vampire bat. Last, in spite of a scholarly consensus that *Dracula* was the first example of a vampire monster turning into a bat, I concluded it was not so. Yet *Dracula* causes the previous ones to pale in comparison. As I write in the conclusion of the paper: "Stoker's use of the contemporary large and menacing bat—to spy, to sedate, to hypnotize, to prey upon, to escape—as one weapon in an arsenal to be wielded by a relentless, foreign, imperial monster bent on conquest in the very heart of the British Empire at the time is quite staggering."[15]

Kevin Dodd
Vanderbilt University, USA

BIBLIOGRAPHY

Azara, Félix de [Félix d'Azara]. *Essais sur l'histoire naturelle des quadrupedes de la province du Paraguay*. 2 vols. Paris: Charles Pougens, 1801. Hathi Trust Digital Library.

Baring-Gould, Sabine. "Margery of Quether." In Eighteen-Bisang and Dalby, *Vintage*, 59–103. Originally published in *Cornhill Magazine*, April 1884, 337–60; May 1884, 466–85.

Bowen, H. Courthope, ed. *Simple English Poems: English Literature for Junior Classes; In Four Parts*. London: C. Kegan Paul, 1879. Google Play Books.

D'Azara, Félix. *See* Azara, Félix de.

Dodd, Kevin. "'Blood Suckers Most Cruel:' The Vampire and the Bat in and Before Dracula." *Athens Journal of Humanities & Arts* 6, no. 2 (April 2019): 107–32. https://doi.org/10.30958/a jha.6-2-1. Originally published ahead of print, August 22, 2018, https://www.athensjourn als.gr/humanities/2018-1-X-Y-Dodd.pdf.

Eighteen-Bisang, Robert, and Richard Dalby, eds. *Vintage Vampire Stories*. New York: Skyhorse Publishing, 2011.

French, Barbara. "False Vampires and Other Carnivores." *Bats*, Summer 1997. http://www.ba tcon.org/resources/media-education/bats-magazine/bat_article/796.

Lydekker, Richard, ed. *The Royal Natural History*. 6 vols. London: Frederick Warne, 1893–96. Internet Archive.

Kingston, William H. G. "The Vampire; or, Pedro Pacheco and the Bruxa." In Eighteen-Bisang and Daly, *Vintage*, 9–18. Reprinted from *Tales for All Ages* (London: Bickers &

---

[15] Dodd, "Blood Suckers Most Cruel," 125.

Bush, 1863), 72–80.

Marshall County (IN) Republican. "Attacked by Vampires." February 26, 1876, 7. https://newsp apers.library.in.gov/cgi-bin/indiana?a=d&d=MCR18740226.1.7.

Mataura Ensign. "A Human Vampire." October 5, 1894, 7. https://paperspast.natlib.govt.nz/n ewspapers/ME18941005.2.31.

May, Karl. "Ein Vampir." In *Lasst die Toten ruhen: Deutsche Vampirgeschichten aus dem 19 Jahrhundert,* edited by Oliver Kotowski, 189–217. Stolberg: Atlantis Verlag, 2012.

Miles, Alfred H., ed. *Natural History in Anecdote: Illustrating the Nature, Habits, Manners and Customs of Animals, Birds, Fishes, Reptiles, Insects, etc., etc., etc.* New York: Dodd, Mead, 1895. https://archive.org/details/naturalhistoryin00mile.

Schomburgk, Richard. *Reisen in Britisch-Guiana in den Jahren 1840—1844.* 3 vols. Leipzig: J. J. Weber, 1847–48.

Spix, Jean de. *See* Spix, Johann von.

Spix, Johann von [Jean de Spix]. *Simiarum et vespertilionum Brasiliensium species novae, ou Histoire naturelle des espèces nouvelles de singes et de chauves-souris observées et recueillies pendant le voyage dans l'intérieur du Brésil exécuté par ordre de S.M. le Roi de Bavière dans les années 1817, 1818, 1819, 1820.* Munich: Typis Francisci Seraphi Hybschmanni, 1823. https://archive.org/details/simiarumetvespe00spix.

[Tenniel, John]. "The Irish 'Vampire.'" Cartoon. *Punch, or The London Charivari,* October 24, 1885, 199. https://doi.org/10.11588/diglit.17759.17.

Veckenstedt, Edm[und]. *Wendische Sagen, Märchen und abergläubische Gebräuche.* Graz: Leuschner & Lubensky, 1880. https://archive.org/details/wendischesage nm01veckgoog.

Wallace, Alfred R. *A Narrative of Travels on the Amazon and Rio Negro, with an Account of the Native Tribes, and Observations on the Climate, Geology, and Natural History of the Amazon Valley.* London: Reeve, 1853. https://archive.org/details/narrativeoftrav00wall.

Nina Auerbach (1943–2017)

Nina Joan Auerbach was born in New York City on May 24, 1943 and received her B.A. at the University of Wisconsin in Madison in 1964 and a MA (1967), and PhD in English Literature from Columbia University in 1970. After teaching at Hunter College and Cal State University, she spent most of her academic career at the University of Pennsylvania, where she was the John Welsh Centennial Professor of English until her retirement in 2010. As both teacher and scholar, she was known for her work on Victorian literature, theater history, feminist criticism, and horror. Among her numerous awards, she received the Lindback Award for Distinguished Teaching at Penn in 1983 and the annual Distinguished Scholarship Award from the International Association of the Fantastic in the Arts in 2000. When she died on February 3, 2017 in New York City of respiratory failure, she was working on *Lost Lives*, a study of ghosts.

Readers of Gothic literature are likely to be most familiar with her penetrating work on vampires and other supernatural figures in *Our Vampires, Ourselves* (1995) and the Norton Critical Edition of *Dracula* (1996), which she co-edited with David J. Skal, as well as her appearance in three short documentary films: *The Blood Tide* (1998), *The Road to Dracula* (1999), and *The Gothic World of Daphne du Maurier* (2008). The film on du Maurier stems from her critical study, *Daphne du Maurier: Haunted Heiress* (2000).

Auerbach's study of vampires and other supernatural figures is grounded in her scholarly study of Victorian literature. She began her career studying women writers in books such as *Communities of Women: An Idea in Fiction* (1978) and *Woman and the Demon: The Life of a Victorian Myth* (1982), which examined the way that mainstream literature such as George Eliot's *The Mill on the Floss* incorporated creatures from popular culture, and she also examined the lesser-known field of Victorian theater in her biographical study, *Ellen Terry: Player in Her Time* (1987) and *Private Theatricals: The Lives of the Victorians* (1990).

That same scholarly rigor is evident in the Norton Critical Edition of *Dracula* she co-edited with Skal, which includes excerpts from material that influenced Stoker, contemporary reviews of *Dracula*, and modern criticism. Her scholarship also paved the way for her studies of popular culture, including *Our Vampires, Ourselves* (1995), which combines sound literary criticism and cultural study of Anglo-American culture with her own sometimes quirky observations of current events. Noting that vampires generally reveal the fears of the cultures that produced them, she explores famous literary vampires: Polidori's Lord Ruthven, Varney, Christabel and Carmilla, and Dracula, and also looks at the way these literary figures were adapted in the twentieth century, touching on links between vampires and the AIDS epidemic and the Queer community. *Our Vampires, Ourselves* concludes with very sensitive readings of contemporary vampire literature and film, including *The Gilda Stories* by Jewelle Gomez (about a black lesbian vampire) and *Near Dark* (directed by Kathryn Bigelow), which she describes as the "best vampire work to come out of the Reaganesque years" (p. 187). The reference to Reagan reinforces the political connection with which she opens her study, noting "that the book took shape between 1989 and 1992 and thus comments on an historical period "of manipulated hate that came to define our national life" (p. 2). One wishes that Auerbach, who saw the connection between the vampire and the popular culture that influenced its producers, were around to comment on politics today. She knew that the fear of vampires is steeped in "political and ideological ambience" (p.3) and concluded *Our Vampires, Ourselves* with a note of caution, however, noting that vampires at the end of the twentieth century "are wearing down and vampires need a long restorative sleep. They will awaken; they always have" because "time is on their side." (p. 192)

Carol A Senf

Georgia Institute of Technology, USA

BIBLIOGRAPHY

Inquirer (Philadelphia). "Nina Auerbach." March 5, 2017. http://www.legacy.com/obituaries/philly/obituary.aspx?n=nina-auerbach&pid=184353073.

New York Times. "Nina Auerbach (1943 - 2017)." February 19, 2017. https://www.legacy.com/obituaries/nytimes/obituary.aspx?n=nina-auerbach&pid=184181437.

Timpane, John. "Vampire-Loving Bicyclist Professor to Be Remembered at Writers House." *Inquirer* (Philadelphia), April 17, 2017. http://www2.philly.com/philly/entertainment/arts/Vampire-loving -bicyclist-professor-to-be-remembered-at-Writers-House.html

University of Pennsylvania. "Nina Auerbach." Department of English. 2018. https://www.english.upenn.edu/people/nina-auerbach.

University of Pennsylvania Almanac. "Nina Auerbach, English." February 28, 2017, 2. https://almanac.upenn.edu/uploads/media/022817-issue.pdf.

University of Pennsylvania Press. "In Memoriam: Nina Auerbach." *Penn Press Log* (blog), February 21, 2017. https://pennpress.typepad.com/pennpresslog/2017/02/in-memoriam -nina-auerbach.html.

Works Cited

Auerbach, Nina. *Our Vampires, Ourselves*. Chicago: University of Chicago Press, 1995.

———. *Communities of Women: An Idea in Fiction*. Cambridge, MA: Harvard University Press, 1978.

———. *Daphne du Maurier: Haunted Heiress*. Philadelphia: University of Pennsylvania Press, 2000.

———. *Ellen Terry: Player and Her Time*. New York: W.W. Norton, 1987.

———. *Private Theatricals: The Lives of the Victorians*. Cambridge, MA: Harvard University Press, 1990.

———. *Woman and the Demon: The Life of a Victorian Myth*. Cambridge, MA: Harvard University Press, 1982.

Cork, John, dir. *The Gothic World of Daphne du Maurier*. Los Angeles: 20th Century Fox Home Entertainment, 2008.

Ricketts, Susan, and Mark Rance, prods. *The Blood Tide*. Burbank, CA: New Line Cinema, 1998.

Skal, David J., dir. *The Road to Dracula*. Los Angeles: Universal Studios Home Video, 1999.

Stoker, Bram. *Dracula: Authoritative Text, Contexts, Reviews and Reactions, Dramatic and Film Variations, Criticism*. Edited by Nina Auerbach and David J. Skal. Norton Critical Editions. New York: W. W. Norton, 1997. [Published 1996]

Candace R. Benefiel (1957–2017)

Candace Renee Benefiel was born on July 7, 1957 in Freeport, Texas. She received a Bachelor's in Classics from Rice University in 1979, a Master's in Library Science from the University of Texas at Austin in 1981, and a Master's in English from West Texas University in 1989. She was completing her doctoral dissertation, "Stakeholders in a New Tradition: Vampires and the American Woman at the Beginning of the Twenty-First Century," at the time of her death. After a brief battle with cancer, she passed away on August 1, 2017 in College Station, Texas. Benefiel was also a tenured professor and Humanities Reference Librarian at Texas A&M University Libraries, where she taught various courses, including several on the vampire in literature and popular culture.

Benefiel's work on the vampire was both expansive and impactful. Her 2004 essay, "Blood Relations: The Gothic Perversion of the Nuclear Family in Anne Rice's *Interview with the Vampire*," is one of her most cited texts in the field, analyzing Rice's revision of the vampiric figure from gothic villain to gothic hero. She would later expand on this idea in both her lectures and published work, describing "the new American vampire" as a figure of romance across multiple genres and media, and by extension, the vampire "fan" as a problematic and highly-gendered critique of media consumers. Her 2010 essay, "Willing Freshies: Blood, Sex, and Vampires in *Moonlight* and Related Fan Fiction," looked at these issues both as portrayed on the short-lived TV series *Moonlight* (2007–2008) and in the fanfiction concerning the show, which portrayed a subculture of "freshies" who were (more than) willing blood donors. Benefiel was also an acafan, a term meant to broadly encompass the relationships between academic work and fan work; she was a long-time moderator for the fan forum *Moonlightaholics* and herself published a great deal of fanfiction for the show, stories which were read in high numbers across the world. As she delved more into fan studies, her work developed to reconceive the textual relationships between popular vampire literature and historical literature. She collaborated on several essays examining fan works and textual relationships, including "We Have Met the Fans, and They Are Us" (2010), "The Hunter Hunted: The Portrayal of the Fan as Predator on *Supernatural*" (2014) and "Fifty Shades of *Twilight*: Transforming Genre and Publishing in Fan Contexts" (2016).

Her book-length study, *Reading Laurell K. Hamilton*, was published by Libraries Unlimited, an ABC-Clio imprint, in 2011. Part of the Pop Lit Book Club series, the volume broadly analyzes and contextualizes Hamilton's numerous novels. It especially emphasizes Hamilton's influence on the vampire genre since the 1990s while drawing connections between modern work and classics of the genre like

John Polidori's *The Vampyre* (1819). A prolific scholar, Benefiel's final, posthumous essay "Biting, Sex, and Blood: The New American Vampire Narrative" was recently published in *The Global Vampire: Essays on the Undead in Popular Culture Around the World* (2020). This final essay has been pieced together and condensed from Benefiel's unfinished doctoral dissertation. Benefiel, a frequent presence at national meetings of the Popular Culture Association and the American Libraries Association, left behind a significant body of scholarly work that is likely to continue influencing our field for many years to come.

Cait Coker
University of Illinois at Urbana-Champaign, USA

BIBLIOGRAPHY

Hillier Funeral Home. "Candace Benefiel." Accessed August 12, 2018. https://www.hillierfun eralhome.com/tributes/Candace-Benefiel.

Legacy.com. "Candace Benefiel." Accessed August 12, 2018. https://www.legacy.com/obituar ies/name/candace-benefiel-obituary?pid=18632845.

Works Cited

Benefiel, Candace. *See* Benefiel, "Willing Freshies."

Benefiel, Candace R. "Biting, Sex, and Blood: The New American Vampire Narrative." In *The Global Vampire: Essays on the Undead in Popular Culture around the World*, edited by Cait Coker, 11–22. Jefferson, NC: McFarland, 2020.

———. "Blood Relations: The Gothic Perversion of the Nuclear Family in Anne Rice's *Interview with the Vampire*." *Journal of Popular Culture* 38, no. 2 (November 2004): 261–73.

———. *Reading Laurell K. Hamilton*. Santa Barbara, CA: Libraries Unlimited, 2011

———. "Willing Freshies: Blood, Sex and Vampires in *Moonlight* Fan Fiction." In *Fanpires: Audience Consumption of the Modern Vampire*, edited by Gareth Schott and Kirstine Moffat, 223–38. Washington, DC: New Academia Publishing, 2011.

Coker, Cait, and Candace Benefiel. "Fifty Shades of *Twilight*: Transforming Genre and Publishing in Fan Contexts." In *Fan Phenomena: The Twilight Saga*, edited by Laurena Aker, 152–61. Bristol: Intellect Books, 2016.

———. "The Hunter Hunted: The Portrayal of the Fan as Predator on *Supernatural*." In *"Supernatural", Humanity, and the Soul: On the Highway to Hell and Back*, edited by Susan A. George and Regina M. Hansen, 97–110. New York: Palgrave MacMillan, 2014.

———. "We Have Met the Fans, and They Are Us: In Defense of Aca-Fans and Scholars." In "Revisiting Aca-Fandom," edited by R. Colin Tait. Special issue, *Flow* 13, no. 5 (2010). https://www.flowjournal.org/2010/12/we-have-met-the-fans.

Coker, Catherine, and Canadace Benefiel. *See* Coker and Benefiel, "We Have Met the Fans."

Re: Vampire Etymology Article

EDITOR'S NOTE *On the strength of his article, "The Evil That Lives After Them: A Cultural and Linguistic Exhumation of the Vampire Myth" (Academia.edu, 2017, https://www.acade mia.edu/35327558), I asked Michael Dilts to peer review a draft of Kamil Stachowski's "Etymologies of* vampire *with* pirъ *'a feast,'" (Journal of Vampire Studies 1, no. 1 [2020]: 5–18). Dilts sent his peer review to me (email message to Anthony Hogg, July 30, 2018), and, in accordance with our open peer review policy, I forwarded the review to Stachowski. I did not anticipate that Stachowski would then address the review in his own article, but doing so highlighted the value of the process as a method of scholarly correspondence. Therefore, to provide a common reference point for readers, I have reproduced Dilts' emailed peer review, below. The only changes made to Dilts' text is the removal of spaces between paragraphs and the inclusion of Dilts' status as an independent scholar beneath his byline. Reprinted with permission from Michael Dilts.*

Section 2.2[1] seems to accept McClelland's 15th Century dating for the *"Oration of St. Gregory"* (also known as *"The Sermon of St. Gregory, devised with commentary on it. On how firstly the pagans were heathens, worshiped idols and brought them sacrifices and now do this."*) However, the date of this item is disputed, with some scholars (e.g. Boris Rybakov) dating it to the beginning of the 12th Century. According to Stella Rock (*"Popular Religion in Russia"*) the comments which mention *upiri,* bereginas, vilas, Mokoš, Perun, etc., were interpolated by a Russian scribe into a poorly translated South Slavic translation of the original "Oration" or an intermediate (possibly garbled) version of it. McClelland insists on the 15th Century date and dismisses the evidence of the "Sermon" for the same reason he ignores Sjöberg's very convincing argument regarding the non-Slavic identity of the supposed 1047 attestation - because of his zeal to promote his "heretic" hypothesis."

On the other hand, the proposed connection of the word for vampire with Slavic *pirъ* and ultimately with the root meaning "to drink," may have more merit than is acknowledged in this article or in the previous festschrift paper by Stachowsi and Stachowski. The word *pirъ* meaning "feast, libation" is semantically very suggestive. The identification of a divinity with the offerings it receives is not at all limited to Christianity (in which Christ is the sacrificed "lamb of god" who identifies his body with the offered bread and his blood with the wine drunk by the celebrant). In the Egyptian tradition, Osiris is the sacrifice as well, torn to pieces and scattered over the land. The Graeco-Thracian myth of Dionysos is another parallel - the god is sacrificed and eaten by the Titans, but his divine spirit survives in the intoxicating beverage which is sacred to his godhead.

An even more closely related parallel comes from the Germanic language

---

[1] The "Bruce A. McClelland" subheading in Stachowski's article; numbered headings were used in earlier drafts. — Ed.

family, where a convincing etymology of the word for "god" (English *god*, Gothic *guth*, Old Norse *gudh*, German *Gott*) derives it from the Proto-Indo-European root **gheu-* "to pour, to libate." A "god" is the one for whom the libation is poured, and is at the same time distinct from the older, more traditional generation of gods, the Aesir, whose name derives from Proto-Germanic **ansu-*, and is related to Vedic *asura-* and Avestan *ahura-*. Perhaps the *upiri*, like the Germanic "gods," were spirits of the ancestors who frequented the gravesites where their remains were laid to rest, and libations kept them satisfied so that they did not harass the living. (Note that in pre-Christian times, the Proto-Germanic word **guthan* was neuter and thus less animate and more impersonal.)

Homer's Odyssey provides evidence that in the Indo-European tradition the spirits of the dead craved blood - it restored consciousness of their prior lives. So perhaps a libation of liquor and/or blood would keep the predations of the *upiri* in check. Note that libation is still a universally valid offering to disembodied spirits of all kinds, especially among the shamanic cultures of Siberia. There is one final piece of evidence to consider. The prefix *u-* actually does appear in combination with the root **pi-* "to drink" in the Old Russian phrase оупити са "become inebriated, get drunk" and survives in modern Russian упиться (*upit'sya*) "get drunk." So, is an *upirь* the one who "gets drunk" from the libation, or the one who regains its mortal consciousness when offered libations by the living?

Michael Dilts
Independent scholar, USA

Contributors

MICHAEL E. BELL is the retired Consulting Folklorist for Rhode Island's State Preservation Commission. He has researched, lectured and written about New England's vampire tradition since delving into it in 1981. His book, *Food for the Dead: On the Trail of New England's Vampires* (2001), received the 2002 Lord Ruthven Award for Non-Fiction. Email: vampirefolklore@gmail.com

ELEANOR BRYAN is an Associate Lecturer and PhD student at the University of Lincoln. Her PhD thesis concerns dramatic adaptations of *Frankenstein* and *Dracula*. and her wider research interests include Romanticism, Edwardian literature, and cinematic adaptation. Eleanor is curator of the BARS Romantic Reimaginings Blog and is Communications Fellow for the K-SAA. Email: ebryan@lincoln.ac.uk

STU BURNS is an independent scholar and historical preservationist living in Omaha. He is a past Regents Fellow at the University of Nebraska – Lincoln. His work has appeared in *eTropic, European Studies Conference Selected Proceedings*, and *Dictionary of Literary Biography*. His current project is a book examining vampire folklore and world history. Email: stu.burns@huskers.unl.edu

MARGARET L. CARTER is an independent scholar, author of *Shadow of a Shade: A Survey of Vampirism in Literature* (1975), *Different Blood: The Vampire as Alien* (2001), edited *Dracula: The Vampire and the Critics* (1988) and *The Vampire in Literature: A Critical Bibliography* (1989). She lives in the United States with her husband. Email: mlcvamp@aol.com

CAIT COKER is an Associate Professor and Curator of Rare Books and Manuscripts at the University of Illinois at Urbana-Champaign. Her research focuses include genre history, women's writing and vampires in popular culture. She edited her first book, *The Global Vampire: Essays on the Undead in Popular Culture around the World* (2020). Email: cait@illinois.edu

MICHAEL DILTS is an independent researcher and online course material developer. He received linguistics degrees from University of California, Berkeley; and Harvard University. Aside from a career in computer speech technology for Wang Laboratories and Apple, he is a student and teacher of world mythology and shamanism. He lives in Southern California. Email: michaeldilts@yahoo.com

KEVIN DODD is a Visiting Scholar at Vanderbilt University in Nashville, Tennessee. He received his doctorate in religion and has taught courses in religion, philosophy, and mythology, including the Faustian pact. In that capacity he has become interested in the nineteenth-century vampire and is devoting himself to a book on the subject. Email: doddblair@bellsouth.net

ÁLVARO GARCÍA MARÍN is a Professor of Modern Greek Studies at the University of

Málaga in Spain. His research focuses on the cultural reception of vampirism (especially Greek), European negotiations of Greekness in modernity, and the uncanny. His most recent monograph, *Historias del vampiro griego* (2017), examines the phenomenon of the Greek *vrykolakas*. Email: agmarin@uma.es

ANTHONY HOGG is Editor of the *Journal of Vampire Studies*; President and founder of the Vampire Studies Association; Editor-in-Chief of Lord Ruthven Award-winning website *Vamped* (https://vamped.org); helped organise There Are Such Things! Vampire Studies Symposium 2015, held at Corinth, Texas; and blogs as *The Vampirologist* (https://thevampirologist.wordpress.com). He lives in Melbourne. Email: thevampirologist@hotmail.com

BRUCE A. MCCLELLAND is a writer and folklorist with emphasis on Russian and Balkan/Slavic ethnography and folklore. He received his PhD in Slavic Studies at the University of Virginia. His book, *Slayers and Their Vampires: A Cultural History of Killing the Dead* (2006), received the Lord Ruthven Award for Non-Fiction in 2007. Email: vampirolog@gmail.com

GERARD P. O'SULLIVAN, Ph.D., wrote "The Continuing Quest for Montague Summers," the prologue to Montague Summers' *The Vampire, His Kith and Kin: A Critical Edition* (2011), edited by John Edgar Browning. In 2008, he recovered the archives of Summers, which had been missing since 1948. They are now housed at Georgetown University's Library. Email: gosullivan@yahoo.com

NIELS K. PETERSEN is an upper secondary school teacher, MSc, and blogger who has covered vampires and related topics at http://magiaposthuma.blogspot.com since 2007. His main focus is the historical aspects of the subject with a particular interest in the subject of *magia posthuma* (posthumous magic) in seventeenth- and eighteenth-century Moravia and Silesia. Email: niels@magiaposthuma.com

BENJAMIN RADFORD is the Deputy Editor of *Skeptical Inquirer* and author or co-author of thirteen books including *Tracking the Chupacabra: The Vampire Beast in Fact, Fiction, and Folklore* (2011). He is a Research Fellow with the Committee for Skeptical Inquiry, member of the American Folklore Society, co-founder and co-host of two podcasts. Email: jaminradford@gmail.com

MARTIN V. RICCARDO is the Director of Vampire Studies, an information clearinghouse. His writings include an essay collection, *Lure of the Vampire* (1983), and two books: *Vampires Unearthed: The Complete Multi-Media Vampire and Dracula Bibliography* (1983) and *Liquid Dreams of Vampires* (1996). He lives in a Chicago suburb, and gives lectures on vampires. Email: batbite@msn.com

CLEMENS RUTHNER is a Professor of German and European Studies at Trinity College Dublin, whose research focuses on Central European Studies, Otherness (including vampirism) and cultural theory. His most recent monograph, *Habsburgs ,Dark Continent': Postkoloniale Lektüren zur österreichischen Literatur und Kultur im langen 19. Jahrhundert* (2018), provides postcolonial readings of Austrian literature. Email: ruthnerc@tcd.ie

CAROL A. SENF is a Professor in the School of Literature, Media, and Communication at Georgia Institute of Technology and author of three books on Stoker, one on Dracula, and one on vampires. She has also written articles on Victorian writers. She lives in Atlanta with her husband, a dog, and three cats. Email: carol.senf@lmc.gatech.edu

KAMIL STACHOWSKI is an assistant at the Department of the History of Languages and Linguistics at Jagiellonian University, Kraków. His primary fields of research are historical and quantitative linguistics, especially Turkic and Slavonic. He authored or co-authored four books and thirty-eight papers, including a series on possible oriental elements in Slavonic folklore. Email: kamil.stachowski@uj.edu.pl

WILLIAM TRINGALI is the Law Librarian for Outreach at Emory University School of Law, and Editor-in-Chief of the *Journal of Anime and Manga Studies*, a peer-reviewed open-access journal, first published in 2020. His various research interests include ethics and morality, vampire studies, queerness, outreach and engagement, games studies, and anime/manga studies. Email: william.tringali@emory.edu

Peer Reviewers

"Etymologies of vampire *with* pirъ *'a feast,'" by Kamil Stachowski*

MICHAEL DILTS is an independent researcher and online course material developer. He received linguistics degrees from University of California, Berkeley; and Harvard University. Aside from a career in computer speech technology for Wang Laboratories and Apple, he is a student and teacher of world mythology and shamanism. He lives in Southern California. Email: michaeldilts@yahoo.com

PETER MARIO KREUTER is a Research Associate, History Division, at the Leibniz Institute for East and Southeast European Studies. He is the author of *Der Vampirglaube in Südosteuropa: Studien zur Genese, Bedeutung und Funktion; Rumänien und der Balkanraum* (2001) and a range of articles on vampires, Vlad Tepes, the monstrous and Balkan studies. Email: kreuter@ios-regensburg.

CPSIA information can be obtained
at www.ICGtesting.com
Printed in the USA
LVHW011144311220
675398LV00006B/393

9 781947 181083